InstaEnglish

Student's Book and Workbook

2nd Edition

1

Emma Heyderman
Fiona Mauchline
Patrick Howarth
Patricia Reilly
Olivia Johnston

macmillan education

InstaEnglish

Student's Book and Workbook 2nd Edition

WALKTHROUGH

Check out how your combo edition of the **Student's Book and Workbook** is structured so you can make the most of it!

STUDENT'S BOOK

Your **Student's Book** is made up of a **Starter unit**, **8 regular units**, 4 sets of **review activities**, plus 2 nifty sections: **Digital Literacy** after every 2 units, and **Global Citizenship** after every 4 units.

Starter unit

This two-page unit provides strategic language for you to kick off your studies!

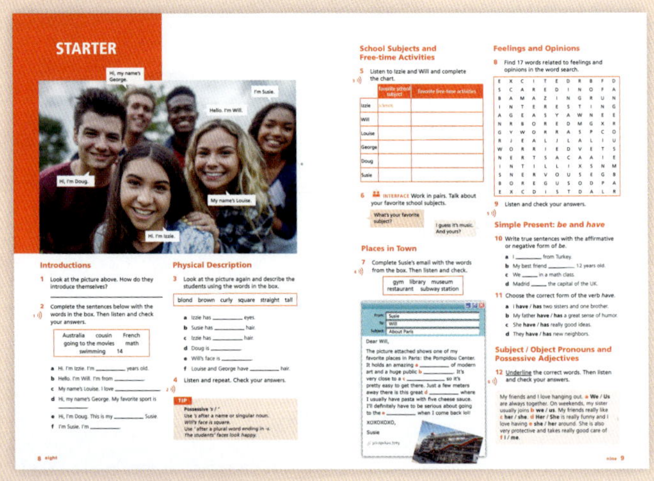

Opener

All regular units open with a visual treat to trigger your first thoughts on the main subject. What's the first thing that pops into your head when you look at it?

VOCABULARY 1

Here you will read, listen to, and look at pictures referring to words or phrases that will help you to explore the unit topic.

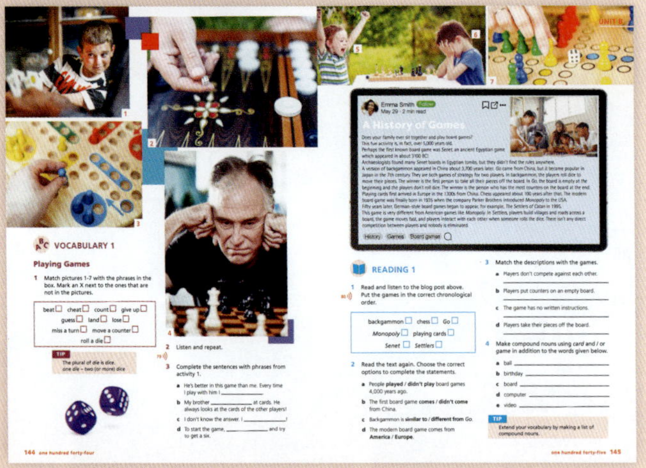

READING 1

Texts of multiple genres provide interesting content to practice your reading skills and introduce relevant language to be explored throughout the unit.

GRAMMAR 1

Grammar topics that were introduced in the reading text are systematically explored so you can easily work out all the rules and patterns.

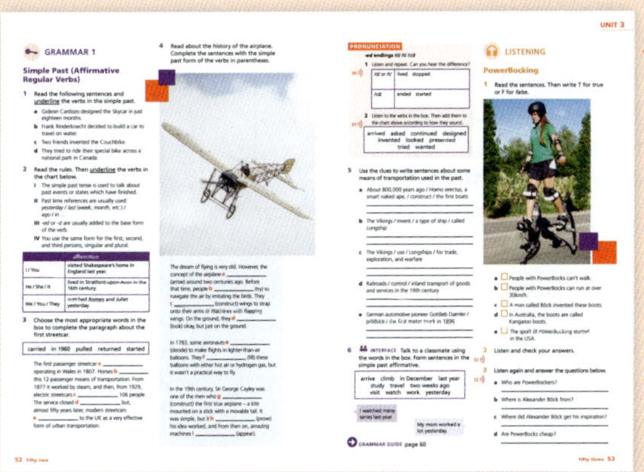

LISTENING

Learn and practice oral comprehension through engaging and contextualized oral texts.

SPEAKING

A clearly guided activity will help you practice your speaking skills using functional language in everyday situations. Throughout the levels, as you improve your ability to communicate orally, you will get increasing contact with real-life oral text genres.

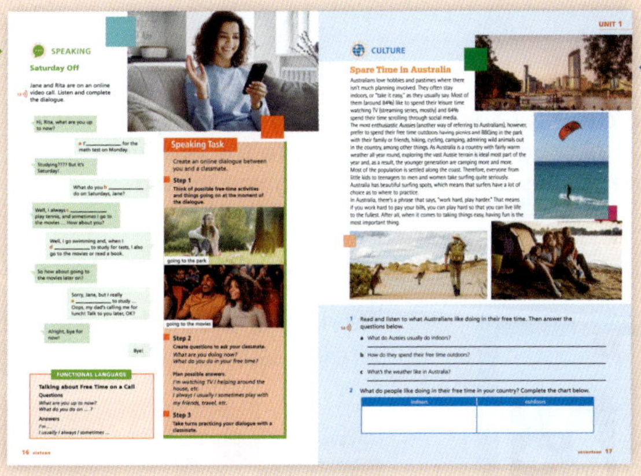

CULTURE

Discover cultural aspects of everyday life in English-speaking countries across the globe!

VOCABULARY 2

The second vocabulary set provides more words and phrases to allow you to go further into the unit topic.

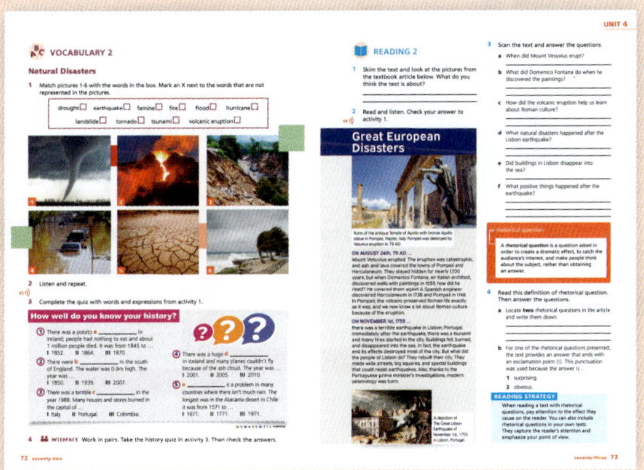

READING 2

The second reading text digs further into the main topic and provides more language to be explored.

GRAMMAR 2

A new grammar topic is introduced in the same contextualized and systematic way seen in **Grammar 1**.

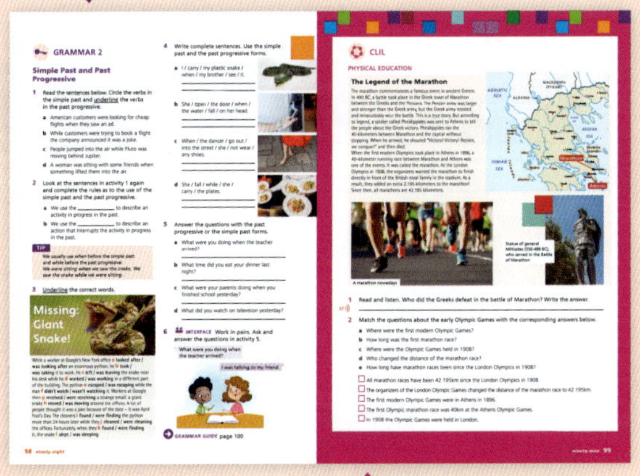

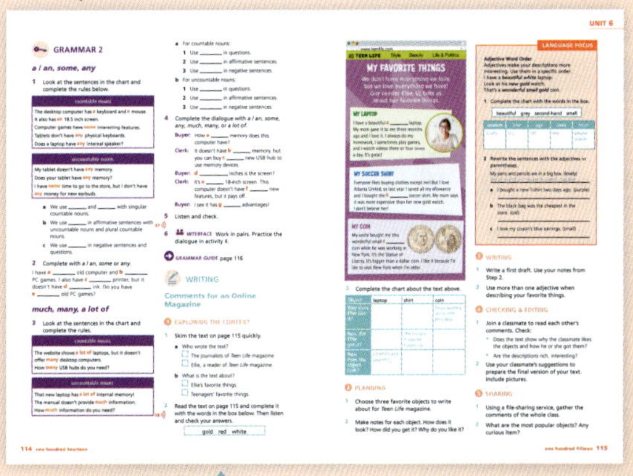

CLIL

In every odd-numbered unit, the **Grammar 2** section is accompanied by the **CLIL** section, for you to integrate your learning of the English language with other school subjects through fun texts and activities.

WRITING

In even-numbered units, the **Grammar 2** section is followed by the **Writing** section, where you are supported every step of the way to practice your writing skills in a range of text genres.

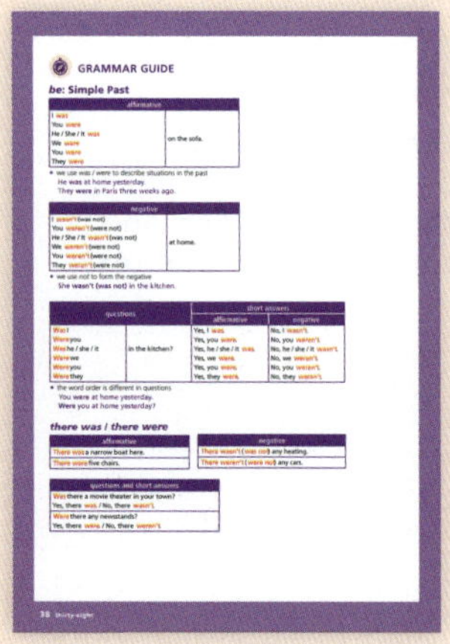

GRAMMAR GUIDE

This is a reference section for all the grammar topics explored in the unit.

VOCABULARY IN PICTURES

Have fun reviewing all the words and phrases learned in the **Vocabulary** sections, all richly illustrated!

PROGRESS CHECK

Once you complete the unit, cut this page out and close your book. Do the activities and check your overall progress. Then go back to the **Grammar Guide** and the **Vocabulary in Pictures** pages and revise anything you missed.

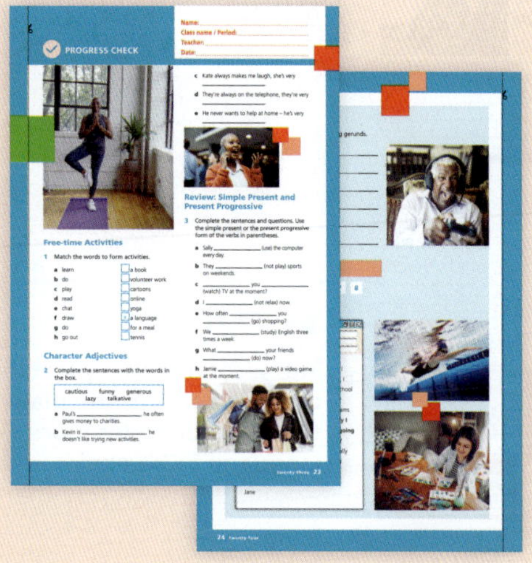

Review

Review the vocabulary and grammar from the previous two units starting with a game!

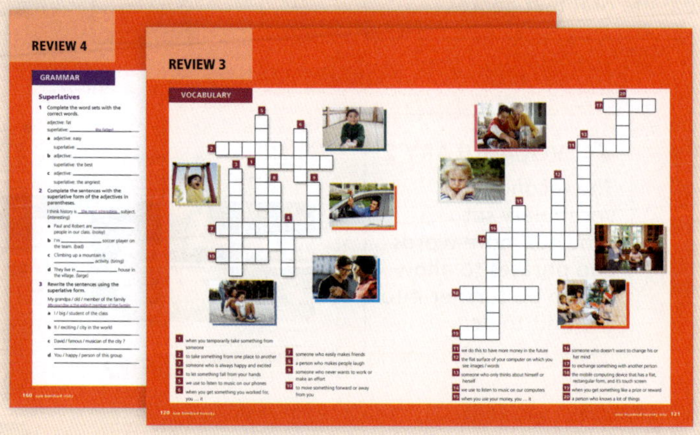

DIGITAL LITERACY

Do you think you use digital technology wisely? Follow siblings Lily and Daniel in a manga-style comic and see how they interact *with* and *through* the digital universe while reflecting about their (and your) relationship with the "digital."

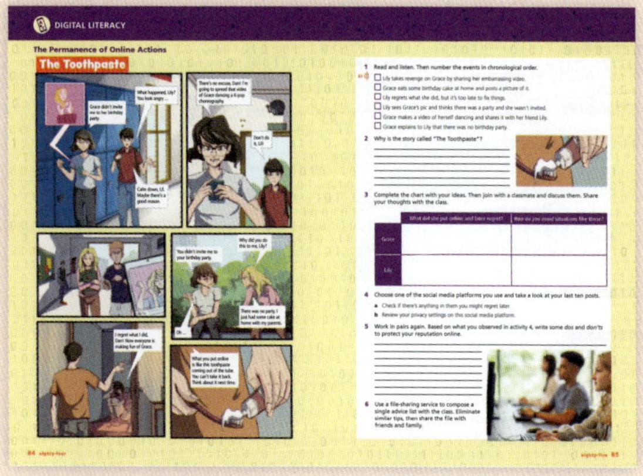

GLOBAL CITIZENSHIP

All of us need to nurture the perception that we are part of the same world. We need to build knowledge and develop skills to live together in the best possible way. That's what this section is all about!

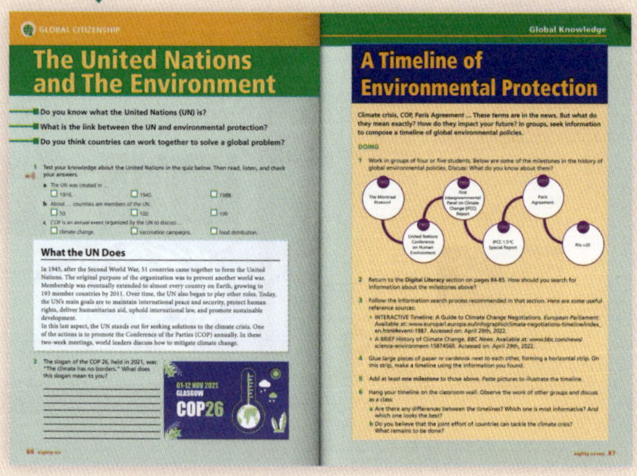

The **TIP, READING STRATEGY, PRONUNCIATION, CULTURAL FACT, FUNCTIONAL LANGUAGE, LANGUAGE FOCUS, CLASS VOTE,** and **INTERFACE** features will make your learning process more practical and effective.

WORKBOOK

The **Workbook** offers target-language practice and additional study material (consolidation and extension). It can be used as homework, independent study, or extra classroom practice. Some of the sections correspond to sections in the **Student's Book**:

VOCABULARY 1

GRAMMAR 1

GRAMMAR CHECK
A text with interesting and curious facts helps you check your reading and language skills.

VOCABULARY 2

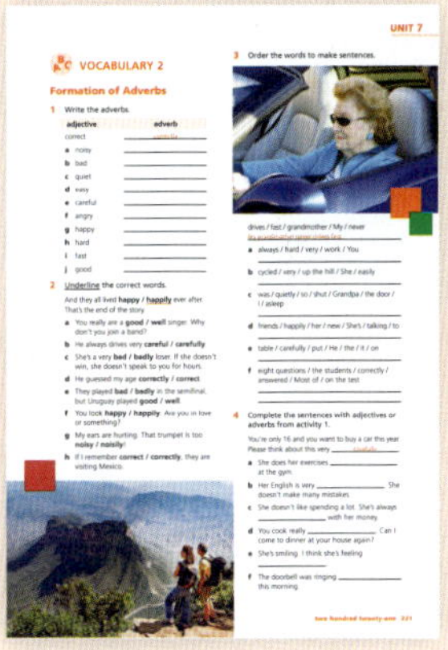

GRAMMAR 2

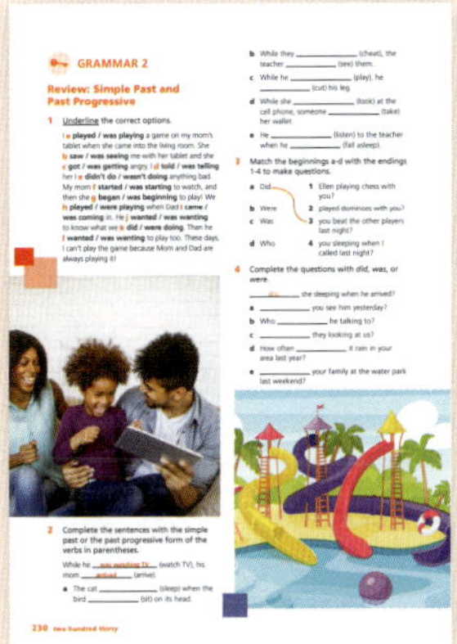

LISTENING

EXTENSION
This engaging section offers an extra challenge on grammar and vocabulary items.

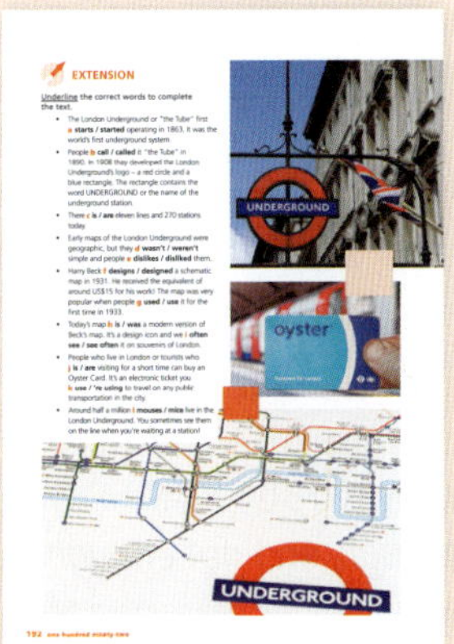

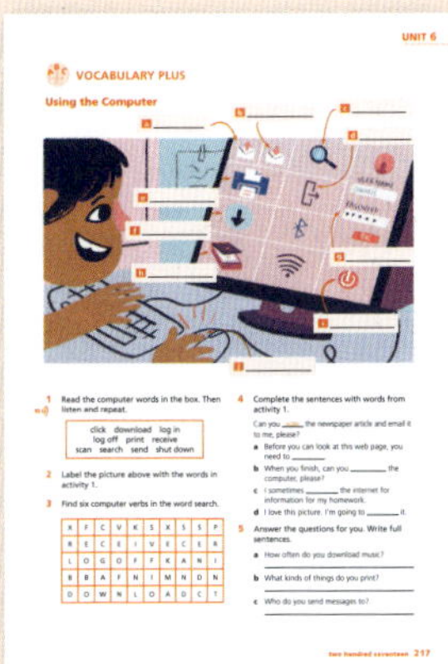

VOCABULARY PLUS
Learn more words related to the unit topic in a fun way! All words are illustrated.

Wordlist

This offers an alphabetical list of the key vocabulary in the **Student's Book** and from the **Vocabulary Plus** sections. It includes phonetic transcriptions and audio recordings.

DIGITAL OFFERINGS

InstaEnglish **2nd Edition** is a fully flexible course, which means you can study using your physical or your digital books and have access to the exact same content and activities. The digital books contain all the audio tracks and videos embedded. The digital offerings include the **On-the-go Practice** feature, for you to keep learning wherever you are!

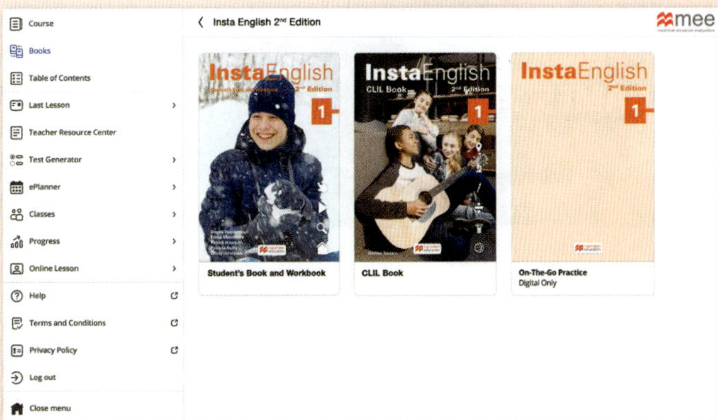

CONTENTS

Feelings and Opinions | Simple Present: *be* and *have* | Subject / Object Pronouns and Possessive Adjectives

STARTER

Introductions

1 Look at the picture above. How do they introduce themselves?

____

2 Complete the sentences below with the words in the box. Then listen and check your answers.
1

Australia cousin French going to the movies math swimming 14

a Hi. I'm Izzie. I'm __________ years old.

b Hello. I'm Will. I'm from __________.

c My name's Louise. I love ______________.

d Hi, my name's George. My favorite sport is __________.

e Hi, I'm Doug. This is my __________ Susie.

f I'm Susie. I'm __________.

Physical Description

3 Look at the picture again and describe the students using the words in the box.

blond brown curly square straight tall

a Izzie has __________ eyes.

b Susie has __________ hair.

c Izzie has __________ hair.

d Doug is __________.

e Will's face is __________.

f Louise and George have __________ hair.

4 Listen and repeat. Check your answers.
2

TIP

Possessive *'s / '*
Use *'s* after a name or singular noun.
Will's face is square.
Use *'* after a plural word ending in *-s*.
The students' faces look happy.

School Subjects and Free-time Activities

5 Listen to Izzie and Will and complete
3 the chart.

	favorite school subject	favorite free-time activities
Izzie	science,	
Will		
Louise		
George		
Doug		
Susie		

6 INTERFACE Work in pairs. Talk about your favorite school subjects.

What's your favorite subject?

I guess it's music. And yours?

Places in Town

7 Complete Susie's email with the words
4 from the box. Then listen and check.

gym library museum restaurant subway station

From: Susie
To: Will
Subject: About Paris

Dear Will,

The picture attached shows one of my favorite places in Paris: the Pompidou Center. It holds an amazing **a** __________ of modern art and a huge public **b** __________. It's very close to a **c** ______________ so it's pretty easy to get there. Just a few meters away there is this great **d** __________ where I usually have pasta with five cheese sauce. I'll definitely have to be serious about going to the **e** __________ when I come back lol!

XOXOXOXO,

Susie

pompidou.jpeg

Feelings and Opinions

8 Find 17 words related to feelings and opinions in the word search.

E	X	C	I	T	E	D	R	B	F	D
S	C	A	R	E	D	I	N	O	F	A
B	A	M	A	Z	I	N	G	R	U	N
I	N	T	E	R	E	S	T	I	N	G
A	G	E	A	S	Y	A	W	N	E	E
N	R	B	O	R	E	D	M	G	X	R
G	Y	W	O	R	R	A	S	P	C	O
R	J	E	A	L	J	L	A	L	I	U
W	O	R	R	I	E	D	V	E	T	S
N	E	R	T	S	A	C	A	A	I	E
I	N	T	I	L	L	I	X	S	N	M
S	N	E	R	V	O	U	S	E	G	B
B	O	R	E	G	U	S	O	D	P	A
E	X	C	D	I	S	T	D	A	L	R

9 Listen and check your answers.
5

Simple Present: *be* and *have*

10 Write true sentences with the affirmative or negative form of *be*.

a I __________ from Turkey.
b My best friend __________ 12 years old.
c We ______ in a math class.
d Madrid ______ the capital of the UK.

11 Choose the correct form of the verb *have*.

a I **have** / **has** two sisters and one brother.
b My father **have** / **has** a great sense of humor.
c She **have** / **has** really good ideas.
d They **have** / **has** new neighbors.

Subject / Object Pronouns and Possessive Adjectives

12 Underline the correct words. Then listen
6 and check your answers.

My friends and I love hanging out. **a** **We** / **Us** are always together. On weekends, my sister usually joins **b** **we** / **us**. My friends really like **c** **her** / **she**. **d** **Her** / **She** is really funny and I love having **e** **she** / **her** around. She is also very protective and takes really good care of **f** **I** / **me**.

1

FREE TIME

1

2

3

4

VOCABULARY 1

Free-time Activities

1 Read the words and phrases in the box. Then write the ones that correspond to the activities represented in pictures 1-6.

chat online	hang out with friends
do a martial art	learn a language
do volunteer work	play an instrument
do yoga	play video games
draw	read a book
go to the movies	relax

1 ______________________

2 ______________________

3 ______________________

4 ______________________

5 ______________________

6 ______________________

2 Listen and repeat.

7

3 Complete the sentences with the words and phrases from activity 1.

a I'm trying to ____________ to study abroad next year. I go to German classes twice a week.

b I ____________ on Mondays, Wednesdays, and Fridays in the morning.

c I do a lot of exercise. I often ____________ or ____________.

d I ____________ once a week. I visit people in hospital.

e I sometimes ____________ with my friends. We love pizza!

f I love technology. I often ____________ or ____________.

4 Listen to Megan and Dan. What is Megan's favorite free-time activity?

8

____

PRONUNCIATION

/ɑ/ /ɔ/ /oʊ/

1 Listen and repeat the words.

9

/ɑ/ v**o**lunteer, h**o**spital, **o**nline

/ɔ/ dr**aw**, sp**o**rt, b**o**ring

/oʊ/ g**o**, disc**o**, d**o**n't

2 Listen and repeat the sentences.

10

a I volunteer at a sports club.

b I don't want to go to the movies. It's boring.

c I often draw cartoons online.

d I don't play video games.

5

6

READING 1

1 Read the title and headings in the news article below. What do you think is the main idea of the text?

a Teen boys spend their free time differently than girls.

b Teen boys have more leisure time than girls.

READING STRATEGY

Use titles and headings to help you guess what the text is about.

The "leisure gap" between boys and girls

USA teenage girls do more homework and household chores than boys, says a new study by The Pew Research Center. According to the researchers, females do 38 minutes of housework daily, while boys spend about 24 minutes helping around the house. Girls also spend more time running errands, such as shopping for groceries (21 minutes *vs.* 11 minutes for boys). As a result, boys enjoy an average of about six hours a day in leisure time, while girls enjoy only five.

A busy teen girl speaks

Rebecca Snow, 15, is one of those girls with no time to have fun or play sports. "I'm always busy," says Rebecca. "When I get home from school, I usually prepare a meal for myself and my brother. In the afternoon, I sometimes vacuum the floor or do the laundry ... He never helps me! I hardly ever have free time. When I do, I usually practice judo. I wish I had more time to take guitar lessons or help at an animal shelter."

Need for gender equality

Sociologist Georgia Roberts, coordinator of the study, argues that a more equal division of household chores can benefit both male and female teenagers.

"Boys need to learn to cook and clean the house to gain autonomy. Girls need less pressure on them," Roberts explains.

2 11 Read and listen. According to the text, why do teen girls have less leisure time?

a Because they devote more time to homework and housework than boys.

b Because they are less interested in sport and entertainment than boys.

3 Read the text again. Then write T for *true* or F for *false*.

a ☐ Teen boys spend more time on homework than girls.

b ☐ Teen girls spend 14 minutes longer than boys doing housework.

c ☐ Teen boys have five hours more leisure time daily than girls.

d ☐ Rebecca Snows cooks for herself and her brother.

e ☐ In her free time, Rebecca takes guitar lessons.

4 According to Georgia Roberts' opinion, why does housework need to be shared equally?

____

____

5 CLASS VOTE In your home, are household chores shared equally?

GRAMMAR 1

Review: Simple Present and Present Progressive

	simple present
+	I often **meet** my friends on Saturdays. She **is** always tired after school.
–	She **doesn't** usually **have** time.
?	**Do** you usually **do** activities after school?

1 Complete the simple present rules below with the information in the box.

Do Does doesn't / does not don't / do not -s

a We add ______________ to the verb in the third person singular affirmative form.

b We make the negative form by adding ______________ before *I / you / we / they*.

c We make the negative form by adding ______________ before *he / she / it*.

d ______________ is used in questions before *I / you / we / they*.

e ______________ is used in questions before *he / she / it*.

2 When do we use the simple present? Check (✓) the correct definition.

☐ The simple present is used for actions and routines.

☐ The simple present is used for actions happening at the moment the person is speaking.

Adverbs of Frequency

3 Read the news article on page 13. Circle the words that describe how often people do things.

4 Look at the graphic below. Complete it with the following adverbs of frequency.

always ~~hardly ever~~ never often sometimes usually

100%

____

____

____

____

hardly ever

____

0%

5 Underline the correct words to complete the rules for the position of adverbs of frequency.

a Adverbs of frequency go **before / after** the main verb, except with the verb *be*.

b Adverbs of frequency go **before / after** the verb *be*.

6 Complete the sentences with the adverbs of frequency and the correct form of the verbs in parentheses.

I often play sports. (play / often)

a Jane ______________ her friends on weekends. (meet /always)

b My friends ______________ busy with homework. (be / sometimes)

c We ______________ to music. (listen / hardly ever)

d He ______________ to parties. (go / never)

e I ______________ at the mall with my friends. (not / hang out / usually)

f Daniel ______________. (volunteer / often)

g Do you ______________ to the gym? (go / sometimes)

	present progressive
+	I'm **watching** TV at the moment.
–	She **isn't studying** math this week.
?	**Are** you **chatting** online now?

7 Look at the sentences in the chart above. Then underline the correct option below to complete the rule for when we use the present progressive.

We use the present progressive for actions **happening now / habits and routines**.

Time Expressions

8 Complete the chart below with the time expressions used with the simple present and the present progressive.

~~always~~ at the moment every day now often this week twice a week usually

simple present	present progressive
always	

9 Complete the sentences with the correct form of the verbs in parentheses.

a I ________ (play) video games every day.

b At the moment, we ____________ (draw).

c He ________ (play) tennis twice a week.

d My mom and dad always ________ (relax) on Sunday evenings.

10 Complete the sentences with the correct form of the verbs in parentheses. Use the simple present or the present progressive.

Simon _isn't talking_ (not talk) about his free-time activities now.

a At the moment Karen ___________ (learn) French, she ___________ (not study) Spanish.

b He ________________ (not usually play) an instrument, but he often ___________ (go) to the gym.

c They ___________ (not do) anything complex at the moment, they ___________ (relax).

d I ___________ (not meet) my friends every day, I usually ___________ (see) them on weekends.

11 Read about what Meryl Streep does in her spare time. Underline the most appropriate verb form: simple present or present progressive.

The award-winning actor Meryl Streep **a loves / is loving** knitting. She says she hand knitted the shawl for the movie *Doubt*. Meryl **b is admitting / admits** that she usually **c spends / is spending** a lot of her free time on set knitting. She **d is believing / believes** the hobby is therapeutic. In her opinion, it is a way of gathering her thoughts and contemplating life. In fact, many actors, especially those who have spare time on set between takes, **e love / are loving** to spend their free time knitting. Some of them are Julia Roberts and Ryan Gosling.

12 INTERFACE Work in pairs. Use the prompts below to ask and answer questions.

a What / you / usually / do / on weekends?

____

b Where / you / usually / meet your friends?

____

c What / you / wear / now?

____

GRAMMAR GUIDE page 22

LISTENING

Sport

1 Look at the pictures and answer the questions.

a What sports are these?

____

b What equipment do you need to do each sport?

____

____

c Do you practice any of these sports?

____

2 12 Listen to an interview on free-time activities and underline the correct answers.

a Lucas is **12 / 13** years old.

b His favorite sport is **tennis / running**.

c He **always / sometimes** feels better after running really fast.

d At the moment things are going really **well / badly** for Lucas.

e Lucas meets his friends every **day / weekend**.

3 12 Listen again and write T for *true* or F for *false*.

a ☐ Lucas doesn't often go running.

b ☐ Lucas plays tennis every day.

c ☐ Lucas isn't feeling stressed now.

d ☐ Lucas plays tennis when he feels stressed.

e ☐ Lucas and his parents usually talk about any problems.

SPEAKING

Saturday Off

13 Jane and Rita are on an online video call. Listen and complete the dialogue.

Hi, Rita, what are you up to now?

a I'____________ for the math test on Monday.

Studying???? But it's Saturday!

What do you **b** ____________ do on Saturdays, Jane?

Well, I always **c** ____________, play tennis, and sometimes I go to the movies … How about you?

Well, I go swimming and, when I **d** ____________ to study for tests, I also go to the movies or read a book.

So how about going to the movies later on?

Sorry, Jane, but I really **e** ____________ to study … Oops, my dad's calling me for lunch! Talk to you later, OK?

Alright, bye for now!

Bye!

FUNCTIONAL LANGUAGE

Talking about Free Time on a Call

Questions

What are you up to now?
What do you do on … ?

Answers

I'm …
I usually / always / sometimes …

Speaking Task

Create an online dialogue between you and a classmate.

Step 1

Think of possible free-time activities and things going on at the moment of the dialogue.

going to the park

going to the movies

Step 2

Create questions to ask your classmate.

What are you doing now?
What do you do in your free time?

Plan possible answers.

I'm watching TV / helping around the house, etc.
I always / usually / sometimes play with my friends, travel, etc.

Step 3

Take turns practicing your dialogue with a classmate.

CULTURE

Spare Time in Australia

Australians love hobbies and pastimes where there isn't much planning involved. They often stay indoors, or "take it easy," as they usually say. Most of them (around 84%) like to spend their leisure time watching TV (streaming series, mostly) and 64% spend their time scrolling through social media.

The most enthusiastic *Aussies* (another way of referring to Australians), however, prefer to spend their free time outdoors having picnics and BBQing in the park with their family or friends, hiking, cycling, camping, admiring wild animals out in the country, among other things. As Australia is a country with fairly warm weather all year round, exploring the vast Aussie terrain is ideal most part of the year and, as a result, the younger generation are camping more and more.

Most of the population is settled along the coast. Therefore, everyone from little kids to teenagers to men and women take surfing quite seriously. Australia has beautiful surfing spots, which means that surfers have a lot of choice as to where to practice.

In Australia, there's a phrase that says, "work hard, play harder." That means if you work hard to pay your bills, you can play hard so that you can live life to the fullest. After all, when it comes to taking things easy, having fun is the most important thing.

1 Read and listen to what Australians like doing in their free time. Then answer the questions below.

14

a What do Aussies usually do indoors?

____

b How do they spend their free time outdoors?

____

c What's the weather like in Australia?

____

2 What do people like doing in their free time in your country? Complete the chart below.

indoors	outdoors

VOCABULARY 2

Character Adjectives

1 Listen and repeat the adjectives. Then underline the adjectives that describe the pictures.

15

a

cautious / adventurous

b

talkative / quiet

c

friendly / unsociable

d

generous / selfish

e

energetic / lazy

f

serious / funny

g

shy / confident

h

honest / dishonest

i

absentminded / observant

j

patient / impatient

2 Complete the description with the correct adjectives from activity 1.

My brother Pete has a lot of energy – he's very ___energetic___. I suppose that's why he's **a** ________ and loves exploring places like the Amazon. He has a lot of friends because he's very **b** ________ and he often pays for things for them because he's **c** ________ – he isn't **d** ________ at all. Sometimes he doesn't stop talking, he's very **e** ________. He isn't shy like me, he's very **f** ________, and he can make people laugh because he's **g** ________. We have some differences: while he's very **h** ________ and notices things around him easily, I'm a little **i** ________ and forget a lot of things. Besides, he's a **j** ________ person because he doesn't get upset in difficult situations, but I'm very **k** ________ and get annoyed when something doesn't happen the way I want.

READING 2

1 Look at the hobbies below. In your opinion, what characteristics does a fan of these hobbies have? Use the words from the **Vocabulary 2** section to write your ideas.

skydiving

a adventurous

fencing

b ______________

solving a Rubik's cube

c ______________

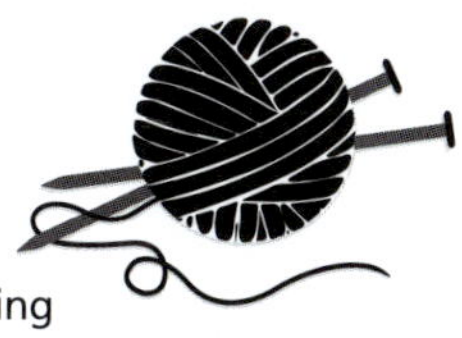
knitting

d ______________

doing magic

e ______________

2 Now look at the pictures in the magazine article in this page. Guess which celebrity does which hobby in activity 1.

a Fernando Alonso: ______________
b Justin Bieber: ______________
c Ryan Gosling: ______________
d Will Smith: ______________
e Nicole Kidman: ______________

3 Read and listen. Check your answers in activity 2.
16 🔊

CELEBRITY HOBBIES

You probably have a lot of hobbies, but what about these stars? What do they like doing in their free time? Read on and find out!

A magician needs to be confident and charismatic to gain the audience's attention. It seems that race car driver **Fernando Alonso** has these traits in spades. In his free time, he likes doing magic to entertain his friends.

This may surprise you, but Canadian singer **Justin Bieber** is an observant person who loves solving logical problems. His favorite game is the Rubik's cube. Through a lot of practice, Bieber is now able to completely solve a Rubik's cube in under 2 minutes.

Knitting is a relaxing hobby that teaches us to be patient and persevering. For actor **Ryan Gosling**, another advantage of practice is that you get something of it at the end. He learned how to knit on the set of *Lars and the Real Girl* and is now good at making scarves.

Actor **Will Smith** is a fencing enthusiast and often trains with his good pals Tom Cruise and David Beckham. Fencing is an ideal activity for energetic people, as well as developing coordination and balance. But you need to be well protected to avoid sword accidents!

Movie star **Nicole Kidman** is an adventurous and audacious person. She's really into practicing sports and she often goes skydiving. "I don't want to miss out on anything just because it's dangerous," she says. "I love skydiving, it's fantastic."

4 Go back to activity 1. Are the adjectives you chose mentioned in the text? What other character adjectives are mentioned?

____

____

5 CLASS VOTE Which of these celebrities' hobbies do you want to practice too?

GRAMMAR 2

Gerunds

1 Read the charts which show when we usually use gerunds.

after preference verbs
He **likes playing** tennis. She **hates going** skydiving.
after prepositions
I'm (not) **into drawing** cartoons. They're (not) interested **in reading** books. He's good / bad **at playing** the piano.

2 Read the sentences in activity 1 again. Check (✓) the correct information as to the use of gerunds.

a ☐ Gerunds are used after preference verbs such as *enjoy*, *like*, and *love*.

b ☐ Gerunds are used before prepositions such as *at*, *about*, *on*, *in*.

c ☐ Gerunds can be used after prepositions such as *at*, *about*, *on*, *in*.

3 Write sentences and questions using gerunds.

Peter / like / play tennis.
Peter likes playing tennis.

a Kate / good at / draw cartoons.
____

b you / enjoy / listen to music?
____

c We / not like / run.
____

d you / good at / learn languages?
____

e She / not interested in / go to the movies.
____

f you / love / do sports?
____

4 **INTERFACE** Work in pairs. Use the cues below to ask and answer questions.

Do you like playing tennis?

Yes, I do.

a you / enjoy / listen to music?
____

b you / like / play sports?
____

c you / good at / play / team sports?
____

d what / you / love / do / in your free time?
____

5 Read the text and underline the correct answers.

Kate and her friend Sam **a love traveling / love travel** all over the world. They like **b meet / meeting** people. Sam **c enjoys / hates** talking to everyone he meets. What does Kate like **d doing / do**? She's a history teacher so she **e doesn't like visiting / loves visiting** museums and ancient monuments. She's also very good at **f learning / learn** languages – she can speak four! She likes **g study / studying** science in her free time. Sam is not much **h into / bad at** doing a lot of activities – he enjoys relaxing!

GRAMMAR GUIDE page 22

CLIL

ART

BRINGING DRAWINGS INTO LIFE

Everyone is into animation movies or cartoons, but do you ever wonder how they are made?

To begin with, cartoons are a series of drawings or frames. Each frame is different, but only in a very small way. For example, imagine a stick figure whose hand changes position over six frames. When the frames are presented one after another very quickly, the stick figure waves its hand. This is *animation*, which literally means "bringing to life." However, the hand doesn't actually move. It just appears to move. This is because of an optical illusion called persistence of vision. Experts believe that an image persists in your vision for a split second after the original image disappears.

Making an animated movie is an incredibly long and laborious process. If you need 24 frames to film a second of a movie, you can imagine how long it takes to make a full-length animated movie like *Toy Story*!

1 Read and listen to the text above. What does the word *animation* mean? Write your answer.

17

____

2 Complete these sentences about animation with the words in the box.

different	drawings	long
moving	one	quickly

a A cartoon is a series of ______________.

b Each drawing is ______________ in a very small way.

c The drawings are shown one after the other very ______________.

d This gives the illusion that the drawing is ______________.

e You need 24 drawings to film ______________ second of a movie.

f It takes a ______________ time to make a full-length animated movie.

GRAMMAR GUIDE

Simple Present

- we use the simple present for habits and routines
- we form the simple present with the base form (e.g., *play, watch*) of the verb
- we add *-s* or *-es* to the verb with *he*, *she*, or *it*
- we form the negative with *do not (don't)* + the verb
- we use *does not (doesn't)* + the verb (without *-s* or *-es*) with *he*, *she*, or *it*

+	I / You **play**	tennis.
	He / She / It **plays**	
	We / You / They **play**	
–	I / You **don't play**	tennis.
	He / She / It **doesn't play**	
	We / You / They **don't play**	
?	**Do** I / you **play** tennis? Yes, I **do**. No, I **don't**.	
	Does he / she / it **play** tennis? Yes, he **does**. No, he **doesn't**.	
	Do we / you / they **play** tennis? Yes, we **do**. No, we **don't**.	

Present Progressive

- we use the present progressive to describe what is happening at the moment
- we form the present progressive with *be* + verb + *-ing*

+	I**'m drawing**.
	You**'re drawing**.
	He / She / It**'s drawing**.
	We / You / They**'re drawing**.
–	I**'m not drawing**.
	You **aren't drawing**.
	He / She / It **isn't drawing**.
	We / You / They **aren't drawing**.
?	**Is** he / she / it **drawing**? Yes, he **is**. No, he **isn't**.

Adverbs of Frequency

- adverbs of frequency go before the verb, but after the verb *to be*

100% always
usually
often
sometimes
hardly ever
0% never

Time Expressions

- with the simple present and the present progressive, time expressions (e.g., *once a week*, *every day*, *now*) usually go at the end of the phrase, but they can also go at the beginning

at the moment	everyday	now
on weekends	this year	twice a week

She never does homework **on weekends**.

We usually chat online **twice a week**.

On Mondays I do volunteer work.

Gerunds

- we use the gerund (*-ing* form) after verbs for like or dislike, and after prepositions

after preference verbs
He **likes playing** tennis. She **hates going** skydiving.
after prepositions
I'm (not) **into drawing** cartoons. They're (not) interested **in reading** books. He's good / bad **at playing** the piano.

PROGRESS CHECK

Name: ____________________

Class name / Period: ____________________

Teacher: ____________________

Date: ____________________

Free-time Activities

1 Match the words to form activities.

a	learn	[ ]	a book
b	do	[ ]	volunteer work
c	play	[ ]	cartoons
d	read	[ ]	online
e	chat	[ ]	yoga
f	draw	[a]	a language
g	do	[ ]	for a meal
h	go out	[ ]	tennis

Character Adjectives

2 Complete the sentences with the words in the box.

cautious	funny	generous	lazy	talkative

a Paul's ____________________, he often gives money to charities.

b Kevin is ____________________, he doesn't like trying new activities.

c Kate always makes me laugh, she's very ____________________.

d They're always on the telephone, they're very ____________________.

e He never wants to help at home – he's very ____________________.

Review: Simple Present and Present Progressive

3 Complete the sentences and questions. Use the simple present or the present progressive form of the verbs in parentheses.

a Sally ______________ (use) the computer every day.

b They ______________ (not play) sports on weekends.

c ______________ you ______________ (watch) TV at the moment?

d I ______________ (not relax) now.

e How often ______________ you ______________ (go) shopping?

f We ______________ (study) English three times a week.

g What ______________ your friends ______________ (do) now?

h Jamie ______________ (play) a video game at the moment.

Gerunds

4 Write sentences and questions using gerunds.

a Simon / interested in / play football?

____

b Simon / into / play video games.

____

c Maggie / like / play tennis?

____

d Maggie / not into / read books.

____

e Tim and Sue / hate / go shopping.

____

f What / Tim and Sue / enjoy / do?

____

Grammar Buildup 1

1 2 3 4 5 6 7 8

5 Choose the correct words.

To: Sam
From: Jane
Subject: All about me

Hi! My name's Jane. I'm American, but I **a don't live / doesn't live** in the USA, I **b lives / live** in Canada. I go to high school in my town. At the moment I **c study / 'm studying** a lot because we have exams soon. What **d do I usually / do usually I** do in my free time? Well, I **e go / am going** swimming once a week. I love **f meet / meeting** my friends on weekends. I really enjoy **g draw / drawing** and I'm good **h in / at** art.

Write soon!

Jane

VOCABULARY IN PICTURES

Free-time Activities

chat online

do a martial art

do volunteer work

do yoga

draw

go out for a meal

go to the gym

go to the movies

hang out with friends

learn a language

play an instrument

play video games

read a book

relax

Character Adjectives

adventurous

cautious

friendly

unsociable

energetic

lazy

shy

confident

talkative

quiet

generous

selfish

serious

funny

honest

dishonest

absentminded

observant

patient

impatient

2

HOUSE AND HOME

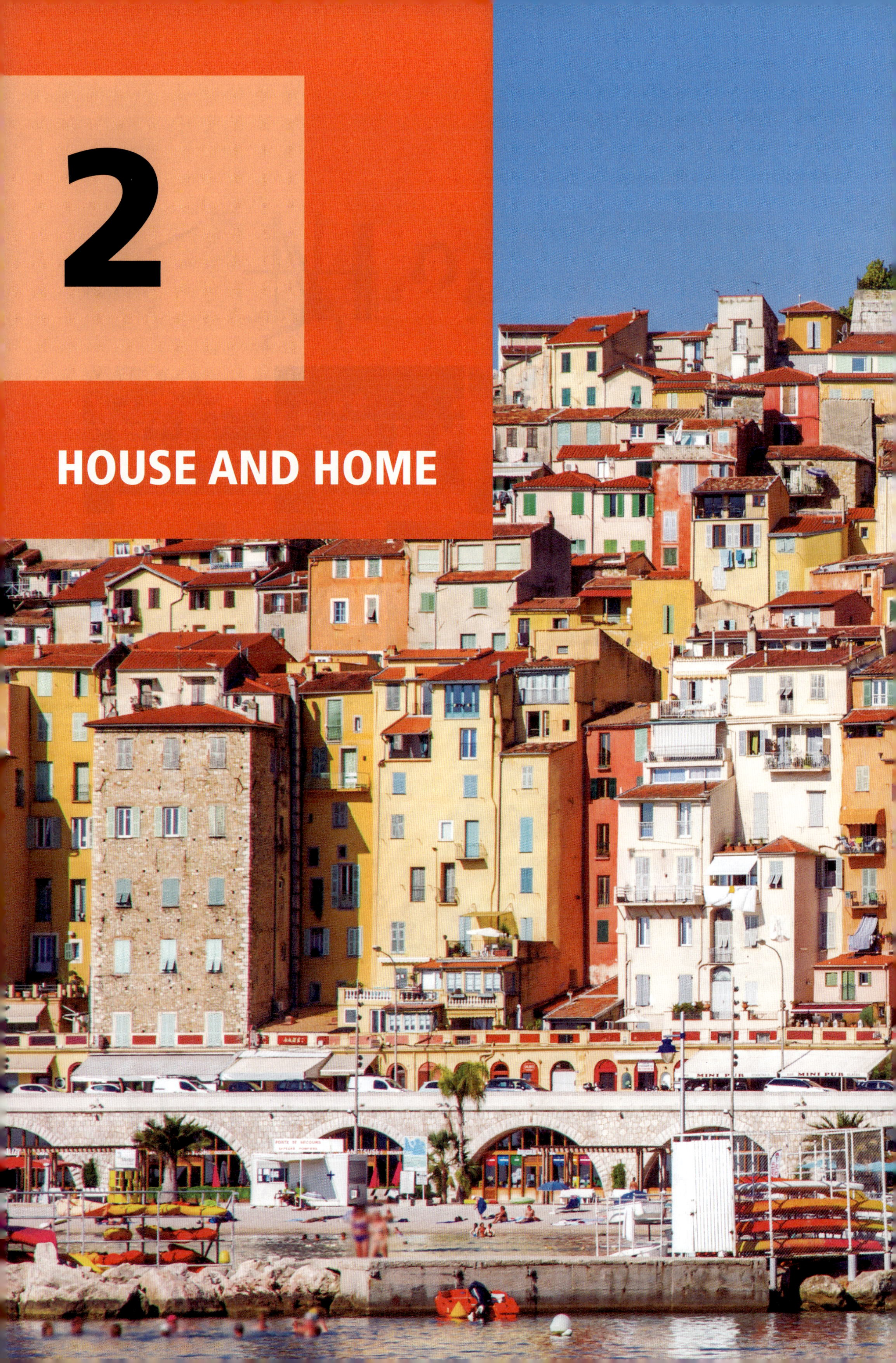

VOCABULARY 1

Rooms and Furniture

1 Match pictures 1-8 with the words in the box. Mark an X next to the words that are not in the pictures.

armchair ☐ bed ☐ bookcase ☐
cabinet ☐ chair ☐ desk ☐ lamp ☐
mirror ☐ sofa ☐ stove ☐
table ☐ toilet ☐ wardrobe ☐

2 Listen and repeat.

18

3 Which piece of furniture in activity 1 goes in each room below?

a bathroom: ______________________

b bedroom: ______________________

c dining room: ______________________

d kitchen: ______________________

e living room: ______________________

____

6

7

8

READING 1

1 Skim the text and match headings a-c with paragraphs 1-3.

a The 1980s apartments
b The 1850s Victorian terrace
c The 1950s semi

2 The text is a / an:

a opinion article. **b** textbook article.

3 Read and listen to the text. Choose the correct options below.

19

a The houses on a street are …
1 often different. **2** very similar.

b Victorian houses usually have …
1 short windows. **2** big rooms.

c The 1950s semi often has …
1 neighbors on one side. **2** a garage.

d A 1980s apartment normally has …
1 a bathroom. **2** a balcony.

4 Scan the text and answer the questions.

a Why do Victorian terraces have fireplaces?

____

____

b What type of house is popular in three countries?

____

c Why were apartments popular in the 1980s?

____

5 CLASS VOTE Which type of house would you prefer to live in?

HISTORY ON THE STREETS

On a street, there is often a variety of houses from very different periods of history.

1 ______________________

The Victorian era was the start of industrial Britain, and industry and jobs were in the cities. There are millions of terraced houses in Britain from that era. They're popular because they often have big rooms with large windows. There's a fireplace in each room because, in the 1850s, there wasn't any electric or gas heating. In a "two-up-two-down" house, there were two bedrooms upstairs, a kitchen and a living room downstairs. The toilet was outside. Victorian terraces have neighbors on both sides.

2 ______________________

Semi-detached houses have neighbors on one side only. They are a popular type of home in England, Australia, and Canada. A 1950s semi usually has a kitchen, a large living room, and dining room downstairs. Upstairs, there are two or three bedrooms, and a bathroom with a toilet and bath. There were cars on the roads in the 1950s, so these houses usually have a garage too.

3 ______________________

In the 1980s, there were more young people who weren't married and didn't live with their parents. Their jobs were stressful, it wasn't an easy life, so they didn't want a garden to work on during the weekend. As a consequence, apartments were popular. In these apartments, there are normally one or two bedrooms, a living room, a bathroom, and a kitchen. There isn't a garden or a balcony, but in the 1980s everyone had a car, so there's usually a garage.

GRAMMAR 1

be: Simple Past

1 Read the sentences below. Underline the verb *be* in the simple past in each sentence.

a The Victorian era was the start of industrial Britain.

b The toilet was outside.

c Their jobs were stressful.

d Many young people weren't married.

e It wasn't an easy life.

2 Match items a-c with the options below to complete the rules about the simple past of *be*. Then complete the chart.

a *Was* is the simple past affirmative form of *be* with ...

b *Were* is the simple past affirmative form of *be* with ...

c The negative simple past forms of *be* are ...

☐ *we, you, they*.

☐ *was not* or *wasn't* / *were not* or *weren't*.

☐ *I, he, she, it*.

affirmative
I ________ outside.
You ________ at home.
He / She / It ________ in the kitchen.
We / You / They ________ popular.

negative
I ________ at school.
You ________ in the living room.
He / She / It ________ inside.
We / You / They ________ in the garden.

3 Complete the sentences with *was* or *were*.

a Igloos ________ the traditional houses of the Inuit people.

b Snow ________ the traditional material for igloos in Canada and Greenland.

c In other Arctic areas, bone ________ the main material.

d Small igloos ________ temporary houses.

e A big, permanent igloo ________ traditionally the home of about twenty people!

4 Complete the text with the simple past form of *be*.

Historically, the tepee **a** ________ the traditional home of Native Americans from the Great Plains. They **b** ________ dry during the rain, and they **c** ________ (not) hot in summer.

The tepee **d** ________ perfect for these nomadic tribes because it **e** ________ durable and it **f** ________ (not) heavy.

5 Read the sentences in the chart below. How do you form the short answers?

____

questions and short answers
Was I at home at 3pm? Yes, I **was**. / No, I **wasn't**.
Were you here last week? Yes, you **were**. / No, you **weren't**.
Was he / she / it in the kitchen? Yes, he / she / it **was**. / No, he / she / it **wasn't**.
Were we / you / they at school? Yes, we / you / they **were**. / No, we / you / they **weren't**.

6 Choose the correct information to complete the rules.

a In questions, *was* and *were* come **before** / **after** the subject.

b In short answers, sentences end with **the subject** / ***was, were, wasn't,*** **or** ***weren't***.

7 Complete the questions with the simple past form of *be*. Then answer the questions below.

a ________ the toilet inside the house during the Victorian era?
(✗) ______________________________

b ________ jobs and industry in the cities?
(✓) ______________________________

c ________ most young people married?
(✗) ______________________________

PRONUNCIATION

was / were

20 **1** Listen to the sentences. Do you hear *was* or *were*?

a ________ **c** ________

b ________ **d** ________

20 **2** Listen again and repeat.

8 **INTERFACE** Work in pairs. Ask and answer questions using *be* in the simple past and the cues below.

Yesterday at 9pm …

a you / at home? ______________________________

b you / in bed? ______________________________

c your parents / in the living room?
____

d your best friend / at school?
____

TIP

Use these time expressions with the simple past: *last* (*week, Saturday*), *ago* (*a year, one month*), *on* (*Monday, Tuesday*), *in* (*the winter, 2009*).

9 Complete the sentences with time expressions so that they are true for you. Use *last*, *ago*, *on*, and *in*.

a I was at home ______________________________.

b My family and I were in the kitchen together
______________________________.

c My best friend wasn't in class
______________________________.

d My friends and I weren't at school
______________________________.

GRAMMAR GUIDE page 38

LISTENING

16th-century Houses

1 Alex and Emily are talking about houses for rich and poor people in the 16th century. Before you listen, complete the chart below with the words in the box.

beds carpets chairs clocks toilets

	there were	there weren't
rich houses		
poor houses		

2 Listen and check your answers.

21

3 Listen again. Then write T for *true* or F for *false*.

21

a ☐ There were two rooms in a poor family's house.

b ☐ The beds were comfortable in all houses.

c ☐ Chairs were very expensive.

d ☐ There were carpets on the floor in rich people's houses.

e ☐ Poor children were often late for school.

Cultural fact

In the 16th century, glass was very expensive. If there were a lot of glass windows in a house, the family was very rich!

SPEAKING

At the Library

22 Samuel and Rick are doing a school research project about Aboriginal houses in the past. Listen and complete the dialogue.

They say here that Australian Aborigines were **a** ______________ a long time ago.

Yeah, they **b** _______ kind of campers. Some of their **c** _______ were usually leaning branches against each other like a dome. They were called *gunyas*.

The info here is that this **d** _______ common in the arid interior.

And in wet seasons? Were shelters different?

Yes, they were. In wet seasons, **e** _______ in sandstone were the most common Aboriginal **f** __________.

Look at this: **g** _______ was always present around *gunyas* as it **h** _______ used to drive away snakes and mosquitoes and other insects as well as for cooking and heating.

To sum up, the climate, the natural environment, and the family size **i** __________ all factors to consider when building a house.

They **j** __________ really city people ...

FUNCTIONAL LANGUAGE

Talking about a School Research

Speaker 1

They say here that ...
They were called ...
This was common in ...
Were houses different / big / small / made of ... ?

Speaker 2

Look at this. Fire was always ...
It was / wasn't used to ...
They were / weren't really ...

Speaking Task

Join a classmate and plan a conversation about a school research project.

Step 1

Think about one of these subjects.

Cities in your country.
Home types in your city / country.
Farm houses in your city / country.

Step 2

Plan what you ask. Take notes of statements / questions about the subject.

Farm houses were made of ...
They were ...
The toilet was ...
Was (the kitchen) ... ?
Were the rooms of the house ... ?
A wood burning stove was ...

Step 3

Talk to your classmate about your school research project. Change roles asking and answering questions.

CULTURE

Scotland's Blackhouses

Thatched buildings are an iconic part of Scotland's heritage and historic environment, especially in rural areas such as the Highlands.

Hundreds of years ago, thatched houses were called blackhouses in Scotland. They were built with stones packed with earth. They were not high: the corners of the construction were rounded, and the thatch was secured by a rope netting and weighed down with stones because of the windy weather in the area. Usually, there was just one door.

The thatched roof, the first roofing material in Scotland, was made with heather (a flowering plant) or broom (a tall and robust shrub). Along with a central hearth (fireplace), it helped keep the house warmed. There was no chimney for the smoke to escape through so it made its way through the roof and contributed to making the walls turn black, and therefore the adoption of the name blackhouse.

The blackhouse was used to accommodate people and animals. People lived at one end and animals at the other end, with a partition between them. Part of the blackhouse was also used to store grains and other products.

Nowadays, there are several restored blackhouses in some parts of Scotland and others which were turned into museums.

1 Read and listen to the information about Scottish blackhouses. Then write T for *true* or F for *false*.

23

a ☐ Hundreds of years ago there were blackhouses in the southeast of England.

b ☐ The roofs of blackhouses were built with stones, just like the walls.

c ☐ The thatched roof of blackhouses was made with heather or broom.

d ☐ All blackhouses had a central hearth which helped warm the house and whose smoke turned the walls black.

e ☐ People and animals shared the same space inside a blackhouse. They were only separated by a partition.

2 What were country houses like in your country 200 years ago?

To answer the question, take into account:

- The material used to build them.
- The size of country houses.
- The number of people who lived in the house.
- The heating system.

____

____

____

____

3 Share your findings with the class and compare them to your classmates' answers. Write down any new information.

____

____

____

VOCABULARY 2

Gadgets

1 Match pictures 1-6 with the words in the box. Mark an X next to the words that are not represented by the pictures.

dishwasher ☐	electric toothbrush ☐	fridge ☐	headphones ☐	laptop ☐
microwave ☐	remote control ☐	smartphone ☐	smartwatch ☐	washing machine ☐

1

2

3

4

5

6

2 Listen and repeat.

24

3 Complete the sentences using words from activity 1.

a A ______________ cleans clothes.

b You use a ______________ to change channels on the TV.

c A __________ is a portable computer.

d In addition to making calls like a telephone, the ______________ has many other functions.

e You use a __________ to heat or cook food.

f You use ______________ to listen to music without disturbing others.

4 Read the words in activity 1 again. In your opinion, which gadgets are the most useful? Why?

____

____

____

____

5 **INTERFACE** Work in pairs. Compare your lists of useful gadgets.

What do you think of the remote control?

I think it's very useful! What about the microwave? Personally I don't use it very often.

READING 2

1 Skim the text quickly and answer the following questions.

a This text is an example of:

1 ☐ an online wiki encyclopedia entry. **2** ☐ a blog post.

b The words in blue are:

1 ☐ keywords. **2** ☐ hyperlinks.

scholarpedia.org/toothbrush

SCHOLARPEDIA

the peer-reviewed open-access encyclopedia

Main page
About
Propose a new article
Instructions for authors
Random article
FAQs
Help
Blog

Contents [hide]

Toothbrush

A **toothbrush** is a device composed of bristles set into a handle that is used for cleaning the teeth. It is usually used with toothpaste.

History

Toothbrushes existed thousands of years ago in Egypt, but they were very different. There wasn't any plastic or nylon, so the ancient Egyptians collected pieces of wood from trees and used them to brush their teeth.
The modern toothbrush appeared in the 15th century. First, the Chinese invented brushes with hair from pigs, then Europeans copied this idea but with horse hair.
In 1935, the chemist Wallace Carothers invented nylon, and the first nylon toothbrushes arrived in Europe from the USA in 1938.
Switzerland produced an experimental electric toothbrush in 1939, but there weren't any electric toothbrushes in stores until the 1960s.
Modern electric toothbrushes appeared in 1987.

Types of toothbrush

The main types of toothbrush are:

- **Manual toothbrush** – it is the most common type worldwide. There are differences in the stiffness of the bristles, which can be hard or soft.
- **Electric toothbrushes** – these brushes are usually costlier, but in return they promote more efficient cleaning.
- **Interdental brush** – it is a brush designed specifically for cleaning between teeth and between the wires of dental braces and teeth.
- **Eco-friendly toothbrush** – they appeared in the 2010s to reduce the plastic waste generated by common toothbrushes. They are made using biodegradable materials such as bamboo and natural bristles.

2 Read and listen. Then label with words from the text.

25

a ______________

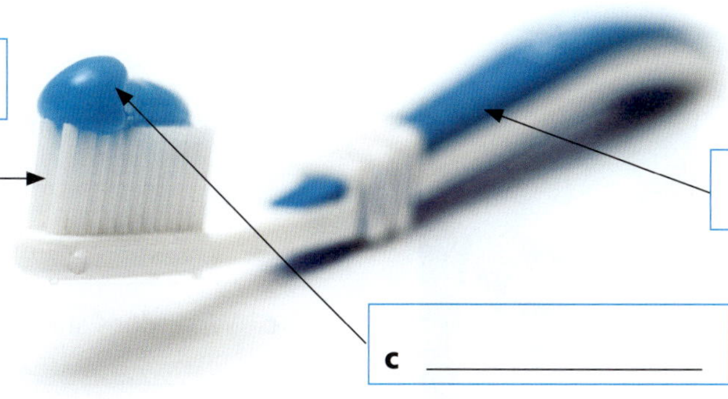

b ______________

c ______________

3 Read the text again. Who invented the modern toothbrush?

____
____
____

4 Underline the correct words. Return to the text whenever necessary.

a There **were** / **weren't** toothbrushes thousands of years ago.

b The first toothbrush **was** / **wasn't** made of plastic and nylon.

c There **were** / **weren't** modern toothbrushes in the 15th century.

d There **were** / **weren't** nylon toothbrushes in Europe before 1938.

e There **were** / **weren't** electric toothbrushes in stores in the 1960s.

f There **were** / **weren't** eco-friendly toothbrushes in the 20th century.

GRAMMAR 2

there was / there were

1 Read the sentences below and circle the nouns that come after *there was*, *there wasn't*, *there were*, and *there weren't*.

a There wasn't plastic or nylon thousands of years ago.

b There was a toothbrush which was made of wood in ancient Egypt.

c There weren't electric toothbrushes in stores until the 1960s.

d There were brushes with hair from pigs in the 15th century.

2 Complete the rules for the use of *there was* and *there were*. Use the words in the box.

plural singular uncountable

After *there was* and *there wasn't*, use a countable noun in the ______________ or an ______________ noun. After *there were* and *there weren't*, use a countable noun in the ______________.

3 Read the article about the invention of the telephone. Complete it with *there was*, *there wasn't*, *there were*, or *there weren't*.

www.greatinventions.com

At the beginning of the 1800s, **a** ________________ a very successful communication system: the telegraph. However, **b** ________________ the possibility of sending and receiving more than one message at a time. Around 1870, **c** ________________ a man who noted the possibility of transmitting more than one message along the same wire at one time: Alexander Graham Bell. **d** ________________ lots of attempts and **e** ________________ many people who believed it could be possible, but, finally, on March 10th, 1876, the first telephone call was a success.

4 Underline the correct forms of *there was / there were* in the questions and answers provided.

a **Was there / There was** a successful communication system at the beginning of the 1800s?

Yes, **there were / there was**.

b **Was there / There was** the possibility of sending and receiving more than one message at a time?

Yes, **there were / there was**.

c **Were there / Was there** a lot of attempts?

Yes, **there were. / there wasn't**.

GRAMMAR GUIDE page 38

WRITING

An Interview for a Magazine

1 EXPLORING THE CONTEXT

1 Skim the text on page 37 quickly. Who is Molly Dale?

2 26 Now read and listen. Then answer the questions.

a What is Molly's favorite room?

____

____

b What is there in her room?

____

____

____

c What does she usually do in there?

____

____

____

3 Read the interviewer's first line again: "Molly, tell us about your new apartment." How does the interviewer know that Molly's living in a new apartment? Circle the most likely reason.

a They are friends.

b They exchanged some information before the interview.

My Favorite Room

We want to know from our readers what their favorite room is! To participate, write to contact@houseandhomemagazine.com

This week's interviewee is Molly Dale, 16, from New Haven (Connecticut). She and her family now live in a spacious apartment downtown.

House and Home Magazine: Molly, tell us about your new apartment.

Molly Dale: My favorite room is my bedroom. When I was little, we lived in a small apartment. There wasn't a dining room and there were only three bedrooms so I shared a bedroom with my sister. Now I have my own room because our new apartment has four bedrooms. I love it!

House and Home Magazine: Can you describe your bedroom?

Molly Dale: I have the usual things in my bedroom such as a big desk, a green chair, and an enormous wardrobe. I also have fantastic posters on the wall. My favorite piece of furniture is my bed, of course. I often sit in my bedroom on my own and I listen to music. I also read magazines, but I don't like studying on my own – it's boring.

2 PLANNING

1 Imagine you work for *House and Home Magazine*. You will interview a classmate for the "My Favorite Room" section.

2 You will conduct the interview via email or a messaging app. Plan questions on the following to get information from your classmate:

- where he or she lives (apartment or house, in which neighborhood, for how long);
- what his or her favorite room is;
- what the room is like.

3 You will also be interviewed by your classmate. So think about how you will answer these questions and make notes.

3 WRITING

1 Write the questions for your classmate. On your turn to be interviewed, write down your answers.

2 In both situations, use your notes from Step 2 and the interview on this page to help you. When describing your favorite room, try to include some adjectives.

3 Ask your classmate to send you a picture of his or her favorite room and send him or her a picture too.

4 CHECKING & EDITING

1 Make a clean copy of your questions and your classmate's answers.

2 Correct spelling mistakes and insert your classmate's picture next to the text.

5 SHARING

1 Using a file-sharing service, gather all the interviews.

2 Read and comment on your classmates' interviews. What's the most popular room in the house among classmates? What's the most common furniture?

LANGUAGE FOCUS

Using Adjectives in a Description

Use adjectives in your writing to give more detail about what you are describing:

*We lived in a **small** apartment.*

*… a **big** desk, a **green** chair, an **enormous** wardrobe …*

1 Look at the adjectives above. Then answer the questions.

a Do adjectives go before the noun? ________

b Do adjectives have a plural form? ________

2 Rewrite the sentences including the adjectives in parentheses.

a I also have two lamps. (small)

____

____

b There are two bookcases. (white)

____

____

GRAMMAR GUIDE

be: Simple Past

affirmative	
I **was** You **were** He / She / It **was** We **were** You **were** They **were**	on the sofa.

- we use *was* / *were* to describe situations in the past
  He **was** at home yesterday.
  They **were** in Paris three weeks ago.

negative	
I **wasn't** (was not) You **weren't** (were not) He / She / It **wasn't** (was not) We **weren't** (were not) You **weren't** (were not) They **weren't** (were not)	at home.

- we use *not* to form the negative
  She **wasn't (was not)** in the kitchen.

questions		short answers	
		affirmative	negative
Was I **Were** you **Was** he / she / it **Were** we **Were** you **Were** they	in the kitchen?	Yes, I **was**. Yes, you **were**. Yes, he / she / it **was**. Yes, we **were**. Yes, you **were**. Yes, they **were**.	No, I **wasn't**. No, you **weren't**. No, he / she / it **wasn't**. No, we **weren't**. No, you **weren't**. No, they **weren't**.

- the word order is different in questions
  You **were** at home yesterday.
  Were you at home yesterday?

there was / there were

affirmative
There was a narrow boat here.
There were five chairs.

negative
There wasn't (**was not**) any heating.
There weren't (**were not**) any cars.

questions and short answers
Was there a movie theater in your town? Yes, there **was**. / No, there **wasn't**.
Were there any newsstands? Yes, there **were**. / No, there **weren't**.

Name: ______________________

Class name / Period: ______________________

Teacher: ______________________

Date: ______________________

PROGRESS CHECK

Rooms and Furniture

1 Name the room depicted in the room plan below. Then name each piece of furniture.

____

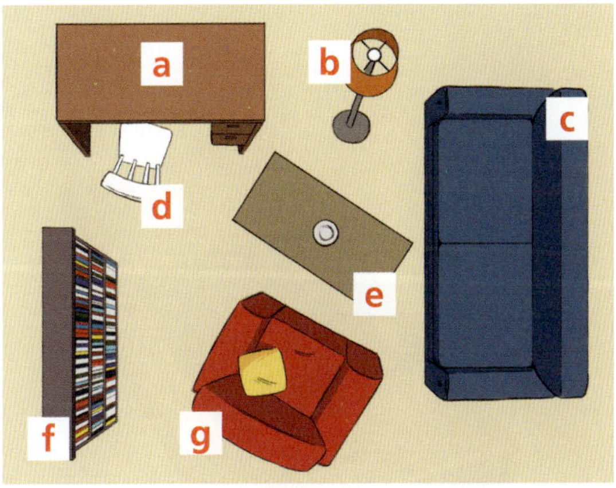

a ______________________

b ______________________

c ______________________

d ______________________

e ______________________

f ______________________

g ______________________

Gadgets

2 Match the columns to make words for gadgets.

a	micro	☐	phone
b	remote	☐	top
c	smart	☐	watch
d	lap	☐	wave
e	washing	☐	phones
f	dish	☐	control
g	electric	☐	toothbrush
h	head	☐	washer
i	smart	☐	machine

3 Label the gadgets below with words from activity 2.

a 

____

b 

____

c 

____

d 

____

be: Simple Past (*there was / there were*)

4 Complete the dialogue with *was / were* or *wasn't / weren't*.

Penny **a** ______________________ houses very different in the 16th century?

Graham Yes, they **b** ______________________.

Penny **c** ______________________ there any rooms?

Graham Yes, there **d** ______________________ a kitchen.

Penny Anything else? **e** ______________________ there a living room?

Graham Yes, there **f** ______________________, but there **g** ______________________ any toilets.

Penny Oh, dear. **h** ______________________ there any bedrooms?

Graham No, there **i** ______________________. The beds **j** ______________________ in the living room.

Penny Oh, so it **k** ______________________ really different times!

Grammar Buildup 2

1 2 3 4 5 6 7 8

5 Complete the dialogue with the correct form of the verbs in parentheses in simple present or simple past.

Charlotte What's that on your desk? It **a** ____________ (not be) there last week.

William This? It **b** ____________ (be) a telephone.

Charlotte But it's got a cable and there **c** ____________ (not be) any buttons!

William I know. There **d** ____________ (not be) any phones without cables in the past and there **e** ____________ (be) a dial on the phone, not buttons.

Charlotte Great!

William There **f** ____________ (be) also an old remote control on my desk. My dad says he watched a lot of TV when he **g** ____________ (be) young. He remembers the day the remote control arrived. He changed the channel every five seconds until his dad shouted at him. His dad **h** ____________ (be) really angry.

Charlotte I can imagine!

VOCABULARY IN PICTURES

Rooms and Furniture

bathroom

mirror

toilet

bedroom

bed

wardrobe

dining room

chair

table

kitchen

cabinet

stove

living room

armchair

bookcase

desk

lamp

sofa

Gadgets

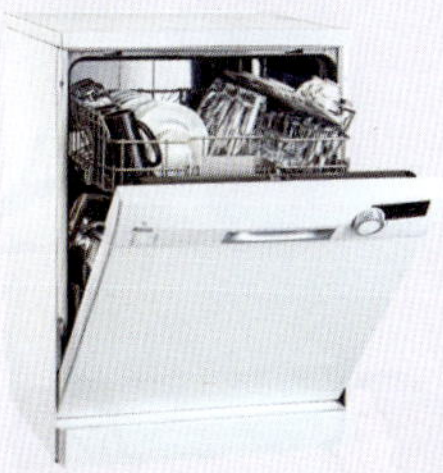
dishwasher

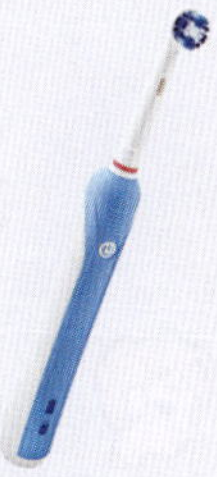
electric toothbrush

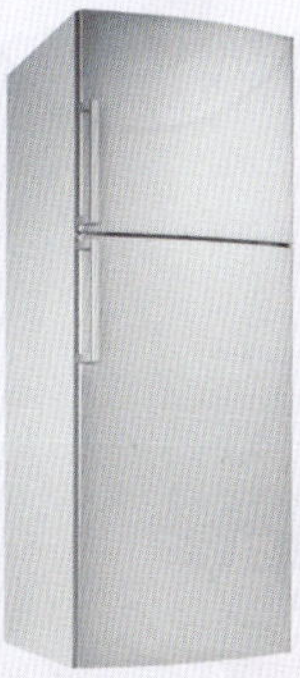
fridge

headphones

laptop

microwave

remote control

smartphone

smartwatch

washing machine

REVIEW 1

VOCABULARY

1 e ___ ___ ___ g e t ___ c
2 h ___ n ___ ___ t
3 t ___ ___ k ___ ___ ___ ___ e
4 s ___ y
5 q ___ ___ ___ t
6 d ___ m ___ ___ ___ ___ ___ l ___ ___ t
7 r ___ ___ ___ x
8 d ___ ___ w
9 d ___ ___ k
10 l ___ ___ p
11 b ___ ___ k s h ___ ___ f
12 c h ___ ___ o ___ l ___ n ___
13 t ___ ___ t h b ___ ___ s h
14 m ___ ___ ___ ___ r
15 p ___ ___ ___ an i ___ ___ t r ___ ___ ___ n t
16 b ___ ___
17 w ___ ___ d ___ ___ b ___
18 r ___ ___ d a b ___ ___ k
19 p ___ ___ y v ___ ___ ___ o g ___ ___ ___
20 w ___ s h ___ ___ g m ___ ___ ___ ___ ___ e
21 c ___ b ___ ___ ___ t
22 s t ___ ___ e

7
8
9
10
11
12
13
14
15
16
17
18
19
20
21
22

REVIEW 1

GRAMMAR

Simple Present

1 Complete the sentences with the simple present form of the verbs in parentheses.

Leo ___watches___ (watch) the news at 10pm.

a I __________ (not eat) meat.

b My father __________ (relax) on weekends.

c __________ her friend __________ (speak) English? Yes, she __________.

d Emma __________ (do) volunteer work.

e Fernando __________ (not eat) curry.

f __________ your mom __________ (speak) French? No, she __________.

g My grandparents __________ (play) video games.

Adverbs of Frequency

2 Rewrite the sentences using the adverbs of frequency in parentheses.

You play tennis after school. (often)
You often play tennis after school.

a I walk to school. (always)
____

b They go to the movies. (rarely)
____

c Clara is unsociable. (sometimes)
____

d We chat online. (every day)
____

e She walks to school. (hardly ever)
____

f Tom eats dairy products. (never)
____

Present Progressive and Time Expressions

3 Underline the correct options.

They **is** / **<u>are</u>** driving to the movies.

a She **'m** / **'s** listening to music now.

b You **are** / **am** playing an old violin.

c Ben **am** / **is** sleeping at the moment.

d I **'s** / **'m** having lunch right now.

e Max and I **am** / **are** doing our homework.

4 Rewrite the sentences in activity 3 using the negative form.

They aren't driving to the movies.

a __________

b __________

c __________

d __________

e __________

5 Write the missing words.

"Are ___you___ having a good time?"
"Yes, I am."

a "Is he watching a movie?"
"No, he __________."

b "Are your parents chatting?"
"Yes, __________ are."

c "__________ Tanya swimming?"
"Yes, she is."

d "Are you enjoying the movie?"
"No, I'm __________."

e "__________ you and Dan relaxing?"
"Yes, we are."

Gerunds

6 Write the gerund (*-ing* form) of the verbs below.

play playing

a make ______

b draw ______

c chat ______

d learn ______

e go ______

f try ______

be: Simple Past

7 Complete the sentences with the simple past form of *be*.

I was in the kitchen at 8am.

a My sister ______ in the bathroom at 1am.

b They ______ at school yesterday.

c We ______ at the beach last weekend.

d Mick ______ behind the classroom door.

8 Rewrite the sentences in the negative form.

I was in the kitchen.
I wasn't in the kitchen.

a We were on the table.
______

b My friends were at the movies.
______

c My cousin was in Omaha.
______

d I was in front of the bank.
______

e We were across from the restaurant.
______

f We were in the park.
______

9 Write questions in the simple past. Then write short answers.

you / at home last night ? ✓
Were you at home last night?
Yes, I was.

a your classmates / at the movies yesterday ✓
______
______

b Paula / in the mall at 10am? ✗
______
______

c we / in our math class at 12pm? ✗
______
______

d Oscar / at the gym two days ago? ✓
______
______

there was / there were

10 Underline the correct options.

There was / **There were** two big cabinets.

a **There was** / **There were** a bookcase.

b **There wasn't** / **There weren't** any cell phones.

c **Was there** / **Were there** a beautiful beach there?

d **Was there** / **Were there** a movie theater in my town?

e No, **there wasn't** / **there weren't** any movie theaters in my town.

f **There was** / **There were** a headphone in my bag.

g **Was there** / **Were there** some gadgets in this store?

h No, **there wasn't** / **there weren't** a smartphone in my bed.

i Yes, **there was** / **there were** a smartwatch on the desk.

Information Seeking Strategies

A Compass To Find Your Way

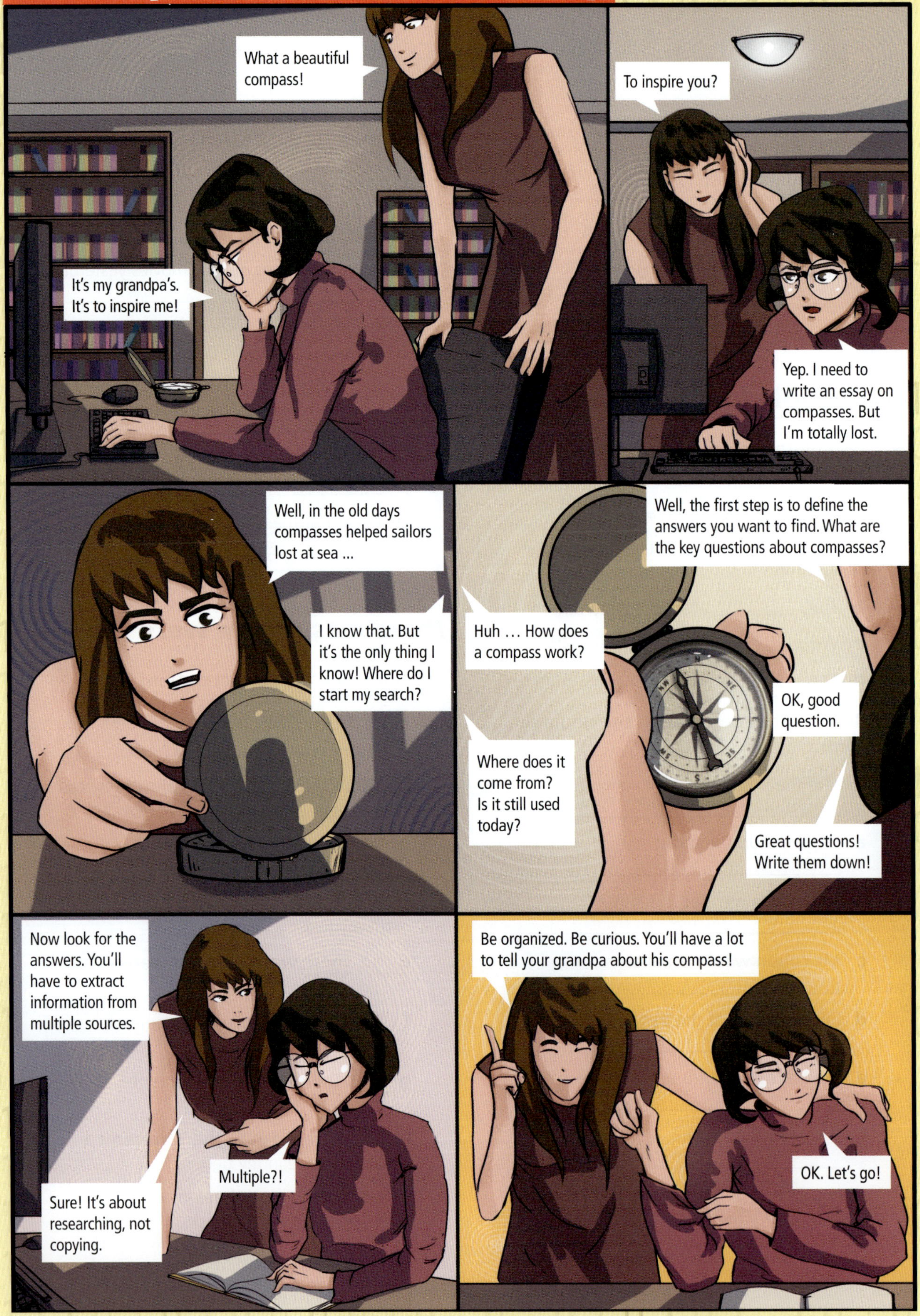

1 Read and listen. Then match the sentences.

27

a Lily is in the library because …

b Lily has her grandpa's compass …

c The librarian helps Lily by …

d According to the librarian, the first step is …

e At first, Lily doesn't like …

f At the end of the story, …

☐ to define the information you need.

☐ guiding her on how to seek information.

☐ the idea of searching for multiple sources.

☐ she needs to write an essay.

☐ Lily is excited about the task.

☐ for inspiration.

2 The librarian encourages Lily to be **organized** and **curious**. What other skills does a student need to have when seeking information to complete a school assignment? Circle all that apply.

creativity	critical thinking	hurry
indifference	laziness	persistence

3 Work with a classmate. Number the steps below for an effective information search process.

☐ Locate and select appropriate sources.

☐ Check and edit your work.

☐ Extract relevant information from multiple sources.

1 Define the information you need.

☐ Write your own text, without copying.

4 Now discuss the questions below. Present your ideas to your classmates.

a When looking for information for a school assignment, do you usually follow the process in activity 3? If not, what do you do differently?

b In your opinion, what is the biggest challenge for a student when searching for information?

c Can the process in activity 3 help? Why? Why not?

3

TRAVEL

1

2

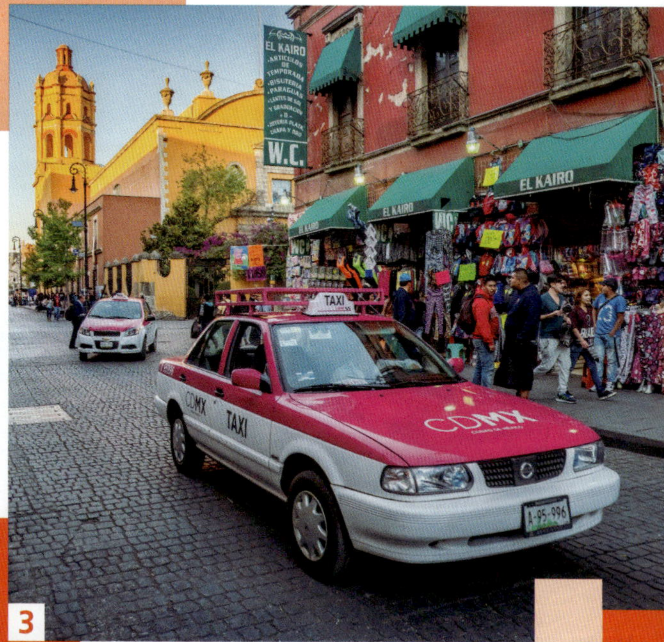

3

4

VOCABULARY 1

Transportation

1 Complete the chart below with the words in the box. Write each word under the corresponding topic.

~~bike~~ boat bus car motorcycle plane streetcar taxi train truck

land	water	air
bike		

2 Listen and repeat.

28

3 INTERFACE Work in pairs. Ask and answer questions about how you go to different places. Use the words in the box or your own ideas.

school the movies your favorite store your friends' houses

How do you go to school?

I go to school by bus. How about you?

I walk to school.

TIP

We go **by** train, bus, boat, etc., but we go **on** foot or we say "I **walk** to …"

4 Complete the sentences with words from activity 1. Then match them with the pictures above.

In Mexico, pink ___taxis___ are for women only. [3]

a In big cities, people can rent a ___________ to travel around the place. [ ]

b In Bangladesh, people often travel on the roof of a ___________. [ ]

c One of the best ways to get around San Francisco is to get the historic ___________. [ ]

d The first ___________ was from the USA and was in the air for 12 seconds. [ ]

e A ___________ in Hong Kong usually has two floors. [ ]

5

6

READING 1

1 Read and listen. What is the article about?

29

a A journey to school **b** Unusual transportation **c** Transportation in the 19th century

THE SKYCAR

You can drive the Skycar or fly it like a plane. Gideon Cardozo, a British engineer, designed the Skycar in just eighteen months. In 2009, Cardozo decided to take the Skycar from the UK to Africa, but he didn't travel alone. He went with Neil Laughton, who is a driver and a pilot. They drove along roads and they flew over mountains and seas. Finally, they arrived in Timbuktu, Mali, more than two months later.

THE SQUBA SUBMARINE

When Frank Rinderknecht saw his hero James Bond drive his car into the sea, he decided that he wanted to build a similar car. The result was the SQuba submarine. The SQuba can travel at 120km/h on land, 6.5km/h on water, and 3.25km/h underwater. This machine is completely ecological, but it is also very expensive: it costs nearly US$1.5 million!

THE COUCHBIKE

Two friends invented the Couchbike.* They tried to ride their special bicycle across a national park in Canada, but two police officers stopped them and inspected their Couchbike. Why? Well, it was more than two meters wide, it was very slow, and the cyclists didn't have helmets. But the police officers didn't know what to do – Couchbikes weren't in their manual – so the two friends continued their journey!

*couch: sofa

2 Scan the article and underline the correct options.

a Gideon Cardozo traveled from the UK to **Asia / Africa** in his Skycar.

b The journey to Timbuktu lasted two **months / years**.

c The SQuba reached **80 / 120** km/h on land.

d It costs around **half / one and a half** million dollars to have a SQuba.

e A Couchbike is made of **chairs / a sofa**.

f The police stopped the Couchbike because it was too **big / strange**.

TIP

Make a note in your notebook of collocations – words which often go together, such as *to fly a plane*.

3 Match the columns to make collocations.

a drive	a plane
b sail	a bike
c fly	a boat
d ride	a car

4 CLASS VOTE Which of the means of transportation in the article is the most unusual in your opinion?

GRAMMAR 1

Simple Past (Affirmative Regular Verbs)

1 Read the following sentences and underline the verbs in the simple past.

- **a** Gideon Cardozo designed the Skycar in just eighteen months.
- **b** Frank Rinderknecht decided to build a car to travel on water.
- **c** Two friends invented the Couchbike.
- **d** They tried to ride their special bike across a national park in Canada.

2 Read the rules. Then underline the verbs in the chart below.

- **I** The simple past tense is used to talk about past events or states which have finished.
- **II** Past time references are usually used: *yesterday* / *last* (*week*, *month*, *etc.*) / *ago* / *in* …
- **III** *-ed* or *-d* are usually added to the base form of the verb.
- **IV** You use the same form for the first, second, and third persons, singular and plural.

affirmative	
I / You	visited Shakespeare's home in England last year.
He / She / It	lived in Stratford-upon-Avon in the 16th century.
We / You / They	watched *Romeo and Juliet* yesterday.

3 Choose the most appropriate words in the box to complete the paragraph about the first streetcar.

carried	in 1960	pulled	returned	started

The first passenger streetcar **a** ______________ operating in Wales in 1807. Horses **b** ______________ this 12-passenger means of transportation. From 1877 it worked by steam, and then, from 1929, electric streetcars **c** ______________ 106 people. The service closed **d** ______________ but, almost fifty years later, modern streetcars **e** ______________ to the UK as a very effective form of urban transportation.

4 Read about the history of the airplane. Complete the sentences with the simple past form of the verbs in parentheses.

The dream of flying is very old. However, the concept of the *airplane* **a** ______________ (arrive) around two centuries ago. Before that time, people **b** ______________ (try) to navigate the air by imitating the birds. They **c** ______________ (construct) wings to strap onto their arms or machines with flapping wings. On the ground, they **d** ______________ (look) okay, but just on the ground.

In 1783, some aeronauts **e** ______________ (decide) to make flights in lighter-than-air balloons. They **f** ______________ (fill) these balloons with either hot air or hydrogen gas, but it wasn't a practical way to fly.

In the 19th century, Sir George Cayley was one of the men who **g** ______________ (construct) the first true airplane – a kite mounted on a stick with a movable tail. It was simple, but it **h** ______________ (prove) his idea worked, and from then on, amazing machines **i** ______________ (appear).

PRONUNCIATION

-ed endings /d/ /t/ /ɪd/

1 Listen and repeat. Can you hear the difference?

30

/d/ or /t/	lived stopped
/ɪd/	ended started

2 Listen to the verbs in the box. Then add them to the chart above according to how they sound.

31

arrived asked continued designed
invented looked presented
tried wanted

5 Use the clues to write sentences about some means of transportation used in the past.

a About 800,000 years ago / *Homo erectus*, a smart naked ape, / construct / the first boats

b The Vikings / invent / a type of ship / called *Longship*

c The Vikings / use / Longships / for trade, exploration, and warfare

d Railroads / control / inland transport of goods and services in the 19th century

e German automotive pioneer Gottlieb Daimler / produce / the first motor truck in 1896

6 INTERFACE Talk to a classmate using the words in the box. Form sentences in the simple past affirmative.

arrive climb in December last year
study travel two weeks ago
visit watch work yesterday

I watched many series last year.

My mom worked a lot yesterday.

GRAMMAR GUIDE page 60

LISTENING

PowerBocking

1 Read the sentences. Then write T for *true* or F for *false*.

a ☐ People with PowerBocks can't walk.

b ☐ People with PowerBocks can run at over 30km/h.

c ☐ A man called Böck invented these boots.

d ☐ In Australia, the boots are called Kangaroo boots.

e ☐ The sport of PowerBocking started in the USA.

2 Listen and check your answers.

32

3 Listen again and answer the questions below.

32

a Who are PowerBockers?

b Where is Alexander Böck from?

c Where did Alexander Böck get his inspiration?

d Are PowerBocks cheap?

SPEAKING

A Visit to a Museum

33 Mark and Adam visited the Riverside Museum of Transport in Glasgow. Listen and complete the dialogue.

I **a** ________________ the Riverside Museum of Transport!

Yeah, I climbed into an old **b** ________________ there. It was awesome!

And The Tall Ship, the Glenlee, as they say here in Glasgow! She **c** ________________ the globe four times and survived with no incident … all that before 1969.

I **d** ________________ around the old prams, streetcars, trains, and buses, bicycles, old cars … oh so many interesting things to see! I also listened to the fascinating stories behind the objects on those big screens.

How about the replica Street? They **e** ________________ it with more stores displaying a fascinating Glasgow shopping street in the 1930s.

The old yellow **f** ________________ called my attention! I imagined myself riding on it fifty years ago!

Yeah. The Riverside Museum of Transport is really worth visiting.

What next now?

FUNCTIONAL LANGUAGE

Talking about a Visit to a Museum

I / my family visited …
I climbed / walked / listened to …
They constructed / reconstructed …

Speaking Task

Create a dialogue between you and a classmate about a museum.

Step 1

Join a classmate and plan what museum you would like to visit. Here are some examples:

The Museum of The Future – Dubai, United Arab Emirates

Guggenheim Museum – Bilbao, Spain

Step 2

Plan sentences asking and answering questions about items in the museum.

Step 3

Take turns practicing the dialogue with your classmate.

CULTURE

Double-decker Buses in London

London's red double-decker bus is practically a national symbol. But how did it all start?

The first commercial double-decker bus was introduced in London in 1829. At that time, the buses were pulled by two or three horses as there were no combustion engines and animal power was the only available source for moving vehicles. The name given to those buses was *Omnibuses*, which means "for all" in Latin. The first omnibuses were free of charge; however, passengers soon started paying a fee to cover maintenance costs, especially to feed the horses.

The design was primitive at first as omnibuses looked like modified horse carriages. The top deck was reached by a staircase or ladder on the outside of the vehicle and the second level didn't have a roof, so it wasn't very popular at first. The passengers who sat in the lower deck had to pay twice the price of the ones on the upper deck.

Horse-drawn buses were used until the 1930's, when the first motorized double-decker bus, with a fully covered top, was introduced and soon gained popularity.

London buses had different colors to indicate their route. However, to stand out from the competition, the London General Omnibus Company, which came to be the biggest bus operator in the city at the time, decided to paint its fleet of buses red and use numbers to indicate different bus routes. And the red buses came to stay ...

1 34 **Read and listen to the information about double-decker buses in London. Choose the most appropriate ending for the information provided.**

a The first double-decker buses ...

☐ were pulled by horses.

☐ had combustion engines.

b The Omnibuses ...

☐ had expensive fares.

☐ were free of charge at first.

c Passengers reached the top deck ...

☐ by a staircase or ladder on the outside of the vehicle.

☐ by a staircase inside the vehicle.

d Passengers who sat in the lower deck ...

☐ paid more than those who sat on the upper deck.

☐ paid less than those who sat on the upper deck.

e London buses ...

☐ were designed to be red since the beginning.

☐ were painted red by the London General Omnibus Company for competition reasons.

2 **What means of public transportation was commonly used in your country in the beginning of the 20th century?**

____

____

____

____

3 **What kind of buses are common in your city? Which routes do they take? What color are they?**

____

____

____

____

VOCABULARY 2

Travel

1 Match pictures 1-6 with some of the words in the box.

climb mountains	1
explore new places	
have a good time	
lay out in the sun	
make friends	
relax	
rent a bike	
take pictures	
taste local food	
visit	

1

2

3

4

5

6

2 Listen and repeat.

35

3 Complete the sentences using the phrases in activity 1.

a Remember to wear sunscreen (minimum of SPF 30) to ________________.

b Staying in hostels is a good way to ________________ when traveling as you share a bedroom with other young people.

c For my next vacation, I plan to just ________________ and stay in a very calm and easy place, far from the city's noise and traffic.

d One of the best things to do when traveling to Asia is to ________________. The aromas and colors of their cuisine are just amazing!

e To ________________ in a foreign country, it is recommended you have a travel guide and a map, or GPS!

READING 2

1 Skim the interview and answer: Who is Bear Grylls?

____

____

2 Skim the interview again and circle the correct option. Who answered the questions?

a Bear Grylls himself.

b The *Teen Explorer* magazine staff.

3 Read and listen to the interview. Does Bear Grylls go on typical holidays?

36

____

____

4 Read the text again. Then write T for *true* or F for *false*.

a ☐ Bear Grylls climbed mountains when he was young.

b ☐ He didn't go exploring again after his accident.

c ☐ He wrote the book *Facing Up*.

d ☐ He laid out in the sun after climbing Everest.

e ☐ He traveled to the Sahara Desert alone.

f ☐ He never engaged in military activities.

g ☐ In addition to being a writer and presenter, he is also a businessman.

5 INTERFACE Work in pairs. Do you prefer an adventurous holiday, like Bear Grills, or a relaxing one?

I prefer an adventurous holiday. I like climbing mountains.

This is not my thing. I prefer to simply relax and lay out in the sun by the pool.

Question and Answer: Bear Grylls

Bear Grylls is a British adventurer, writer, and TV presenter who is admired by many. Last week, *Teen Explorer* magazine told us more about him!

Q Why is he called Bear?

A Bear is a nickname. His sister invented that nickname for him when he was a baby!

Q Obviously, he loves exploring new places. When did he start?

A At an early age, he climbed mountains with his father.

Q Was that dangerous?

A Not as dangerous as when he was in the Special Forces and had a serious parachuting accident. He fractured his back in three places.

Q Did he stop his adventures?

A No, quite the opposite: at the age of 23, he was the youngest British man to climb Everest.

Q What did he do next?

A He released the book *Facing Up*, describing his experiences.

Q And then did he have a holiday? Did he relax and lay out in the sun like us?

A No, he didn't. First he circumnavigated the United Kingdom on jet skis, then he crossed the North Atlantic Ocean on an open, inflatable boat to support a charity.

Q What did he do next?

A Next he and a group of men joined the French Foreign Legion in the Sahara Desert. Maybe that was a holiday for Bear – it depends on what you call a holiday!

Q And what is he up to now?

A He continues to film more adventure episodes for TV and has his own gym brand, *BG Fitness Center*!

GRAMMAR 2

Simple Past: Regular Verbs (Spelling)

1 **Read these sentences about Bear Grylls. Underline the simple past endings: *-d / -ed / -ied*.**

a In 1998, Grylls achieved his childhood dream of climbing to the summit of Mount Everest in Nepal.

b Grills prepared to climb Mount Everest. In 1997, he climbed Ama Dablam, a mountain in the Himalaya range.

c He rowed naked in a homemade bathtub along the River Thames. He tried to raise funds for a friend who lost his legs in a climbing accident.

d He also planned the highest open-air dinner party under a hot-air balloon at 7,600 meters.

e He employed survival strategies for his dangerous adventures.

2 **Read the spelling rules for the simple past of regular verbs. Then write in the box what rule applies to each verb in activity 1.**

achieve ☐	climb ☐	employ ☐	
plan ☐	prepare ☐	row ☐	try ☐

a For most verbs, add *-ed*.

b For verbs that end in *-e*, add *-d*.

c For verbs that end in a consonant + *-y*, omit the *-y* and add *-ied*.

d For verbs that end in a vowel + *-y*, just add *-ed*.

e For verbs that end in a stressed vowel + a consonant (except *w*, *x*, or *y*), double the final consonant and add *-ed*.

3 **Complete the sentences with the correct forms of the verbs in parentheses.**

a My mom __________ (work) for a huge software company in California.

b The airline company __________ (apply) a discount to my ticket.

c The police __________ (stop) the Couchbike inventors in a park.

d We __________ (shop) at street markets when we were in New York last year.

e My sister always __________ (prefer) cookies to donuts, but I'm a donut person!

GRAMMAR GUIDE page 60

CLIL

MATH

Read and listen. Then answer the questions.

37

Titanic in Figures

In 1912, the Titanic was the biggest passenger ship in the world. When it hit an iceberg and went down on its first voyage, it was also the greatest maritime tragedy in history, with the loss of 1,517 lives.
Here are some facts and figures: **do the math!**

Titanic Visitor Center – Belfast, Northern Ireland

Computer-generated Titanic's 3D illustration

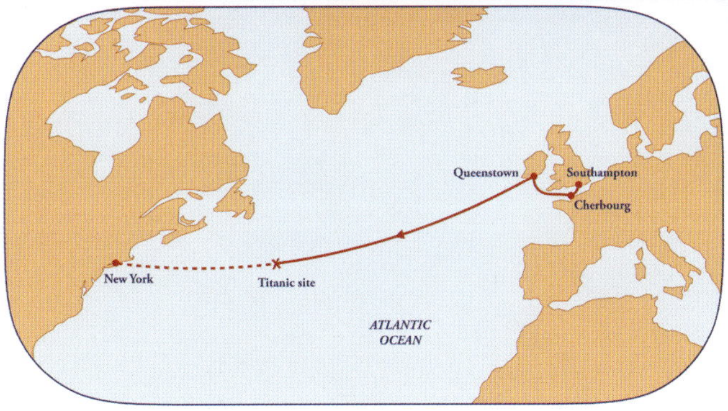

The Titanic route

a The Titanic's capacity was for 3,547 people. There were lifeboats for 1,178 people. What approximate percentage of the passengers could go on a lifeboat?

1 25%
2 33%
3 45%
4 50%

b There are 2.54 centimeters in an inch and there are 12 inches in a foot (ft). Work out these measurements of the Titanic in meters.

1 length = 882 ft 9 inches ________

2 height (waterline to deck) = 59 ft ________

c There were lifeboats for 1,178 people. Lifeboats 1 and 2 were for 40 people. Lifeboats 3 to 16 were for 65 people. How many people were each of the remaining 4 lifeboats for? ________

GRAMMAR GUIDE

Simple Past (Affirmative Regular Verbs)

- is used to talk about past events or states which have finished
- past time references are usually used:
  yesterday / last (week, month, etc.) / ago / in ...
- *-ed* or *-d* are usually added to the base form of the verb.
  I **prepared** dinner **yesterday.**
  We **planned** a travel **last week.**
  They **married** two years **ago.**
- we use the same form for the first, second, and third persons, singular and plural.

affirmative	
I **traveled** You **traveled** He / She / It **traveled** We **traveled** You **traveled** They **traveled**	around Australia.

Simple Past: Regular Verbs (Spelling)

- for most verbs add *-ed*
  invent → **invented**
- for verbs that end in *-e*, add *-d*
  arrive → **arrived**
- for verbs that end in a consonant + *-y*, omit the *-y* and add *-ied*
  study → **studied**
- for verbs that end in a vowel + *-y*, add *-ed*
  employ → **employed**
- for verbs that end in a stressed vowel + a consonant (except *w*, *x*, or *y*), double the final consonant and add *-ed*
  stop → **stopped**
  permit → **permitted**

FOR THE IRREGULAR VERBS LIST, see page 166

Name: ______________________
Class name / Period: ______________________
Teacher: ______________________
Date: ______________________

PROGRESS CHECK

Transportation

1 Identify the types of transportation.

a ______________________

b ______________________

c ______________________

d ______________________

e ______________________

f ______________________

Travel

2 Match the words to form activities.

a taste	mountains
b explore	friends
c climb	pictures
d have	museums
e make	new places
f take	local food
g visit	a good time

Simple Past (Affirmative Regular Verbs)

3 Complete the sentences with the simple past form of the verbs in activity 2.

a In the capital of Greece, Athens, we __________ museums.

b I __________ some local food, such as *moussaka*.

c We __________ mountains, including Mount Olympus.

d We __________ the island of Crete with its amazing historic sites.

Simple Past: Regular Verbs (Spelling)

4 Complete the text with the simple past form of the verbs in parentheses.

Last Saturday I **a** ______________ (visit) my grandparents. I **b** ______________ (arrive) in town early – at 8am. They live in a seaside town nearby and I love going there! I **c** ______________ (travel) by bus with my sister. We **d** ______________ (enjoy) ourselves a lot. It's really fun to go there! On Sunday we **e** ______________ (walk) on the beach and **f** ______________ (pick) up some shells. I **g** ______________ (taste) some local food, but my sister **h** ______________ (refuse) it, she hates seafood! Then we **i** ______________ (explore) the neighboring town, which has an amazing street market where we **j** ______________ (try) lots of different ice-cream flavors. Sunday was fun!

Grammar Buildup 3

1 2 3 4 5 6 7 8

5 Complete the dialogue. Use the correct form of the verbs in parentheses.

Ben How was your weekend, Emily?

Emily It **a** ________________ (be) really fun!

Ben What **b** ________________ (be) you up to?

Emily Well, you know my sister Natalie? It **c** ________________ (be) her birthday last week, so all the family **d** ________________ (travel) to the countryside.

Ben Fantastic! I love **e** ________________ (go) to the country and getting a break from the city. I was in the country for a day last week.

Emily Really?

Ben Yes, I **f** ________________ (help) a friend who **g** ________________ (rescue) a dog there. We **h** ________________ (arrive) at 10am and we **i** ________________ (stay) there until 7pm!

Emily Wow, you **j** ________________ (be) probably tired by the end of the day, right?

Ben I **k** ________________ (be). But it was totally worth it! Look at how happy Snoopy, the dog, is now!

Emily I bet! Oh, he's so cute!

VOCABULARY IN PICTURES

Transportation

bike

boat

bus

car

motorcycle

plane

streetcar

taxi

train

truck

Travel

climb mountains

explore new places

have a good time

lay out in the sun

make friends

relax

rent a bike

take pictures

taste local food

visit museums

4

HISTORY

1

2

3

VOCABULARY 1

Verbs of Discovery

1 Read the verbs in the box. Then listen and repeat.
38

arrive discover ~~drive~~ explore fly go land leave ride sail take off travel

2 Match the sentences with pictures 1-6.

- [ ] Ferdinand Magellan's ships sail across the Pacific in 1521.
- [ ] Captain Cook and his crew arrive in Australia in 1770.
- [ ] Roald Amundsen and his team go to the South Pole in 1911.
- [ ] Amelia Earhart is the first woman to fly solo across the Atlantic in 1932.
- [ ] Neil Armstrong and Buzz Aldrin are the first men to land on the moon in 1969.
- [ ] Steve Fossett is the first person to travel solo around the world in a hot-air balloon in 2002.

3 Complete the chart with the words in activity 1.

by land	by sea	by air
drive		

4 Which words in the chart above relate to all three contexts?

____

____

5 INTERFACE Work in pairs. Ask and answer questions to reflect about the words in activity 1.

Do you think the word *discover* is appropriate to talk about the arrival in unknown lands?

I think *arrive* is better. We don't know if there were already people in the place.

4

5

6

READING 1

1 Skim the magazine article and complete the sentences with the words in the box. Then listen and check your answers.
39

cookies	fruit	pasta	tomatoes

a Originally, ______________ were from America.

b You need wheat flour to make modern ______________.

c There were ______________ in Spain before other countries in Europe.

d They put ______________ in the snow to make a dessert.

A Discovery of Food

A lot of food started its history in very different countries. European explorers discovered potatoes, tomatoes, chocolate, and vanilla in America in the 16th century, and rice began its journey in China. But what about other favorites?

a. Cookies

Cookies are a favorite with everyone, but where were they discovered? The Persians cooked the first cookies with sugar in the 7th century. The Arabs invaded Persia at that time and they loved them. Later, they took the cookies to the rest of their empire, including Spain. From Spain, traders took cookies to North Europe, and then English colonizers sailed to America and made them there.

b. Pasta

People often say that the explorer Marco Polo discovered pasta in China, but this isn't true. In fact, Greeks ate something similar to lasagna in the 1st century. But it was the Arabs who were responsible for modern pasta because they introduced wheat flour to Sicily, in the south of Italy. Pasta, as we know it, was created in Italy in the 13th or 14th century.

c. Ice cream

Ice desserts were popular a long time ago. The Persians (400 BC) and the Chinese (200 BC) enjoyed snow and ice with fruit and honey. Marco Polo discovered a technique for making ice desserts in China and transported it to Italy. So the first modern sorbets were from Italy, but the first ice cream made with milk and cream appeared in 1718 in England!

2 Scan the text and answer the questions.

a What did European explorers discover in the 16th century?

____

b What did the Persians cook before the Europeans?

____

c Why were the Arabs responsible for modern pasta?

____

d What did Marco Polo really discover?

____

e What dessert did the Italians invent?

____

TIP

Many words used to name people's occupation end in *-er* and *-or*. They often come from verbs.
discover – discoverer
sail – sailor
travel – traveler

3 Read the words ending in *-er* and *-or* and write the verb form of each word.

a colonizer ______________
b driver ______________
c explorer ______________
d inventor ______________
e navigator ______________
f trader ______________

4 CLASS VOTE Which is your favorite story in the magazine article?

GRAMMAR 1

Simple Past (Affirmative and Negative)

1 Read the sentences below. Then write the verbs in the following charts.

affirmative – regular and irregular verbs
A lot of food **started** its history in very different countries.
Rice **began** its journey in China.
Arabs **invaded** Persia at that time and they **loved** the cookies.
From Spain, traders **took** cookies to North Europe.
Greeks **ate** something similar to lasagna in the 1st century.
The Persians and the Chinese **enjoyed** snow and ice with fruit and honey.

verbs ending in *-d* or *-ed*

verbs not ending in *-d* or *-ed*

2 Underline the correct words to complete the rules.

a **Regular** / **Irregular** verbs end in *-d* or *-ed*.

b **Regular** / **Irregular** verbs do not follow an established pattern. They usually have a different form.

3 Match the verbs with their simple past irregular forms.

a	take	☐ went
b	make	☐ took
c	be	☐ rode
d	leave	☐ made
e	go	☐ became
f	become	☐ was, were
g	ride	☐ left

4 Complete the text with the correct form of the verbs in parentheses. Use the simple past affirmative.

The history of the potato

Europeans first discovered (discover) potatoes in Chile. Sailors **a** __________ (take) the potatoes on their ships. They **b** __________ (eat) them as they **c** __________ (sail) across the ocean. They **d** __________ (leave) the potatoes in Ireland. Then potatoes **e** __________ (become) very popular in the rest of Europe.

5 Read the sentences in the chart. Then answer: Is the negative form different for regular and irregular verbs? __________

negative	
He	**didn't introduce** pasta to Italy.
The Americans	**didn't make** cookies.

6 Write sentences in the simple past negative form.

a Marco Polo (discover) pasta in China.

____

____

b The Arabs (eat) cookies before the 7th century.

____

____

c The Chinese (introduce) wheat flour to Sicily.

____

____

d Italians (make) the first ice cream with milk and cream.

____

____

TIP

We often use time expressions with the simple past: *last night, on Monday, yesterday, in 2015, two years ago.*

7 Complete the sentences with the simple past affirmative or negative form of the verbs in parentheses.

a Jules Verne ______________ (write) *Around the World in Eighty Days* in 1873.

b Phileas Fogg, the main character, ______________ (have) a lot of money. He ______________ (bet) his friends he could go around the world in eighty days.

c Fogg ______________ (not go) alone. His employee Passepartout ______________ (go) with him.

d They ______________ (take) trains, sailboats, and steamboats. They even ______________ (ride) an elephant!

e They ______________ (not fly) a hot-air balloon. They ______________ (want) to, but ______________ (not put) it in practice.

f They ______________ (find) many obstacles on the way, but they ______________ (not give up).

g They ______________ (not finish) their journey late.

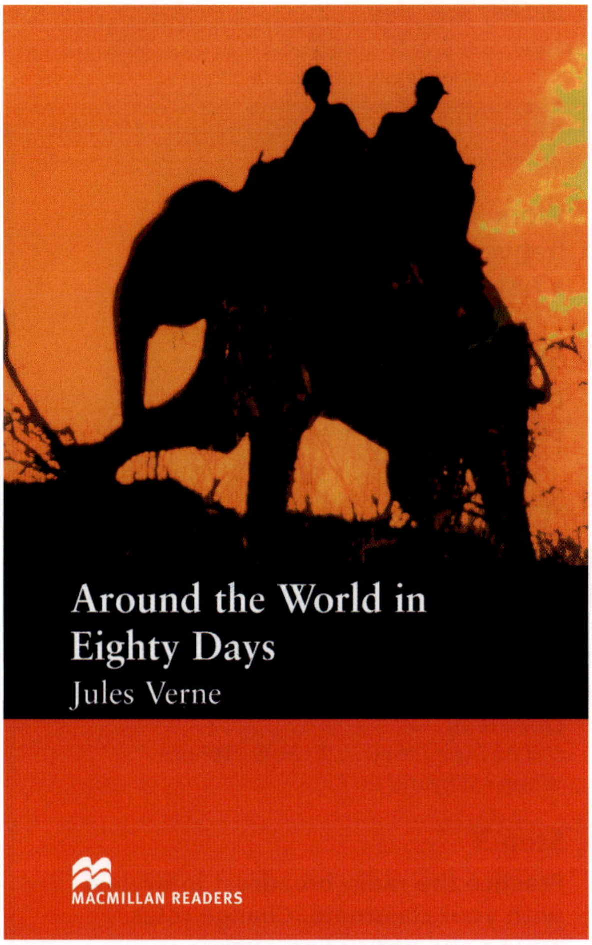

GRAMMAR GUIDE page 76

LISTENING

History Quiz

1 Ashley, Julia, and Grace are watching a quiz show. Read the questions and make a guess on the correct answers.

1 England's first queen was ...
A Elizabeth.
B Mary.
C Victoria.
D Kylie.

2 The first animal in space was a fly, but the second was a ...
A mouse.
B dog.
C rat.
D monkey.

3 Captain Cook arrived in ...
A Alaska.
B Japan.
C Hawaii.
D Chile.

4 Christopher Columbus arrived in the Americas on ... 1492.
A August 3rd
B September 8th
C October 12th
D December 25th

2 Listen and check your answers.

40

3 Listen again and complete the sentences.

40

a Queen Mary ruled in the ______________ century.

b Laika was a ______________ that flew in outer space.

c Captain Cook also arrived in ______________.

d Christopher Columbus left Spain in ______________ because of the currents.

e Gary answers ______________ questions correctly.

4 Do you like history? Which historical figure do you like best?

____

____

Cultural fact

Christopher Columbus took three ships on his first voyage to the Americas: the Santa María, the Pinta and the Santa Clara. The Santa Clara was also called "Niña," because her owner was called Juan Niño de Moguer.

SPEAKING

A Radio Broadcast

41 Patrick (radio broadcaster) is interviewing Dr. Alamis, an expert on American history. Listen and complete the dialogue.

Every October we celebrate *Columbus Day* in the United States, and this **a** ______________ couldn't be any different. Dr. Alamis is here to talk about it.

Thank you, Patrick. Well, Christopher Columbus **b** ______________ at the Americas on October 12th, 1492.

But **c** ______________ he really **d** ______________ his foot in the USA?

In fact, **e** ______________ went as far as the Caribbean. He **f** ______________ to mainland America.

We know that, in recent decades, **g** ______________ is leading to a discussion among the population ...

That's because indigenous people already lived here when Columbus **h** ______________. He simply facilitated its **i** ______________ by Western European powers.

So, *Indigenous People's Day* is a more culturally-sensitive alternative ...

Absolutely! Some American cities **j** ______________ to recognize the **k** ______________ and customs of North America indigenous peoples.

That's good news, Dr. Alamis. Thank you for sharing all this with us.

Thank you for the opportunity!

FUNCTIONAL LANGUAGE

Talking about Explorers in History

He / She / They discovered / facilitated / lived / achieved / arrived in ...
He / She / They didn't ...
Did he / she / they ... ?

Speaking Task

Work in pairs. Plan an interview between a radio broadcaster and a historian.

Step 1

Decide which explorer or historical celebration you are going to talk about.

Step 2

Plan what to say about the explorer or celebration chosen:

Statements
He / She / They arrived in / facilitated / lived / achieved ... / He / She / They didn't ...

Questions
Did he / she / they ... ? / How / Where / When / Why did ... ?

Step 3

Practice the radio broadcast interview with your classmate. Change roles asking and answering questions.

CULTURE

DAVID THOMPSON — THE MAN WHO LOOKED AT THE STARS

DAVID THOMPSON (1770-1857) is remembered as a surveyor, but he was also an explorer, fur trader, and one of the most pioneering geographers in Canadian history. He mapped the main travel routes through around 1,700,000 square miles of the Canadian and American West, journeying some 50,000 miles by canoe, by horse, and on foot. No matter where he traveled, he marked down the latitude and longitude, temperature, and geographical characteristics. For that reason the natives called him "The man who looks at stars."

Thompson was an explorer of First Nations traditions, and he considered the Native peoples to be members of distinct and rich cultures. He mapped not only the land but also the cultural and religious practices of its inhabitants.

His greatest achievement in cartography, his "great map" of 1815, provided an expansive view of the lands from Hudson Bay to the Pacific Ocean and from the Missouri River basin to the Athabasca region. His work was so precise that it was used as the basis for all maps of the west for almost a century.

Thompson traveled with the spirit of inquiry and a sense of wonder, or, crucially, combined these qualities with the ability to communicate his vision to others.

Unfortunately, like many geniuses, his achievements were only recognized after his death.

1 Read and listen to the information about David Thompson. Correct the sentences below. 42

a David Thompson was an explorer, fur trader, surveyor, and a famous geographer in the USA.

____

____

____

b He mapped the main travel routes through around 1,700,000 square kilometers of the Canadian and American West.

____

____

____

c Thompson was not interested in the First Nations, traditions, and culture.

____

____

d The Natives called Thompson "The man who looks at the Moon."

____

____

e Thompson's achievements were fully recognized at the time.

____

____

2 Can you name one explorer that made a difference in your country? Do you consider that he or she contributed to your country? Why? Why not?

____

____

____

____

____

____

____

VOCABULARY 2

Natural Disasters

1 Match pictures 1-6 with the words in the box. Mark an X next to the words that are not represented in the pictures.

drought ☐	earthquake ☐	famine ☐	fire ☐	flood ☐	hurricane ☐
landslide ☐	tornado ☐	tsunami ☐	volcanic eruption ☐		

1

2

3

4

5

6

2 Listen and repeat.

43

3 Complete the quiz with words and expressions from activity 1.

How well do you know your history?

(1) There was a potato **a** _____________ in Ireland; people had nothing to eat and about 1 million people died. It was from 1845 to …
I 1852. **II** 1864. **III** 1870.

(2) There were **b** _____________ in the south of England. The water was 0.9m high. The year was …
I 1850. **II** 1939. **III** 2007.

(3) There was a terrible **c** _____________ in the year 1988. Many houses and stores burned in the capital of …
I Italy. **II** Portugal. **III** Colombia.

(4) There was a huge **d** _____________ in Iceland and many planes couldn't fly because of the ash cloud. The year was …
I 2001. **II** 2005. **III** 2010.

(5) **e** _____________ is a problem in many countries where there isn't much rain. The longest was in the Atacama desert in Chile: it was from 1571 to …
I 1671. **II** 1771. **III** 1971.

Answers: 1. I, 2. III, 3. II, 4. III, 5. III.

4 INTERFACE Work in pairs. Take the history quiz in activity 3. Then check the answers.

READING 2

1 Skim the text and look at the pictures from the textbook article below. What do you think the text is about?

____

____

2 Read and listen. Check your answer to activity 1.

44

Great European Disasters

Ruins of the antique Temple of Apollo with bronze Apollo statue in Pompeii, Naples, Italy. Pompeii was destroyed by Vesuvius eruption in 79 AD.

ON AUGUST 24th, 79 AD ...

Mount Vesuvius erupted. The eruption was catastrophic, and ash and lava covered the towns of Pompeii and Herculaneum. They stayed hidden for nearly 1,700 years, but when Domenico Fontana, an Italian architect, discovered walls with paintings in 1559, how did he react? He covered them again! A Spanish engineer discovered Herculaneum in 1738 and Pompeii in 1748. In Pompeii, the volcano preserved Roman life exactly as it was, and we now know a lot about Roman culture because of the eruption.

ON NOVEMBER 1st, 1755 ...

there was a terrible earthquake in Lisbon, Portugal. Immediately after the earthquake, there was a tsunami and many fires started in the city. Buildings fell, burned, and disappeared into the sea. In fact, the earthquake and its effects destroyed most of the city. But what did the people of Lisbon do? They rebuilt their city. They made wide streets, big squares, and special buildings that could resist earthquakes. Also, thanks to the Portuguese prime minister's investigations, modern seismology was born.

A depiction of The Great Lisbon Earthquake of November 1st, 1755 in Lisbon, Portugal.

3 Scan the text and answer the questions.

a When did Mount Vesuvius erupt?

____

b What did Domenico Fontana do when he discovered the paintings?

____

____

c How did the volcanic eruption help us learn about Roman culture?

____

____

d What natural disasters happened after the Lisbon earthquake?

____

____

e Did buildings in Lisbon disappear into the sea?

____

f What positive things happened after the earthquake?

____

____

____

rhetorical question

A **rhetorical question** is a question asked in order to create a dramatic effect, to catch the audience's interest, and make people think about the subject, rather than obtaining an answer.

4 Read this definition of rhetorical question. Then answer the questions.

a Locate **two** rhetorical questions in the article and write them down.

____

____

____

b For one of the rhetorical questions presented, the text provides an answer that ends with an exclamation point (!). This punctuation was used because the answer is …

1 surprising.

2 obvious.

READING STRATEGY

When reading a text with rhetorical questions, pay attention to the effect they cause on the reader. You can also include rhetorical questions in your own texts. They capture the reader's attention and emphasize your point of view.

GRAMMAR 2

Simple Past (Questions and Short Answers)

1 Read the information in the chart below. Do we use *did* for all subjects in simple past questions?

____

questions and short answers
Did Pompeii and Herculaneum **stay** hidden for nearly 1,700 years? / Yes, they **did**.
Did Domenico Fontana **discover** walls with paintings 1,700 years ago? / No, he **didn't**.
Did the volcano **preserve** Roman life? / Yes, it **did**.

2 Read the text *Great European Disasters* on page 73 again and match the answers below with the following questions.

a Did Portugal go through a terrible earthquake?

b Did many fires start in Lisbon after the tsunami?

c Did people in Lisbon move to another place?

d Did the prime minister investigate the problem?

☐ No, they didn't.

☐ Yes, it did.

☐ Yes, they did.

☐ Yes, he did.

3 Write complete questions using the simple past.

a how many ships / Christopher Columbus / have?

____

____

b when / they / discover / Pompeii?

____

____

c where / Marco Polo / go?

____

____

d when / Hillary and Norgay / climb Everest?

____

____

4 Listen and check your answers in activity 3.

45

Then listen again and write the answers to the questions.

a ______________________

b ______________________

c ______________________

d ______________________

could / couldn't

TIP

We use *could / couldn't* to talk about **ability** and **possibility in the past**:
The buildings could resist earthquakes. They couldn't stop the fires.

5 Complete the sentences with *could* or *couldn't*.

a Many fires occurred in Lisbon in 1755, but the population ______________ rebuilt the city.

b Many people ______________ go back to their old houses because their properties disappeared into the sea.

c Some people ______________ take their things along with them because they were badly injured.

GRAMMAR GUIDE page 76

WRITING

A Biography

1 EXPLORING THE CONTEXT

1 Skim the text on page 75 quickly. Where do you expect to find this text genre? Check (✓) all that apply.

a ☐ On culture websites.

b ☐ In history books.

c ☐ In travel guides.

d ☐ In English dictionaries.

e ☐ In encyclopedias.

2 How do you think the facts are organized?

a From most recent to oldest.

b In chronological order.

3 Read and listen. Then check your answer in activity 2.
46

Leonardo da Vinci

Leonardo da Vinci is remembered as one of the most interesting personalities in history. He was a painter, a sculptor, and an inventor. He studied anatomy and botany, and he liked many other things too. He was born in Vinci, near Florence, on April 15th, 1452. He didn't go to school, but he studied math, Latin, and geometry at home. When he was 14, he started to work. He was very good at art so he worked for a famous painter, Andrea del Verrocchio, and learned techniques from him. Then he went to live in Milan in 1482 and, from this time on, Da Vinci painted his most famous works, for example, *The Last Supper*. He painted *The Mona Lisa*, probably the most famous painting in the world, in about 1505. It is in the Louvre Museum in Paris, France. He was interested in math, science, and anatomy, and he drew people and bodies perfectly. He also drew inventions, for example, a flying machine similar to the modern helicopter. He was the typical Renaissance man. Da Vinci died on May 2nd, 1519, at the age of 67. He left his notebooks and drawings to his faithful apprentice Francesco Melzi. It is because of Melzi's efforts to preserve this treasure that we now know much of Da Vinci's genius.

4 What information about Leonardo da Vinci is presented in the text? Check (✓) all that apply.

- **a** ☐ His job.
- **b** ☐ His education.
- **c** ☐ His date of birth.
- **d** ☐ His daily routine.
- **e** ☐ His main artworks.
- **f** ☐ The date of his death.

5 Complete this description of the biography structure. Use the words from the box.

after	comment	facts	first

The **a** __________ sentences introduce the person and explain how he or she stood out in history. Then the **b** __________ of his or her life are presented in chronological order. At the end, there may be a **c** __________ about what happened **d** __________ the person's death.

2 PLANNING

1 Write a biography about an important person in history.

2 Choose a person you admire and look for information about him or her. Who was he or she? What did he or she do? What were the important events in his or her life? How did this person stand out in history?

LANGUAGE FOCUS

Time Prepositions
Remember to use *on*, *at*, or *in* correctly with times.
Leonardo was born ***on*** *April 15th, 1452* ***at*** *10:30pm. Leonardo died* ***in*** *May. Leonardo died* ***in*** *1519.*
Look at the sentences above. Complete the rules below with *on*, *at*, or *in*.

- **a** We use ______ before months and years.
- **b** We use ______ before times.
- **c** We use ______ before days and dates.

3 WRITING

1 Prepare a first draft. Write a few sentences to introduce the person, then arrange the facts of his or her life in chronological order. End with a comment about his or her legacy or anything else you feel is important.

2 Refer back to your notes from Step 2 and the biography on this page to help you.

4 CHECKING & EDITING

1 Ask a classmate to read your text and check:

- Does the text present basic information about the person's life?
- Were the simple past and time prepositions used correctly?

2 Use your classmate's suggestions to prepare the final version of your text. Don't forget to include a picture of the person being biographed.

5 SHARING

Alphabetize the class's biographies and organize a biographical encyclopedia. It may be available in the school library for other students to refer to.

GRAMMAR GUIDE

Simple Past

affirmative	
I	arrived.
You	arrived.
He / She / It	arrived.
We	arrived.
You	arrived.
They	arrived.

- we use the simple past to describe finished actions or situations in the past
  I **traveled** to France last year.
- the form is the same for all subject pronouns
- the regular simple past ending is *-ed*
  explore → ***explored*** sail → ***sailed***
- many common verbs are irregular
  drive → ***drove*** go → ***went***

FOR THE IRREGULAR VERBS LIST, see page 166

negative	
I	didn't go.
You	didn't go.
He / She / It	didn't go.
We	didn't go.
You	didn't go.
They	didn't go.

- we use *didn't* (*did not*) before the verb to form the negative
  Ferdinand Magellan **didn't discover** Australia.

questions			short answers	
			affirmative	negative
Did	I	go?	Yes, I did.	No, I didn't.
	you		Yes, you did.	No, you didn't.
	he / she / it		Yes, he / she / it did.	No, he / she / it didn't.
	we		Yes, we did.	No, we didn't.
	you		Yes, you did.	No, you didn't.
	they		Yes, they did.	No, they didn't.

- we use *did* with the infinitive to make questions
  Did you **ride** a camel?
- we don't repeat the main verb in short answers
  Did you **read** that biography?
  Yes, **I did**. / No, **I didn't**.

Past Time Expressions

- we often use time expressions with the simple past
- we usually write them at the end of the sentence
  I was at home **on Monday**.
  It was her birthday **three days ago**.

could / couldn't

- we use *could* for ability and possibility in the past
  She **could** swim when she was 3 years old.
- the form is the same for all subject pronouns
  I **could** speak French when I was young.
  My brother **could** speak French when he was young.
- the negative form of *could* is *couldn't* (*could not*)
  They **couldn't** drive.
- we never use *to* after *could / couldn't*
  We **could write** our names.

6

PROGRESS CHECK

Name: ______________________________
Class name / Period: ______________________________
Teacher: ______________________________
Date: ______________________________

Verbs of Discovery

1 Find eight verbs of discovery in the word search.

Q	L	M	V	T	C	I	F	L	Y
W	E	R	D	R	U	F	G	E	F
L	D	G	S	A	I	L	P	A	L
A	R	R	I	V	E	K	Q	V	K
N	P	I	S	E	P	C	E	E	F
D	G	D	J	L	R	B	X	X	T
R	O	E	U	D	Z	T	G	C	Q

Natural Disasters

2 Match pictures 1-6 with the words in the box.

1

2

3

4

5

6

drought ☐ earthquake ☐ famine ☐
fire ☐ flood ☐ tornado ☐

Simple Past

3 Complete the text with the simple past form of the verbs in parentheses.

I **a** ______________ (arrive) home yesterday at 4pm. I **b** ______________ (be) alone in the house so I **c** ______________ (sit) down on the sofa with a book, a biography about Captain Cook. I **d** ___________ (start) to read and I **e** ______________ (read) for seven hours! I **f** ______________ (forget) to have dinner, but I **g** ______________ (finish) the book and it was wonderful.

4 Make the sentences true for you.

a I went to Hawaii last year.

____

b I ate cactus for dinner last night.

____

c My grandpa was an explorer.

____

5 Complete the sentences with *was / wasn't* or *were / weren't*.

a I ________ at home last night. ✓
b My friends ________ in school yesterday. ✗
c She ________ tired so she didn't go to bed. ✗
d You ______ on vacation two days ago. ✓

6 Order the words to make questions.

a you / arrive / What time / home / did / last night ?

____

b study / Did / you / history / on the weekend ?

____

c your dad / did / buy / his first car / When ?

____

d you / English / study / Did / in elementary school ?

____

e Did / three months ago / you / Lisbon / visit ?

____

could / couldn't

7 Complete the sentences with *could* or *couldn't*.

a ☐ The population ________________ escape from the earthquake.

b ☐ Leonardo da Vinci ________________ learn different painting techniques from Andrea del Verrocchio.

c ☐ Francesco Melzi ________________ keep Da Vinci's notebooks and drawings.

d ☐ The firefighters ________________ avoid the fire to spread through the forest.

Grammar Buildup 4

1 2 3 4 5 6 7 8

8 Underline the correct words.

Mom What **a do you do / are you doing**, Stella?

Izzie I **b do / 'm doing** my history homework.

Mom Can I **c help / helping** you?

Izzie Oh, yes, please. I **d find / found** some information in the library yesterday and now I **e write / 'm writing** about Victorian London. But I have some questions. Where **f did / does** Queen Victoria live?

Mom I **g wasn't / weren't** alive then! Let's **h look / looking** on the internet!

Izzie Good idea. Where **i do you usually put / are you usually putting** your laptop?

Mom Oh, no! I **j leave / left** it at work.

Izzie Oh, Mom!

VOCABULARY IN PICTURES

Verbs of Discovery

arrive

discover

drive

explore

fly

go

land

leave

ride

sail

take off

travel

Natural Disasters

drought

earthquake

famine

fire

flood

hurricane

landslide

tornado

tsunami

volcanic eruption

REVIEW 2

VOCABULARY

Start

1 Which F do you do when you travel by air? ________

2 Which C do you do when you go up a mountain? ________

3 Which P do you take when you register the image you see in digital or analogic media? ________

10 Which S means to travel by boat? ________

11 Which R do you do when you need to rest your body and mind? ________

12 Which M is for a motorized bike? ________

13 Which B is for a non-motorized two-wheel vehicle? ________

14 Which F is for a disaster caused by excessive rain? ________

15 Which T and O is when the plane leaves the ground? ________

21 Which B travels over the sea or river? ________

22 Which M and F do you do when you meet new people? ________

Finish

4 Which F is when many people are suffering from no access to food? ____________

5 Which L do you do when the plane arrives at the airport? ____________

6 Which L can you do on the beach when it's hot and sunny? ____________

7 Which D is when someone conducts a car? ____________

8 Which B is a type of public transportation? ____________

9 Which T is a natural disaster caused by a huge wave? ____________

16 Which T is for a means of transportation with wagons? ____________

17 Which R do you do on a bike or motorcycle? ____________

18 Which T is a very strong wind? ____________

19 Which P can you fly to different countries in? ____________

20 Which E is a natural disaster from tectonic origin? ____________

REVIEW 2

GRAMMAR

Simple Past (Affirmative Regular Verbs)

1 Complete the text with the correct form of the verbs in parentheses.

Frida Kahlo's museum and birthplace in Coyoacan, Mexico

The artist Frida Kahlo was born in Mexico in 1907. As a teenager, she __wanted__ (want) to be a doctor. However, one day in September 1925, she **a** ________ (suffer) a terrible bus accident and **b** ________ (fracture) a lot of bones. She **c** ________ (stay) many months in the hospital. During her recovery, she **d** ________ (consider) becoming a medical illustrator, to combine her interests in medicine and art, but in the end she **e** ________ (study) art by herself. In 1929 she **f** ________ (marry) Diego Rivera, another Mexican artist. She **g** ________ (die) in 1954. Her museum in Coyoacan is one of the most visited attractions around Mexico City nowadays.

2 Use the verbs in the box to complete the sentences in the simple past affirmative.

ask ~~explore~~ invent travel visit

He __explored__ the town entering all churches, museums, and cafés mentioned in his tourist guide.

a When we were in Germany, I ________ for information in German to practice the language.

b My mom ________ to Turkey during her last vacation to visit the hometown of her grandparents.

c In 1942 a French designer ________ an electric car in the shape of an egg, the *L'Oeuf Electrique*.

d My history teacher ________ the Museum of Archeology in search of curious facts on Ancient Egypt to teach us in class.

3 Underline the correct time expressions in the past.

We moved to a new town **last year** / **in the last year**.

a My uncle sailed across the Atlantic ocean in a yacht **in 2019** / **on 2019**.

b We bought a new smart TV **three months ago** / **for three months ago**.

c It was my birthday **in Wednesday** / **on Wednesday**.

d I traveled to the seaside **last week** / **the last week**.

e My friends watched the final game **last day** / **yesterday**.

Simple Past: Regular Verbs (Spelling)

4 Write the verbs in the chart in the simple past form according to their spelling rule.

~~appear~~ call challenge design grab invent like marry multiply produce stop try use want weigh

add *-ed*	add *-d*
appeared, ________	________
________	________
________	________
________	________

omit *-y* and add *-ied*	double final consonant and add *-ed*
________	________
________	________
________	________
________	________

Simple Past (Affirmative and Negative)

5 Write the simple past form of the verbs.

begin began

a do ______ e run ______

b come ______ f speak ______

c eat ______ g win ______

d hit ______ h fly ______

6 Complete the sentences with the simple past affirmative form of the verbs in parentheses.

a He ______ a camel in Tenerife. (ride)

b I ______ a great time at your party. (have)

c I ______ your brother for the first time. (meet)

d We ______ some money in the park. (find)

7 Rewrite the sentences in the negative form.

a They rode their bikes yesterday.

______

b We watched a funny movie.

______

c She flew to Paris with her uncle.

______

d Ferdinand Magellan sailed around the world.

______

Simple Past (Questions and Short Answers)

8 Look at the information in the table. Write questions and short answers.

	James	Rachel	Josh and Amy
transportation	by plane	by boat	by train
place	the beach	an island	a city

James / travel / by plane?
Did James travel by plane? / Yes, he did.

a James / go / to an island?

______

b Rachel / travel / by plane?

______

c Rachel / stay / on an island?

______

d Josh and Amy / fly / to a city?

______

9 Order the words to make questions.

you / play / Where / did / tennis ?
Where did you play tennis?

a the boys / did / How / travel ?

______

b Katie / by car / Why / go / did ?

______

c you / arrive / What time / home / did ?

______

d go / Who / he / with / to the movies / did ?

______

could / couldn't

10 Write sentences with *could* or *couldn't*.

a ☐ Mary ______ finish the exercises.

b ☐ Leonardo da Vinci ______ study math, Latin, and geometry at home.

c ☐ My sister ______ read Jules Verne's book.

d ☐ We ______ travel to Europe last year.

The Permanence of Online Actions

The Toothpaste

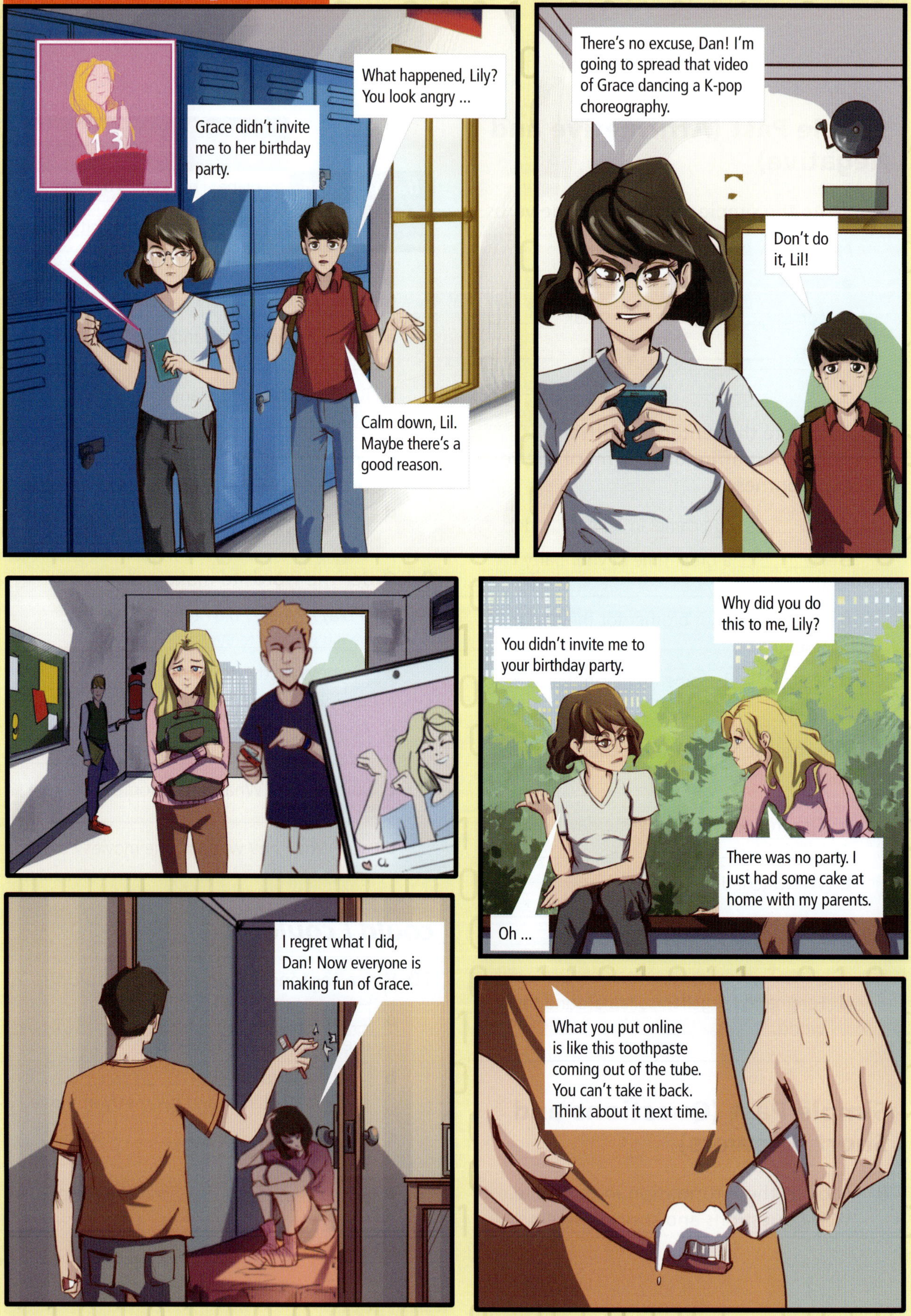

1 Read and listen. Then number the events in chronological order.

47

- ☐ Lily takes revenge on Grace by sharing her embarrassing video.
- ☐ Grace eats some birthday cake at home and posts a picture of it.
- ☐ Lily regrets what she did, but it's too late to fix things.
- ☐ Lily sees Grace's pic and thinks there was a party and she wasn't invited.
- ☐ Grace makes a video of herself dancing and shares it with her friend Lily.
- ☐ Grace explains to Lily that there was no birthday party.

2 Why is the story called "The Toothpaste"?

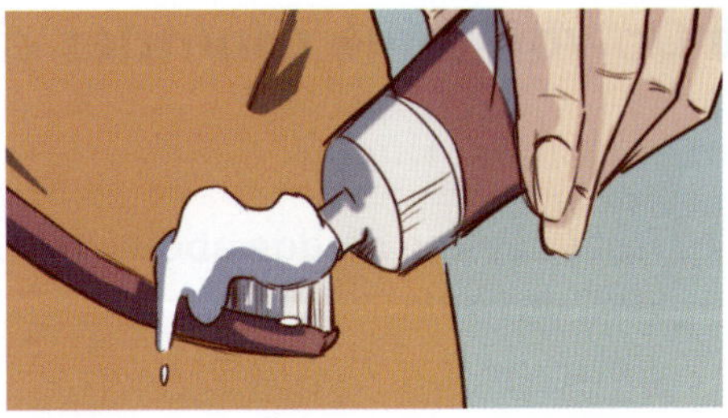

____
____
____
____
____
____

3 Complete the chart with your ideas. Then join with a classmate and discuss them. Share your thoughts with the class.

	What did she put online and later regret?	How do you avoid situations like these?
Grace		
Lily		

4 Choose one of the social media platforms you use and take a look at your last ten posts.

a Check if there's anything in them you might regret later.

b Review your privacy settings on this social media platform.

5 Work in pairs again. Based on what you observed in activity 4, write some *dos* and *don'ts* to protect your reputation online.

____
____
____
____
____
____
____
____

6 Use a file-sharing service to compose a single advice list with the class. Eliminate similar tips, then share the file with friends and family.

The United Nations and The Environment

- Do you know what the United Nations (UN) is?
- What is the link between the UN and environmental protection?
- Do you think countries can work together to solve a global problem?

1 48 Test your knowledge about the United Nations in the quiz below. Then read, listen, and check your answers.

a The UN was created in …

☐ 1916. ☐ 1945. ☐ 1988.

b About … countries are members of the UN.

☐ 50 ☐ 100 ☐ 190

c COP is an annual event organized by the UN to discuss …

☐ climate change. ☐ vaccination campaigns. ☐ food distribution.

What the UN Does

In 1945, after the Second World War, 51 countries came together to form the United Nations. The original purpose of the organization was to prevent another world war. Membership was eventually extended to almost every country on Earth, growing to 193 member countries by 2011. Over time, the UN also began to play other roles. Today, the UN's main goals are to maintain international peace and security, protect human rights, deliver humanitarian aid, uphold international law, and promote sustainable development.

In this last aspect, the UN stands out for seeking solutions to the climate crisis. One of the actions is to promote the Conference of the Parties (COP) annually. In these two-week meetings, world leaders discuss how to mitigate climate change.

2 The slogan of the COP 26, held in 2021, was: "The climate has no borders." What does this slogan mean to you?

____
____
____
____
____
____
____
____

A Timeline of Environmental Protection

Climate crisis, COP, Paris Agreement ... These terms are in the news. But what do they mean exactly? How do they impact your future? In groups, seek information to compose a timeline of global environmental policies.

DOING

1 Work in groups of four or five students. Below are some of the milestones in the history of global environmental policies. Discuss: What do you know about them?

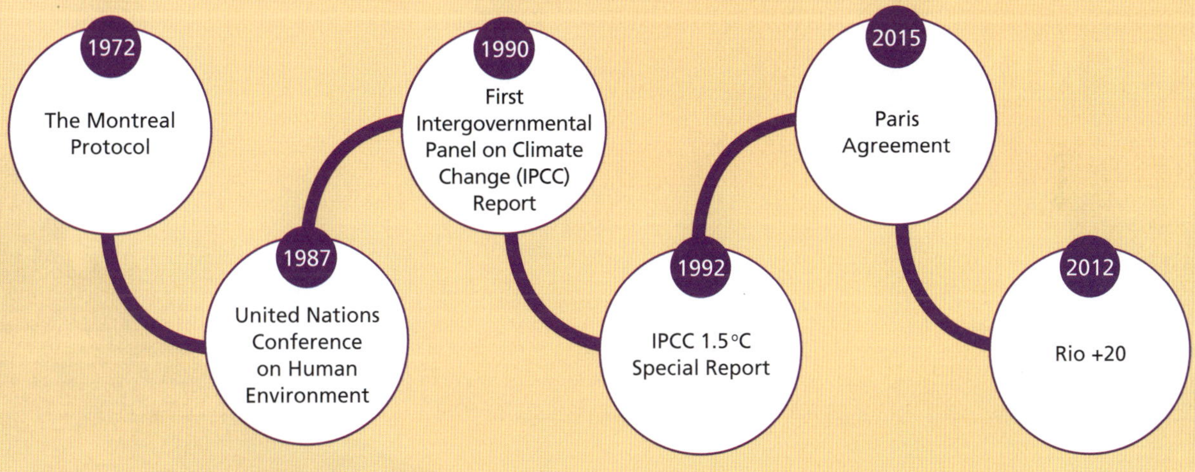

2 Return to the **Digital Literacy** section on pages 84-85. How should you search for information about the milestones above?

3 Follow the information search process recommended in that section. Here are some useful reference sources:

- INTERACTIVE Timeline: A Guide to Climate Change Negotiations. *European Parliament*. Available at: www.europarl.europa.eu/infographic/climate-negotiations-timeline/index_en.html#event-1987. Accessed on: April 29th, 2022.
- A BRIEF History of Climate Change. *BBC News*. Available at: www.bbc.com/news/science-environment-15874560. Accessed on: April 29th, 2022.

4 Glue large pieces of paper or cardstock next to each other, forming a horizontal strip. On this strip, make a timeline using the information you found.

5 Add at least **one milestone** to those above. Paste pictures to illustrate the timeline.

6 Hang your timeline on the classroom wall. Observe the work of other groups and discuss as a class:

a Are there any differences between the timelines? Which one is most informative? And which one looks the best?

b Do you believe that the joint effort of countries can tackle the climate crisis? What remains to be done?

5

MYTHS AND LEGENDS

1

2

3

4

5

VOCABULARY 1

Character Adjectives

1 Read the words in the box below and underline the ones you know. Then check online the ones you don't.

brave cheerful cruel friendly funny kind lazy loyal selfish shy stubborn wise

2 Listen and repeat.

49

3 Look at the characters in pictures 1-6 above and choose the correct words below.

- **a** The White Witch was **cruel** / **funny**.
- **b** Sam Gamgee was **loyal** / **cruel** to Frodo Baggins.
- **c** Sherlock Holmes was **wise** / **cheerful**.
- **d** Merlin the Wizard was **lazy** / **friendly**.
- **e** Robin Hood was **kind** / **selfish**.
- **f** Queen Boudicca was **shy** / **brave**.

TIP

We often use *What's he* or *she like?* or *What was he* or *she like?* to ask about someone's character.

6

4 Listen to Josh and Lane talking. What does Lane say about her first friend and her first teacher?

50

____

5 Write and answer questions about your personal experience. Use the words in the box below and the character adjectives from activity 1.

first classmate	first friend	first teacher

What was your first classmate like?

She was very funny.

____

____

____

____

____

____

READING 1

1 Check online the meaning of the words in the box below.

afraid	conquer	dangerous	fight
pull	rule	stone	sword

2 Look at the names of the people in the text. What do you think they are like? Read and listen.
51

3 Read the online encyclopedia article again. Then write T for *true* or F for *false*.

- **a** ☐ Queen Boudicca was living in London.
- **b** ☐ The Romans killed Boudicca.
- **c** ☐ Arthur went with Merlin to get the sword.
- **d** ☐ We know that Merlin existed.
- **e** ☐ John had control of the country.
- **f** ☐ Robin Hood wasn't kind to rich people.

4 Scan the text and answer the questions.

- **a** What was Boudicca like?

____

- **b** What happened when the Romans were planning to leave Britain?

____

- **c** Why was Arthur the true king?

____

- **d** Why wasn't King Richard ruling England?

____

5 Underline some cognates in the text.

READING STRATEGY

Cognates are words in English that are similar to words in your language and have a similar meaning. These words can help you understand the text as a whole.

6 CLASS VOTE Which legend from the encyclopedia article do you prefer?

www.britishlegends.com

British Legends

Queen Boudicca

In 60 AD, Queen Boudicca was ruling the east of England when the Romans decided to attack her people, the Iceni. Legend says that the queen was incredibly brave and she attacked the Romans in London. The Romans discovered her plan, so she didn't conquer the city. But they were afraid of Boudicca – she was an extremely dangerous enemy. In fact, the Romans were planning to abandon England when suddenly they won a battle and had control of the province again. Legend says Boudicca killed herself.

Merlin the Wizard

After the Romans left Britain, there was chaos. There were different kings and they were rivals, and people from other countries were invading. Britain needed one true and loyal king, and Merlin found Arthur. He took Arthur to see a sword, Excalibur. The legend says only the true king could pull Excalibur out of the stone. Arthur pulled the sword out of the stone and he became King Arthur. But did someone like Merlin really exist? Experts say this is possible, but nobody is sure.

Robin Hood

There are many stories about Robin Hood. He was a popular hero and he lived with his friends, the Merry Men, in Sherwood Forest near Nottingham. At that time, King Richard of England wasn't ruling the country because he was fighting in the Crusades. His cruel, lazy brother John was ruling England. Robin and his Merry Men were kind to poor people. They robbed the rich aristocrats and gave the money to the poor. But is Robin Hood fact or fiction? Nobody knows.

GRAMMAR 1

Past Progressive

1 Read the sentences below and <u>underline</u> the verbs in the past progressive.

a In 60 AD, Queen Boudicca was ruling the east of England.

b The Romans were planning to abandon England.

c King Richard of England wasn't ruling the country.

d He was fighting in the Crusades.

2 Complete the chart with the correct verb forms. Refer to the sentences in activity 1.

affirmative form		negative form	
I / He / She / It	________ ruling the east of England.	I / He / She / It	________ ruling the country.
We / You / They	were ________ in the Crusades.	We / You / They	weren't ________ to abandon England.

3 Choose the correct rule below to form the past progressive.

☐ We form the past progressive with the past form of the verb *to be* (*was / were*) and the *-ing* form of the main verb.

☐ We form the past progressive with the present form of the verb *to be* (*am / is / are*) and the *-ing* form of the main verb.

4 Read the story of the Stanton Drew Circles in England and fill in the blanks with the past progressive form of the verbs in parentheses.

Two young people ___were celebrating___ (celebrate) their wedding. A violinist **a** ________________ (play) and their friends **b** ________________ (dance). It **c** ________________ (get) late and the next day was Sunday so the violinist stopped. But the young wife **d** ________________ (have) fun and she wanted more music. Suddenly, a mysterious musician arrived and started to play. The dancers **e** ________________ (feel) tired, but the music **f** ________________ (not stop). On Sunday morning, there were no dancers, but there were large stones in their place. How did the stones get there? The dancers became stones because they **g** ________________ (dance) on a Sunday.

5 Read about the Loch Ness Monster. Complete sentences a-d with the past progressive negative form. Then match them with the affirmative sentences below.

a The monster ________________ (swim) in the waters of Loch Lomond.

b Nessie ________________ (eat) an animal.

c In the 1960s local farmers ________________ (conduct) an investigation.

d The Bureau ________________ (use) the Air Force during the search.

☐ It was in the waters of Loch Ness.

☐ The Loch Ness Investigation Bureau conducted the investigation.

☐ People saw Nessie eating a local farmer.

☐ Mini-submarines explored the depths of the Loch.

6 Read the questions below and <u>underline</u> the auxiliary verbs.

a Was the queen attacking the Romans in London?

b Were the Romans planning to abandon England?

c Was Robin Hood living with his family in Sherwood Forest?

d Were Robin and his friends robbing the poor?

7 Now, complete the chart with the correct auxiliary forms. Underline the main verbs.

questions and short answers		
was / wasn't / were / weren't		
Was I celebrating a wedding?	Yes, I ______.	No, I ______.
______ you living in Sherwood Forest?	Yes, you were.	No, you ______.
______ he / she / it attacking the Romans?	Yes, he / she / it was.	No, he / she / it ______.
Were we / you / they ruling the country?	Yes, we / you / they ______.	No, we / you / they ______.

8 Read the text *British Legends* from page 91 again and use *was / were / wasn't / weren't* to give short answers to the questions in activity 6.

a ______________ **c** ______________

b ______________ **d** ______________

9 Look at the picture below and write complete questions. Then write short answers.

the group leader / talk?
Was the group leader talking? / Yes, she was.

a the parents / listen ?
____

b the ghost / smile ?
____

c the boy / drop his telephone ?
____

d the girl / look at the ghost ?
____

e the ghost / fly ?
____

GRAMMAR GUIDE page 100

LISTENING

A Highwayman

1 Jesse James was a highwayman. What is a highwayman? Look at the picture and choose the correct answer.

a ☐ A highwayman robs from the rich and gives to the poor.

b ☐ A highwayman steals from people who are traveling.

c ☐ A highwayman steals horses and sheep.

2 52 Listen to Josh and Lane talking about Jesse James. Check your answer to activity 1.

3 52 Listen again and choose the correct answers.

a The real Jesse James was …
☐ brave and kind.
☐ cruel and selfish.

b The police were looking for Jesse James …
☐ and didn't find him.
☐ and found him.

c When Robert Ford killed him he was living …
☐ in Kearney.
☐ in St. Joseph.

d The legend says Jesse James helped an old lady save her …
☐ property.
☐ life.

e But after helping the lady he and his gang robbed the …
☐ governor.
☐ tax collector.

4 What famous legends do you have in your country?

____
____

SPEAKING

Last Weekend

53 Jill and Stacey are talking about their weekend. Listen and complete the dialogue below.

How **a** ______________ your weekend?

It was great! I **b** __________ every minute of it.

What **c** __________ you __________?

Well, many things, but I really loved the **d** __________ I saw on Saturday afternoon.

What movie did you **e** __________?

Rob Roy. It is about Rob Roy MacGregor, an 18th-century Scottish clan chief who battled with an unscrupulous nobleman in the Scottish Highlands.

I think I've read the book about him. He **f** __________ always __________ to live up to his word, even if it meant sacrificing his personal choices.

Yeah, but some people **g** __________ him a thief and a blackmailer. A great story about honest clansmen and corrupt aristocrats.

I think I'm going to watch it next weekend!

Definitely not to be missed!

FUNCTIONAL LANGUAGE

Talking about the Weekend

How was your weekend?
What did you do?
Did you … ?

Speaking Task

Create a dialogue between you and a classmate.

Step 1

Talk to a classmate about what he or she did over the weekend. Here are some examples:

go to the club / swimming pool

go cycling

read / relax

Step 2

Plan what questions to ask.

How was your weekend?
What did you do?
Where did you go?
Did you like it?

Ask your classmate to think about answers.

I went / watched / visited …
I was visiting … when …
I liked it. I didn't like it.

Step 3

Change roles asking and answering questions.

CULTURE

BLARNEY CASTLE

Blarney Castle is a medieval fortress in county Cork, Ireland. The first Blarney Castle, built in the 10th century, was a wooden structure. A stone fortification replaced it two centuries later, around 1210, but, because of foundation problems, it was knocked down and the third medieval structure was constructed in 1446 by Cormac McCarthy. Although the McCarthy clan built Blarney Castle, different families possessed it over the centuries.

Blarney Castle is popular mainly because of the Blarney Stone, which carries many stories. The most accepted, however, is that in 1314 the Irish were supporting the Scots at the battle of Bannockburn so, in gratitude, Robert the Bruce (a Scot who defeated the English) gave a portion of the stone to McCarthy, who installed it at Blarney Castle. It became known as the Blarney Stone.

According to Irish folklore, any person who kisses the stone receives the ability to speak with eloquence, that is, to be a better communicator. They call it "the gift of the gab*." Kissing the stone became popular in the 1800s. Over the past 200 years, rich and poor, young and old, famous and not-so-famous, millions of kissing pilgrims have come looking for one thing in common: the gift of the gab.

*gab: the ability to talk a lot and for a long time about unimportant things.

1 Read and listen to the information above about Blarney Castle and write T for *true* or F for *false*. Correct the false statements.

54

- **a** ☐ Blarney Castle is situated in Cork, Ireland.
- **b** ☐ Around 1210, a third medieval structure was built.
- **c** ☐ The McCarthy clan owns the castle to this day.
- **d** ☐ One of the stories about the Blarney Stone is that Robert the Bruce gave a portion of the stone to McCarthy, who installed it at Blarney Castle.
- **e** ☐ According to Irish folklore, any person who kisses the stone receives the ability to speak different languages.
- **f** ☐ The Irish call this ability "the gift of the gab."

2 Do you know any famous castles or historical sites in your country? Do some online research to find out. Then name one of these sites and mention any fact about it that can attracts visitors.

VOCABULARY 2

Movement Verbs

1 Match pictures 1-8 with the words in the box. Mark an X next to the words that are not in the pictures.

carry ☐	cross ☐	drop ☐	fall ☐	follow ☐	jump ☐	lead ☐
lift ☐	move ☐	pull ☐	push ☐	sit ☐	stand ☐	

2 Listen and repeat.

55

3 Choose the correct words.

a A Serbian woman **fell** / **pushed** 10,160m without a parachute and survived.

b The "Iranian Hercules," Hossein Rezazadeh, **lifted** / **dropped** a total of 472.5kg at the 2004 Olympics.

c A man from Sri Lanka **stood** / **lifted** on one foot for 76 hours.

d Two Brazilians **crossed** / **carried** 8,120km on windsurf boards in the longest windsurfing journey.

e Canadian strongman Kevin Fast **jumped** / **pulled** a house weighing in at 35 tonnes a distance of 11.95 meters.

READING 2

1 Skim the text below quickly. Then match each paragraph with its key idea.

a 1st paragraph ☐ Patrick Moore's example
b 2nd paragraph ☐ What's April Fool's Day?
c 3rd paragraph ☐ "Catflights" example

April Fool!

April Fool's Day is April 1st, and on this day people traditionally play practical jokes. Companies and TV and radio stations often play tricks too, and their customers and audience believe them! Here are two examples of them.

In 2017, many American customers were searching for cheap airline tickets when they saw an ad for "Catflights." The website stated they were launching a filter to look for flights that offered the company of cats for people who were scared of flying. Customers had the option of crossing the Atlantic or Pacific carrying their own cats or sitting next to a pet owned by the airline company. Many people believed the ad and were trying to book a flight, but weren't able to do it. Then they called the company to find out it was an April Fool joke!

Why can't cats cross the country with a window view?

In 1976, Patrick Moore, a famous astronomer, played a trick on the radio. He said that Pluto was moving behind Jupiter and this was affecting Earth's gravity. He told people to jump in the air at exactly 9:47am if they wanted to feel the effect. By 9:49am, the radio station's phones were ringing. The trick was a wonderful success! Hundreds of people believed it and jumped. One woman said, "At exactly 9:47, while I was sitting with some friends, something lifted us into the air! We nearly reached the ceiling!"

2 Read and listen to the text above. Then choose the correct options below.
56

a The text is a …
☐ news story. ☐ magazine article.

b The photo caption intends to be …
☐ funny. ☐ reflective.

c April Fool's Day is a day when people …
☐ play tricks. ☐ tell jokes.

3 Underline the movement verbs in the text.

4 Scan the text and answer the questions.

a What were the customers looking for when they found "Catflights?"
____

b What was the website offering?
____

c According to Patrick Moore, what was Pluto doing?
____

d Why did people call the radio station?
____

e What was the woman doing at 9:47am?
____

5 Complete the sentences with the words from the box below. Then go back to the text and check your answers.

audience	customers	owner

a A cat may have an ______________.
b A company has ______________.
c A radio station has an ______________.

6 CLASS VOTE Do you think people would believe Patrick Moore's story nowadays?

GRAMMAR 2

Simple Past and Past Progressive

1 Read the sentences below. Circle the verbs in the simple past and underline the verbs in the past progressive.

a American customers were looking for cheap flights when they saw an ad.

b While customers were trying to book a flight the company announced it was a joke.

c People jumped into the air while Pluto was moving behind Jupiter.

d A woman was sitting with some friends when something lifted them into the air.

2 Look at the sentences in activity 1 again and complete the rules as to the use of the simple past and the past progressive.

a We use the ______________ to describe an activity in progress in the past.

b We use the ______________ to describe an action that interrupts the activity in progress in the past.

TIP

We usually use *when* before the simple past and *while* before the past progressive:
*We were sitting **when** we saw the snake. We saw the snake **while** we were sitting.*

3 Underline the correct words.

While a worker at Google's New York office **a** **looked after** / **was looking after** an enormous python, he **b** **took** / **was taking** it to work. He **c** **left** / **was leaving** the snake near his desk while he **d** **worked** / **was working** in a different part of the building. The python **e** **escaped** / **was escaping** while the man **f** **didn't watch** / **wasn't watching** it. Workers at Google then **g** **received** / **were receiving** a strange email: a giant snake **h** **moved** / **was moving** around the offices. A lot of people thought it was a joke because of the date – it was April Fool's Day. The cleaners **i** **found** / **were finding** the python more than 24 hours later while they **j** **cleaned** / **were cleaning** the offices. Fortunately, when they **k** **found** / **were finding** it, the snake **l** **slept** / **was sleeping**.

4 Write complete sentences. Use the simple past and the past progressive forms.

a I / carry / my plastic snake / when / my brother / see / it.

____

____

b She / open / the door / when / the water / fall / on her head.

____

____

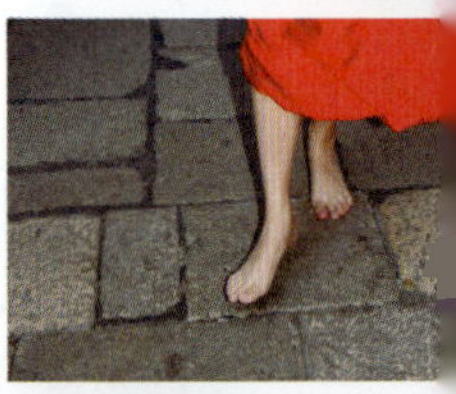

c When / the dancer / go out / into the street / she / not wear / any shoes.

____

____

d She / fall / while / she / carry / the plates.

____

____

5 Answer the questions with the past progressive or the simple past forms.

a What were you doing when the teacher arrived?

____

b What time did you eat your dinner last night?

____

c What were your parents doing when you finished school yesterday?

____

d What did you watch on television yesterday?

____

6 INTERFACE Work in pairs. Ask and answer the questions in activity 5.

What were you doing when the teacher arrived?

I was talking to my friend.

GRAMMAR GUIDE page 100

CLIL

PHYSICAL EDUCATION

The Legend of the Marathon

The marathon commemorates a famous event in ancient Greece. In 490 BC, a battle took place in the Greek town of Marathon between the Greeks and the Persians. The Persian army was larger and stronger than the Greek army, but the Greek army resisted and miraculously won the battle. This is a true story. But according to legend, a soldier called Pheidippides was sent to Athens to tell the people about the Greek victory. Pheidippides ran the 40 kilometers between Marathon and the capital without stopping. When he arrived, he shouted "Victory! Victory! Rejoice, we conquer!" and then died.

When the first modern Olympics took place in Athens in 1896, a 40-kilometer running race between Marathon and Athens was one of the events. It was called the marathon. At the London Olympics in 1908, the organizers wanted the marathon to finish directly in front of the British royal family in the stadium. As a result, they added an extra 2.195 kilometers to the marathon! Since then, all marathons are 42.195 kilometers.

A marathon nowadays

Statue of general Miltiades (550-489 BC), who served in the Battle of Marathon

1 Read and listen. Who did the Greeks defeat in the battle of Marathon? Write the answer.

57

____

2 Match the questions about the early Olympic Games with the corresponding answers below.

a Where were the first modern Olympic Games?
b How long was the first marathon race?
c Where were the Olympic Games held in 1908?
d Who changed the distance of the marathon race?
e How long have marathon races been since the London Olympics in 1908?

☐ All marathon races have been 42.195km since the London Olympics in 1908.
☐ The organizers of the London Olympic Games changed the distance of the marathon race to 42.195km.
☐ The first modern Olympic Games were in Athens in 1896.
☐ The first Olympic marathon race was 40km at the Athens Olympic Games.
☐ In 1908 the Olympic Games were held in London.

GRAMMAR GUIDE

Past Progressive

affirmative	
I **was** You **were** He / She / It **was** We **were** You **were** They **were**	**listening**.

- we use the past progressive to describe activities in progress at a specific time in the past
  They **were walking** to school at 7:30am this morning.
- the form is subject + *was* / *were* + verb + *-ing*

negative	contracted form
I **was not listening**.	**wasn't listening**.
You **were not listening**.	**weren't listening**.
He / She / It **was not listening**.	**wasn't listening**.
We / You / They **were not listening**.	**weren't listening**.

- we use *not* to form the negative form
  He **was not** running. / He **wasn't** running.

questions and short answers
Was I **walking**? Yes, I **was**. No, I **wasn't**.
Were you **walking**? Yes, you **were**. No, you **weren't**.
Was he / she / it **walking**? Yes, he / she / it **was**. No, he / she / it **wasn't**.
Were we / you / they **walking**? Yes, we / you / they **were**. No, we / you / they **weren't**.

- in questions we use *was* / *were* before the subject
  What **were** you doing at 9pm on Monday?
- we don't repeat the verb + *-ing* in short answers
  Were you **running** at 6pm?
  Yes, I **was**.

Simple Past and Past Progressive

- we often use the past progressive with the simple past in the same sentence
  I **was running** to catch the bus when I **fell**.
- we use the past progressive to describe activities which were in progress
  I **was running** to catch the bus ...
- we use the simple past to describe an action which interrupted an activity
  ... when I **fell**.
- we usually use *when* before the simple past and *while* before the past progressive
  He was carrying the box **when** he dropped it.
  While he was carrying the box, he dropped it.

Name: ______________________________

Class name / Period: ______________________________

Teacher: ______________________________

Date: ______________________________

PROGRESS CHECK

Character Adjectives

1 Match the character adjectives with pictures 1-6.

cheerful ☐ cruel ☐ funny ☐

lazy ☐ shy ☐ wise ☐

1

4

2

5

3

6

Movement Verbs

2 Order the letters to make movement verbs.

a prdo ______________

b lpul ______________

c fitl ______________

d woflol ______________

e spuh ______________

f voem ______________

g datsn ______________

h upjm ______________

i srcso ______________

Past Progressive

3 Complete the sentences with the past progressive form of the verbs in parentheses.

a I ______________ (sleeping).

b My brother ______________ (read) a book.

c It ______________ (not rain).

d My parents ______________ (not watch) TV.

e I ______________ (hear) some strange sound in the house.

f A ghost ______________ (move) around the house!

4 Order the words to make questions and negative sentences.

a doing / Were / you / your homework ?

____

____

b working / was / Your / mom / not

____

____

c Your friends / running / not / a marathon / were

____

____

d your teacher / Was / sitting / in the classroom ?

____

____

Simple Past and Past Progressive

5 Complete the sentences with the correct form of the verbs in parentheses.

a While they ________________ (throw) paper, the teacher arrived.

b I was following my friend when I ________________ (lose) him.

c He ________________ (try) to reach the cookies when he fell.

d While my mom was holding the baby, he ________________ (smile) for the first time.

Grammar Buildup 5

1 2 3 4 5 6 7 8

6 Complete the dialogue with the correct form of the verbs in parentheses.

Taylor You look happy. How **a** ________________ (be) your vacation?

Dustin Great! We **b** ________________ (have) a great time.

Taylor Really? **c** ________________ you ________________ (go) anywhere?

Dustin Yes, we **d** ________________ (take) the ferry to Puget Sound. We **e** ________________ (stay) in a little hotel on Bainbridge Island.

Taylor **f** ________________ you ________________ (see) anything interesting?

Dustin Yes! While we **g** ________________ (walk) on the beach I **h** ________________ (see) Bill Gates.

Taylor Really? What **i** ________________ he ________________ (do)?

Dustin He **j** ________________ (swim) in the sea.

Taylor That's incredible!

Dustin Oh, Taylor. It's April Fool's Day!

VOCABULARY IN PICTURES

Character Adjectives

Queen Boudicca was *brave*.

cheerful

The White Witch was *cruel*.

friendly

funny

kind

lazy

Sam Gamgee was *loyal* to Frodo.

selfish

shy

stubborn

Sherlock Holmes was *wise*.

Movement Verbs

carry

cross

drop

fall

follow

jump

lead

lift

move

pull

push

sit

stand

6

WISE SPENDING

1

2

3

4

VOCABULARY 1

Money

1 Look at the words in the box. What's their meaning? Check online.

borrow	☐	save	☐
buy	☐	sell	☐
earn	☐	spend	☐
lend	☐	swap	☐
pay (for)	☐	win	☐

2 Listen and repeat.

58

3 Match the words in activity 1 with pictures 1-7. Mark an X next to the words that are not represented in the pictures.

4 Choose the correct words.

My brother Karl is very bad with money. He **a spends / saves** all of his allowance on PC games and candy. He is always **b buying / winning** new clothes and he already has lots. My sister is the opposite. She **c swaps / pays** her old possessions with her friends so that she always has something new. She has a part-time job so she **d earns / wins** some extra money too.

5 Answer the questions.

a What do you spend your allowance on?

____

b What things do you lend to your friends?

____

c What things do you swap with your friends?

____

5

6

7

READING 1

1 Skim the following pieces of advice taken from a booklet about saving money. Match headings a-d with paragraphs 1-4.

a Do I really need it? ___

b Don't borrow money. ___

c New for old. ___

d Save money now. ___

Smart Tips for Young People

1 Would you like to have $10,000 on your 30th birthday? Well, you need to save either 78 cents a day from the age of 13, $4.47 a day from the age of 25, or $27 a day from the age of 29. Just do the math. It's more intelligent to save money early. So, how can you start saving money?

2 Imagine there's a new gaming console. It's faster and better than yours, but it's very expensive. At home, you have a lot of old games and a very old gaming console. Why don't you swap them for something new? Many games stores have a swapping system. They also sell second-hand games and consoles; they're often much cheaper than new products.

3 If you want to save for something big, use your initiative and do a part-time job on the weekend. You can earn a few dollars a week if you walk your neighbors' dogs or wash their cars, and a few dollars an hour if you look after children. Then you don't need to borrow – and you don't lose friends because you can't pay them back!

4 Before you spend money on something new, think about it. Do you really need the best cell phone in the store? Do you really need the biggest memory card for your camera or the best basketball? If the answer is no, don't buy it!

2 Read and listen to the pieces of advice. Choose the correct answers below.

59

a To have $10,000 you need to save 78 cents a day from …

1 the age of 13. **2** the age of 25.

b Many … sell second-hand games.

1 friends **2** stores

c To save a lot of money it is best to …

1 borrow it. **2** get a part-time job.

d The text advises you to:

1 think before you buy. **2** buy and think after.

3 Answer the questions.

a How can you get a lot of money on your 30th birthday?

____

b How can you get a new gaming console if you don't have much money?

____

c Why is it a good idea to buy second-hand products?

____

d What part-time jobs can you get to earn more money?

____

e Is it a good idea to buy something that you don't really need?

____

TIP

Antonyms are words that mean the opposite of another word. You can improve your vocabulary by learning them.

4 Match words in the text with the antonyms below.

a stupid ______________

b late ______________

c cheap ______________

d none ______________

e lend ______________

f old ______________

5 **CLASS VOTE** Which part of the text is the best piece of advice?

GRAMMAR 1

Comparatives

1 Look at the sentences in the table below.

It's **more intelligent** to save money early.
Some gaming consoles are **faster** and **better** than others.
Second-hand games are often much **cheaper** than new products.
8GB memory cards are **more expensive** than 1GB cards.

2 Use the words in the box to complete the rules of the use of comparative adjectives.

-er *good* irregular *more*
people, things, and places *than*

a We use comparative adjectives to compare ______________.

b We usually add _______ to short adjectives.

c We add _______ before long adjectives.

d *Better* is an _______ comparative. The corresponding adjective is _______.

e We add _______ after the comparative adjective.

3 Check online the meaning of the adjectives below and write the comparative forms.

a heavy ______________
b far ______________
c large ______________
d rich ______________
e fat ______________
f bad ______________
g old ______________
h intelligent ______________

4 Complete the sentences with the comparative form of the adjectives in parentheses.

a In the USA, many soft drinks are __________ (cheap) than mineral water.

b Gold is __________ (expensive) than silver.

c The USA is __________ (old) than Canada.

d A full-time job is ________ (tiring) than a part-time job.

e Getting a small allowance is __________ (good) than nothing.

5 Use some of the adjectives in the box to compare the items below.

expensive fast friendly funny
interesting quiet small

a cars / bicycles

____

b a cell phone / a laptop

____

c a dog / a cat

____

d a village / a city

____

6 Use the clues provided below to write affirmative or negative sentences about you. Use comparatives.

a Saving to shop for clothes / interesting / saving to buy books.

____

b The cell phone I want to buy / cheap / than a bike.

____

c New cheap clothes / nice / second-hand items.

____

d Spending at a mall / expensive / at a regular store.

____

PRONUNCIATION

Comparative *-er* /ər/

1 Listen and repeat.

60 heavier larger newer smaller

2 Listen to the sentences and repeat.

61 **a** My bedroom's **smaller** than his bedroom.
b My bicycle's **heavier** than his bicycle.

7 INTERFACE Work in pairs. Compare your sentences in activity 5.

Cars are more expensive than bicycles, don't you think?

Sure! And they're faster too.

(*not*) *as … as*

8 INTERFACE Join a classmate and look at the sentences in the chart below. Think together about what they indicate.

(*not*) *as … as*
Spending money is **not as good as** saving.
Buying new clothes is **as interesting as** buying second-hand items.
In my town, earning money walking dogs is **as popular as** washing cars.
In my opinion, buying something you don't need is **not as intelligent as** saving for something really important.

9 Look at the sentences in activity 8 again and underline the correct information to complete the rules.

a *As … as* is used to show that two things are **the same** / **different**.

b *Not as … as* is used to show that two things are **the same** / **different**.

c The adjective used **doesn't change** / **changes**.

10 Complete the information about mountain bikes and road bikes. Use *as … as* or *not as … as* and the adjectives in parentheses.

Mountain Bikes vs Road Bikes

The road bike is **a** ________________ for tough terrain **b** ________________ the mountain bike (appropriate / negative). A mountain bike is **c** ________________ a road bike (lightweight / negative). The tires of a road bike are **d** ________________ those of a mountain bike (thick / negative). Mountain bikes are **e** ________________ road bikes (fast / negative). Depending on what your riding plans are, buying a road bike is **f** ________________ a mountain bike (interesting / affirmative). Mountain bikes are **g** ________________ road bikes (nice / affirmative).

GRAMMAR GUIDE page 116

LISTENING

Allowance

1 62 Listen to Madelyn, Gus, and Kylie talking. Answer the questions for each speaker.

a How much allowance do you get?

____

____

b Do you buy your own clothes with this money?

____

c Do you have a part-time job?

____

2 62 Listen again and complete the sentences with the numbers in the box.

10	12	30	32

a Madelyn's friend earns $___ at her uncle's store.

b Gus would like to save $___ a month.

c Gus's best friend earns $___ a month.

d Kylie goes babysitting and earns $___ an hour.

3 Answer the questions.

a How often does Madelyn go shopping?

____

b Why can't she get a part-time job?

____

c How does Gus get his clothes?

____

d What job does his best friend have?

____

____

e What does Kylie spend her money on?

____

f How often does she babysit her neighbor's son?

____

SPEAKING

Going Shopping

Marion and John are shopping for clothes.
63 Listen and complete the dialogue.

Look at this blue hat, John! It's gorgeous!

It really is, but it's **a** ______________ the brown one.

It's **b** ______________ too. I like it, though.

How about this red sweater?

I think it's **c** ______________ than the blue one and it goes well with my black pants.

And you could try these sneakers with that outfit.

Really?

No, I think black shoes are much **d** ______________!

You're right. I'll get the red sweater, then.

Perfect choice!

FUNCTIONAL LANGUAGE

Talking about Shopping

Look at this / these … It's / They're lovely / gorgeous …
It's / They're more expensive / cheaper / nicer than …

Speaking Task

Join a classmate to pratice talking about shopping in a clothing store.

Step 1

Think about what clothing item(s) you want to buy. Your friend should help you with shopping ideas.

Step 2

Think about how you can compare items in a store:

Look at this / these … It's / They're lovely / gorgeous … No, they are not very nice.
It's / They're more expensive / more popular / cheaper / nicer / better than …
It looks good on me. / It doesn't look good on me.
It goes well with …
I'll take it (them).

Step 3

Take turns with your classmate practicing the dialogue.

CULTURE

American Teens' Spending Preferences

Just a few decades ago, the typical American family spent about 50% of its income on food and clothes. Nowadays, Americans spend only about a fifth of their budget on food and clothing. However, there is a group of Americans that spends about half of its cash on eating and clothes: teenagers.

Both middle-income and upper-income teens dedicate 60% of their spending on the "selfie budget" (clothing, accessories, personal care, footwear, and food), although upper-income teens' largest share goes to what is called the "social budget" (food, video games, music, movies, events, and books). Male teens usually spend more on social than selfie budgets, whereas female teens prefer selfie budgets.

With technology on the way, American teens are buying online, and there is a leader in e-commerce destination: Amazon, which is teens' favorite website to purchase from.

Where Do these Kids Get the Money for All That?

Many teens get an allowance from parents, others have after-school jobs, and a lot of them make money buying and selling clothes: they buy something, wear it for a while, and then sell it on sites like Grailed or eBay for more than they had originally paid.

Teens mustn't forget that their teenage years can be a great practice for the adult years to come. It is important to budget responsibly and not "burn through" all their cash. In the USA, one of the suggestions is: go to a 25-cent bin at Goodwill and learn what your must-haves are from a young age.

1 Read and listen to the information about American teens' spending preferences. Match the sentences below.

64

- **a** Teenagers spend half of their cash on ...
- **b** Upper-income teens' largest share goes to a social budget that is ...
- **c** The leader in e-commerce for teens ...
- **d** Teens get money from various sources: ...
- **e** Teens must learn to budget responsibly ...

- ☐ allowances, after-school jobs, and selling their second-hand clothes on sites.
- ☐ clothing and food.
- ☐ and not simply spend all their cash.
- ☐ food, video games, music, movies, events, and books.
- ☐ is Amazon.

2 Look at the chart below. Choose if the information provided is the same or different in your country.

American teens	teens in my country	
	the same	different
Spend 60% of their cash on their selfie budget.		
Male teens usually spend more on social than selfie budgets, whereas female teens prefer selfie budgets.		
The leader in e-commerce is Amazon.		
Many teens get an allowance from parents.		
Many teens have after-school jobs.		
Many teens make money selling second-hand clothes online.		

VOCABULARY 2

Technology Devices

1 Match pictures 1-8 with the words in the box. Mark an X next to the ones that are not in the pictures.

desktop	☐	scanner	☐
earbuds	☐	screen	☐
keyboard	☐	speaker	☐
laptop	☐	tablet	☐
mouse	☐	USB hub	☐
printer	☐	webcam	☐

1

2

3
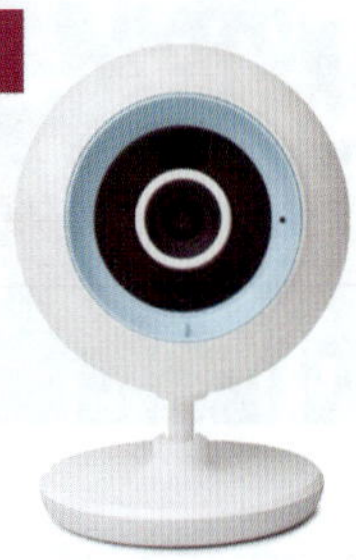

4

5

6

7

8

2 Listen and repeat.

65

3 Complete the definitions below with words from activity 1.

a A ____________ is a small computer you can carry.

b You click on the ____________ to do things on the computer screen.

c A ____________ is a camera which is connected to a computer.

d You need a ____________ to put computer documents or images on paper.

e You use a ____________ to type information into the computer.

f With a Bluetooth ____________, you can listen to your favorite songs.

READING 2

1 Skim the text and answer: How can you get things for free on this website?

____

www.bigswapstore.com

The Big Swap Store

Do you have a laptop or tablet that you no longer use? Did you get earbuds for your birthday but didn't like the model? Do you want any newer or better things? With the Big Swap Store, you can swap your things for free. Just follow these five easy steps:

Step 1: Register your name and address on our website. Are you under 18 years old? Your parents also need to complete the registration form.

Step 2: Make a list of the things you want to swap. Include a short description of each one.

For example:

Laptop. It's less than 6 months old and in excellent condition. It has a 12.5-inch screen and a lot of storage space (SSD 1TB).

Step 3: Our website automatically calculates some points for each thing on your list, for example, a laptop = 12,500 points, a pair of earbuds = 1,000 points, a five-port USB hub = 250 points.

Step 4: Search our website and choose something new. There are more than 15,000 things you can choose from, including a lot of computer games and books.

Step 5: Use your swap points to get products for free!

Happy swapping!

2 Underline the correct option.

The text in activity 1 is **an encyclopedia article / a tutorial**.

3 Read the text and listen. Then write T for *true* or F for *false*.

66

- **a** ☐ First you need to give your name and address.
- **b** ☐ You can't use this website if you are under 18.
- **c** ☐ You need to describe the objects you want to swap.
- **d** ☐ The website gives you money for your unwanted things.
- **e** ☐ This website doesn't have many books.

4 CLASS VOTE Would you use this swap store website?

GRAMMAR 2

a / an, some, any

1 Look at the sentences in the chart and complete the rules below.

countable nouns
The desktop computer has **a** keyboard and **a** mouse.
It also has **an** 18.5 inch screen.
Computer games have **some** interesting features.
Tablets don't have **any** physical keyboards.
Does a laptop have **any** internal speaker?

uncountable nouns
My tablet doesn't have **any** memory.
Does your tablet have **any** memory?
I have **some** time to go to the store, but I don't have **any** money for new earbuds.

a We use _______ and _______ with singular countable nouns.

b We use _______ in affirmative sentences with uncountable nouns and plural countable nouns.

c We use _______ in negative sentences and questions.

2 Complete with *a / an*, *some* or *any*.

I have **a** ________ old computer and **b** ________ PC games. I also have **c** ________ printer, but it doesn't have **d** ________ ink. Do you have **e** ________ old PC games?

much, many, a lot of

3 Look at the sentences in the chart and complete the rules.

countable nouns
The website shows **a lot of** laptops, but it doesn't offer **many** desktop computers.
How **many** USB hubs do you need?

uncountable nouns
That new laptop has **a lot of** internal memory!
The manual doesn't provide **much** information.
How **much** information do you need?

a For countable nouns:

1 Use ________ in questions.

2 Use ________ in affirmative sentences.

3 Use ________ in negative sentences.

b For uncountable nouns:

1 Use ________ in questions.

2 Use ________ in affirmative sentences.

3 Use ________ in negative sentences.

4 Complete the dialogue with *a / an*, *some*, *any*, *much*, *many*, or *a lot of*.

Buyer: How **a** _______ memory does this computer have?

Clerk: It doesn't have **b** _______ memory, but you can buy **c** _______ new USB hub to use memory devices.

Buyer: **d** ___________ inches is the screen?

Clerk: It's **e** _______ 18-inch screen. This computer doesn't have **f** _______ new features, but it pays off.

Buyer: I see it has **g** _______ advantages!

67 **5** Listen and check.

6 INTERFACE Work in pairs. Practice the dialogue in activity 4.

GRAMMAR GUIDE page 116

WRITING

Comments for an Online Magazine

1 EXPLORING THE CONTEXT

1 Skim the text on page 115 quickly.

a Who wrote the text?

☐ The journalists of *Teen Life* magazine.

☐ Ellie, a reader of *Teen Life* magazine.

b What is the text about?

☐ Ellie's favorite things.

☐ Teenagers' favorite things.

68 **2** Read the text on page 115 and complete it with the words in the box below. Then listen and check your answers.

gold red white

www.teenlife.com

TEEN LIFE | Style | Beauty | Life & Politics

MY FAVORITE THINGS

We don't have everything we love, but we love everything we have! Our reader Ellie, 12, tells us about her favorite things.

MY LAPTOP

I have a beautiful **a** ________ laptop. My mom gave it to me three months ago and I love it. I always do my homework, I sometimes play games, and I watch videos three or four times a day. It's great!

MY SOCCER SHIRT

Everyone likes buying clothes except me! But I love Atlanta United, so last year I saved all my allowance and I bought the **b** ________ soccer shirt. My mom says it was more expensive than her new gold watch. I don't believe her!

MY COIN

My uncle bought me this wonderful small **c** ________ coin while he was working in New York. It's the Statue of Liberty. It's bigger than a dollar coin. I like it because I'd like to visit New York when I'm older.

3 Complete the chart about the text above.

Object	laptop	shirt	coin
Why does Ellie like it?			Because she'd like to visit New York.
How did Ellie get it?		She bought it with her allowance.	
How does the object look?	It's white and beautiful.		

2 PLANNING

1 Choose three favorite objects to write about for *Teen Life* magazine.

2 Make notes for each object. How does it look? How did you get it? Why do you like it?

LANGUAGE FOCUS

Adjective Word Order
Adjectives make your descriptions more interesting. Use them in a specific order:
I have a ***beautiful white*** laptop.
Look at his ***new gold*** watch.
That's a ***wonderful small gold*** coin.

1 Complete the chart with the words in the box.

beautiful grey second-hand small

opinion	size	age	color	noun
lovely	big	old	red	phone watch

2 Rewrite the sentences with the adjectives in parentheses.

My pens and pencils are in a big box. (lovely)
My pens and pencils are in a lovely big box.

a I bought a new T-shirt two days ago. (purple)
____

b The black bag was the cheapest in the store. (old)
____

c I love my cousin's blue earrings. (small)
____

3 WRITING

1 Write a first draft. Use your notes from Step 2.

2 Use more than one adjective when describing your favorite things.

4 CHECKING & EDITING

1 Join a classmate to read each other's comments. Check:

- Does the text show why the classmate likes the objects and how he or she got them?
- Are the descriptions rich, interesting?

2 Use your classmate's suggestions to prepare the final version of your text. Include pictures.

5 SHARING

1 Using a file-sharing service, gather the comments of the whole class.

2 What are the most popular objects? Any curious item?

GRAMMAR GUIDE

Comparatives

	adjective	comparative
1 syllable adjectives	big old large	bigger than older than larger than
2 syllables ending *-y*	easy	easier than
2 or more syllables	famous	more famous than
Irregular	good bad far	better than worse than farther / further than

- we use comparative adjectives to compare two things, places, or people
  John is **taller** than David.
- we form comparatives by adding *-er* to adjectives with one syllable or adjectives with two syllables ending in *-y*
  Kansas City is **smaller** than Detroit.
  I think math is **easier** than science.
- for adjectives with more than one syllable, we use *more* + adjective
  Activity 1 is **more difficult** than activity 2.
- we use *than* after comparative adjectives
  Detroit is **bigger than** Phoenix.
- *good*, *bad*, and *far* are irregular adjectives and they have a different comparative form
  Boston Celtics is **better** than Utah Jazz.

(not) as … as

- we use *as* … *as* to show that two things are the same
  New York is **as famous as** London.
- we use *not as* … *as* to show that two things are different
  The Taj Mahal is **not as old as** the Great Pyramid.

a / an, some, any much, many, a lot of

	countable	uncountable
+	It has **a** screen.	
+	There are **some** screens.	There is **some** memory.
+	There are **a lot of** screens.	There is **a lot of** memory.
+	It doesn't have **a** screen.	
–	There aren't **many** screens.	There isn't **much** memory.
–	There aren't **any** screens.	There isn't **any** memory.
?	Does it have **a** screen?	Is there **any** memory?
?	Are there **any** screens?	Does it have **much** memory?

- we use *a / an*, *some*, *any*, *a lot of*, *much*, and *many* to talk about quantities of things
- we use *a / an* with singular countable nouns; we do not use *a / an* with uncountable nouns
  I have **a** laptop.
- we use *some* in affirmative sentences with plural countable nouns and uncountable nouns to talk about a medium quantity
  She has **some** money so she can buy the memory card.
- we use *a lot of* in affirmative sentences with plural countable nouns and uncountable nouns to talk about a large quantity
  James has **a lot of** tablets.
- we use *many* in negative sentences with plural countable nouns to talk about a small quantity
  She doesn't have **many** computer games.
- we use *much* in negative sentences with uncountable nouns to talk about a small quantity
  The laptop doesn't have **much** memory.
- we use *any* in negative sentences with plural countable nouns and uncountable nouns to talk about zero quantity
  He couldn't buy the new computer game because he didn't have **any** money.

Name: ____________________

Class name / Period: ____________________

Teacher: ____________________

Date: ____________________

PROGRESS CHECK

Money

1 Complete the words with letters.

a b ___ r r ___ ___

b ___ w a p

c s ___ ___ n ___

d s ___ ___ e

e e ___ r ___

f ___ i ___

Technology Devices

2 Identify the computer parts in the pictures.

a ____________________

b ____________________

c ____________________

d ____________________

e ____________________

f ____________________

Comparatives

3 Write sentences with the comparative form of the adjectives below comparing the laptop and the desktop.

	weight	price	speed
A laptop	2.68kg	$300	✓
A desktop	12kg	$350	✓✓

a heavy

____

____

b expensive

____

____

c cheap

____

____

d fast

____

____

e slow

____

____

(not) as … as

4 Complete the sentences with the words in parentheses.

My school bag / my pencil case. (small) ✓

My school bag is as small as my pencil case.

a My school bag / my shoes. (heavy) ✗

____

____

b My pen / my pencil. (new) ✗

____

____

c My English book / my math book. (difficult) ✓

____

____

d My hands / my friend's hands. (large) ✓

____

____

e My father / my friend's father. (young) ✗

____

____

a / an, some, any, much, many, a lot of

5 Choose the correct options.

a I have **an** / **a** unwanted laptop.

b It doesn't have **many** / **much** memory.

c It has **a lot of** / **any** accessories, such as a mouse and a keyboard.

d I also have **some** / **any** DVDs and CDs.

e I don't have **many** / **much** computer games.

f Do you have **some** / **any** unwanted items?

g It has **a lot of** / **much** memory.

Grammar Buildup 6

1 2 3 4 5 6 7 8

6 Complete the dialogue with the correct form of the verbs in parentheses.

Will Excuse me, how much **a** ____________ the T-shirt ____________ (cost)?

Assistant It **b** ____________ (be) $8.99.

Will Can I **c** ____________ (try) it on?

Assistant Yes, of course!

Emma That looks great, Will, and it's cheap. I **d** ____________ (buy) a similar T-shirt last week and it **e** ____________ (be) more expensive. How much **f** ____________ these earrings ____________ (cost)?

Assistant They **g** ____________ (be) $6.

Will I'll **h** ____________ (have) the T-shirt and the earrings. I'm paying!

Emma But, Will!

Will It **i** ____________ (be) your birthday last week and I **j** ____________ (forget).

Emma Thanks, Will.

VOCABULARY IN PICTURES

Money

borrow

buy

earn

lend

pay (for)

save

sell

spend

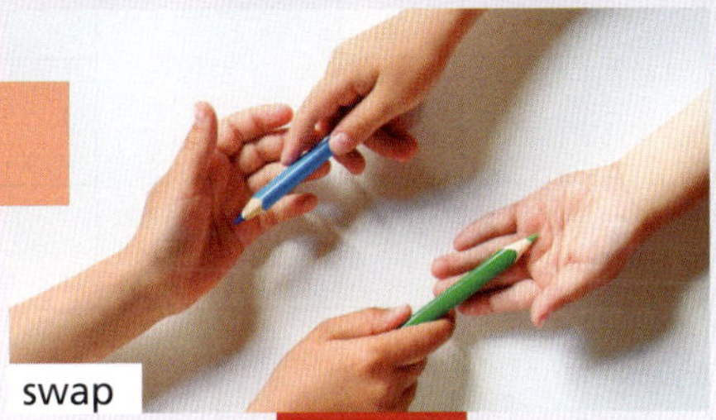
swap

win

Technology Devices

desktop

earbuds

keyboard

laptop

mouse

printer

scanner

screen

speaker

tablet

USB hub

webcam

REVIEW 3

VOCABULARY

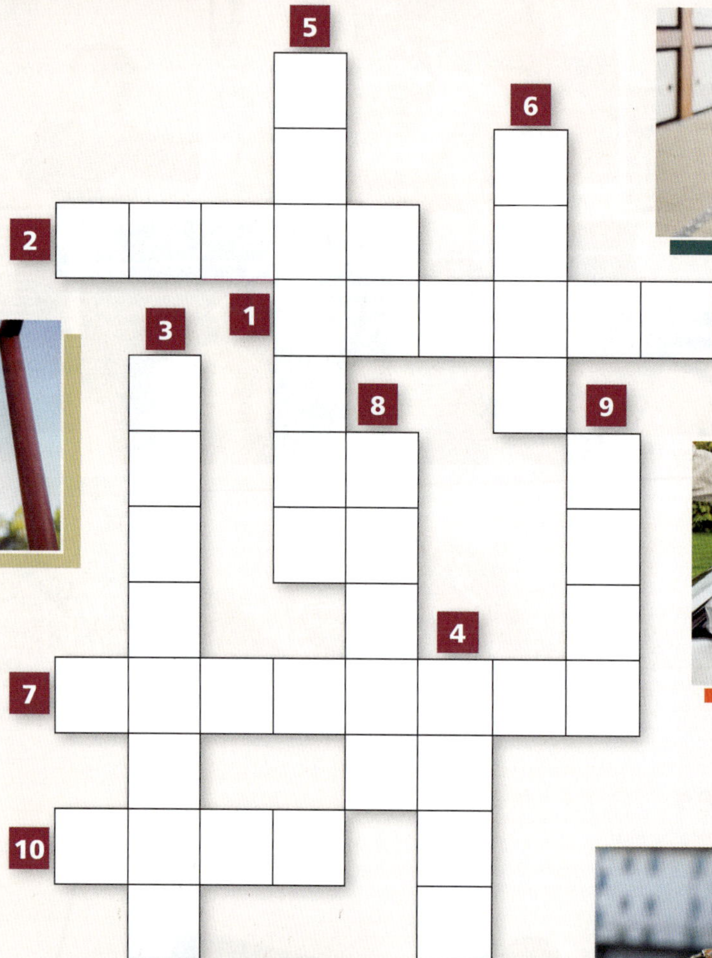

1. when you temporarily take something from someone
2. to take something from one place to another
3. someone who is always happy and excited
4. to let something fall from your hands
5. we use to listen to music on our phones
6. when you get something you worked for, you … it
7. someone who easily makes friends
8. a person who makes people laugh
9. someone who never wants to work or make an effort
10. to move something forward or away from you

11 we do this to have more money in the future

12 the flat surface of your computer on which you see images / words

13 someone who only thinks about himself or herself

14 we use to listen to music on our computers

15 when you *use* your money, you … it

16 someone who doesn't want to change his or her mind

17 to exchange something with another person

18 the mobile computing device that has a flat, rectangular form, and it's touch screen

19 when you get something like a prize or reward

20 a person who knows a lot of things

REVIEW 3

GRAMMAR

Past Progressive

1 Complete the sentences with the past progressive affirmative form of the verbs in the box.

drive	have	listen
~~read~~	swim	watch

I ___was reading___ a comic in bed at 10pm.

a My friends ______________ in the sea.

b Matt ______________ a horror film.

c My dad ______________ his new car.

d You ______________ to music.

e We ______________ a g0reat time.

2 Write negative sentences using the past progressive form.

I / not talk / to my friends
I wasn't talking to my friends.

a we / not win / the match

____

b I / not feel / brave

____

c the children / not fight / in the playground

____

d you / not walk / very fast

____

e my teacher / not smile

____

3 Order the words to make questions.

in the afternoon / Was / swimming / Oliver ?
Was Oliver swimming in the afternoon?

a Sophie / playing cards / at 5pm / Was ?

____

b you / Were / studying / yesterday morning ?

____

c at 6am / she / Was / sleeping ?

____

Simple Past and Past Progressive

4 Complete the sentences with the correct form of the verbs in parentheses. Use the simple past or the past progressive forms.

While I was standing at the bus stop,
I ___saw___ my grandma. (see)

a I was carrying the shopping bag when I __________ the eggs. (drop)

b We arrived home, we __________ dinner, and then we went to bed. (have)

c My friends __________ their homework when I called them. (do)

d When I __________ you for the first time, you were wearing a pink dress. (meet)

5 Underline the correct words.

I was dancing **while / when** the music stopped. (answer: when)

a They heard a strange noise **while** / **when** they were watching TV.

b **While** / **When** I was cleaning my hamster's cage, it escaped.

c **While** / **When** my brother arrived home, my parents were sleeping.

d I was listening to music **while** / **when** the teacher arrived.

e My mom found some old pictures **while** / **when** she was cleaning her desk.

6 Rewrite the sentences with the correct forms of the verbs in parentheses.

Liam was (study) in his bedroom.
Liam was studying in his bedroom.

a We didn't (feel) tired.

____

b What were you (do) yesterday at 9pm?

____

c Were you (read) a book when I called you?

____

d You weren't (dance) in the disco at 2am.

____

Comparatives

7 Write the comparative forms of these adjectives below.

old ___older___
a heavy ______
b rich ______
c busy ______
d big ______
e expensive ______
f intelligent ______
g difficult ______
h good ______
i bad ______
j far ______
k large ______
l fat ______
m funny ______
n friendly ______
o interesting ______
p quiet ______
q small ______

8 Complete the sentences with the comparative form of the adjectives in parentheses.

My sneakers are ___newer___ than my boots. (new)

a The bus station is ______ than the train station. (busy)

b Monkeys are ______ than dogs. (intelligent)

c Ostriches are ______ than humans. (fast)

d Cola is ______ for you than water. (bad)

e Books are ______ than earbuds. (heavy)

(not) as ... as

9 Underline the correct options.

I'm going to eat now. I**'m as** / **'m not as** hungry as a bear.

a I can't see the board, but you can. My eyes **are as** / **aren't as** good as yours.

b Are you OK? You're very pale. You**'re as** / **aren't as** white as a sheet!

c This exercise is simple! It**'s as** / **isn't as** easy as ABC.

d Mexico City **is as** / **isn't as** big as São Paulo.

a / an, some, any, much, many, a lot of

10 Underline the correct options.

We have **some** / **any** computers in our classroom.

a My printer doesn't have **a** / **any** ink.

b **How much** / **How many** tablets do you have?

c There's **some** / **a** milk in the fridge.

d We don't have **a** / **any** homework today.

e **How much** / **How many** money do you need?

11 Complete the sentences with *a lot of*, *not many*, or *not much*.

I love Brad Pitt. I have ___a lot of___ his movies.

a There are ______ children in the park because it's cold and wet.

b We're not pleased. We have ______ homework to do tonight.

c There is ______ water. Let's buy another bottle.

d I'm surprised. It's cold and there are ______ people on the beach.

e There is ______ USB ports. I need a new USB hub.

Digital Footprint

The Product Is You!

1 Read and listen. Complete the statements with the verbs from the box.

69

continued	gave up	left
sold	thought	watched

a Daniel __________ about starting a band.

b Daniel __________ videos on how to start a band.

c In doing so, Daniel __________ a digital footprint.

d Daniel's browsing data was __________ to music stores, and they started sending him advertisements.

e Daniel __________ on starting a band.

f Daniel __________ to receive advertisements for musical instruments.

2 Read about digital footprint. Then answer the questions.

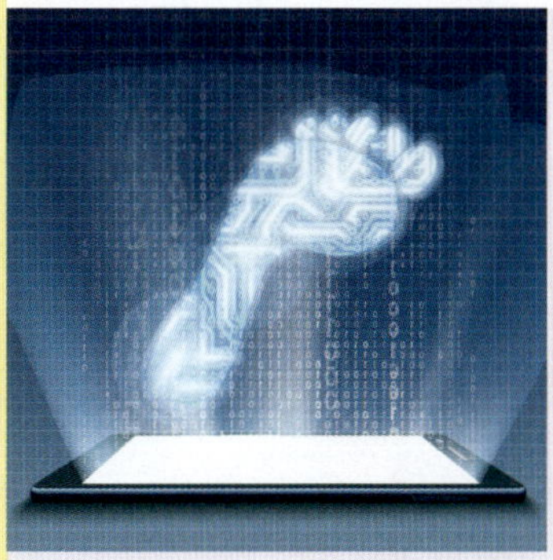

Whenever you use online services, you leave a **digital footprint**. There are two types of footprint: passive footprint and active footprint.

An **active digital footprint** is data you intentionally leave behind. This may include posts on social media sites or a subscription to an online newsletter.

A **passive digital footprint** is data you leave behind without knowing. This occurs, for example, when you watch videos or do an online search.

a In *The Toothpaste* story on page 84, Lily and Grace regretted things they had posted or shared online. In that case, did they leave an active or passive digital footprint?

____

b What about Daniel in *The Product Is You!* story? Did he leave an active or passive digital footprint?

____

3 Read again: "If you're not paying for it, you're the product being sold!" What does this statement mean? Check (✓) all that apply.

a ☐ Daniel will have to pay for the videos he watched.

b ☐ There are no truly free services.

c ☐ A service that appears to be free actually earns money by selling your data.

4 Work with two or three classmates. Complete the charts about pros and cons of digital footprint and how to manage them. If necessary, seek information on digital footprints.

Digital footprints	
Pros	**Cons**
Companies can recommend items based on your preferences.	You may receive unwanted advertising.

How to manage your digital footprint?
Get rid of your unused online accounts.

5 Share your notes with the other groups. Discuss as a class:

a Have you come to similar conclusions?

b Do people have different ways of dealing with their digital footprint?

7

AMAZING PLACES

1

2

3

4

VOCABULARY 1

Places to Visit 1

1 Match pictures 1-7 with the places in the box below. Mark an X in the words not represented in the pictures.

a castle ☐	a rainforest ☐
a cave ☐	a reef ☐
a coastline ☐	a ruin ☐
a lighthouse ☐	a temple ☐
an opera house ☐	a tomb ☐
a pyramid ☐	

2 Listen and repeat.

70

3 Underline the correct options.

a The city of Pompeii is full of Roman **ruins** / **pyramids**.

b La Scala in Milan is the world's most famous **tomb** / **opera house**.

c West Quoddy Light in Maine is an old **castle** / **lighthouse**.

d The most famous **reef** / **cave** in the world is near the coast of Australia.

e The most biodiverse **rainforest** / **opera house** is in Brazil.

f The Tower of London is a famous **lighthouse** / **castle**.

g The Parthenon is an ancient Greek **temple** / **cathedral**.

h Lascaux, in France, has a **ruin** / **cave** with prehistoric paintings.

4 Listen to Rita and Dan. What is Cuzco famous for?

71

____

READING 1

1 Look at the pictures and the title of the newspaper feature on page 129. What do the Great Pyramid of Giza and the Taj Mahal have in common?

____

2 Read the feature and listen. Check your answer.

72

3 Read the newspaper feature again. Match headings a-c with paragraphs 1-3.

a ☐ The Taj Mahal

b ☐ UNESCO Sites

c ☐ The Great Pyramid

5

6

7

A World of Heritage

What do these places have in common? Stonehenge, Notre Dame, Yellowstone National Park, and the Inca ruins of Cuzco. Any ideas? Yes, they are all UNESCO World Heritage sites.

1 There are 1,073 UNESCO (United Nations Educational, Scientific and Cultural Organization) World Heritage sites. Many people think that World Heritage sites are all famous old structures like Stonehenge, but this is not true. Some are natural places, like Yellowstone National Park, not cultural, man-made monuments. Two of the most famous cultural sites are the Great Pyramid of Giza and the Taj Mahal in Agra, India.

2 The Egyptian Pharaoh Khufu ordered his people to build the Great Pyramid as his tomb. It took nearly 100,000 workers twenty years to complete. The builders needed over 2 million granite blocks to make the pyramid, but first they had to transport the blocks over 500 miles. They used boats to bring the blocks down the River Nile from Aswan, and the result was the biggest pyramid in the world.

3 The Taj Mahal is not as old as the Great Pyramid. In the seventeenth century, the Mughal emperor Shah Jahan had a favorite wife called Mumtaz Mahal. When she died, he wanted to build an everlasting monument for her. He ordered 20,000 workers to build an enormous white marble tomb decorated with gold and precious stones. The builders needed more than 1,000 elephants to bring the marble to the site. It took over twenty years to build and it looks more like a palace than a tomb. Many people think the Taj Mahal is more beautiful than the Great Pyramid. Some people even call it the loveliest building in the world.

Why not look at the UNESCO website and find out if there are any World Heritage sites near you?

4 Choose the correct options.

a The Taj Mahal and the Great Pyramid are both …
1 in India. **2** cultural sites. **3** natural sites.

b How did the builders move the granite to build the Great Pyramid?
1 by elephant **2** by chariot **3** by boat

c Why did Shah Jahan build the Taj Mahal?
1 because his favorite wife died **2** as a palace for his family **3** as a present for his wife

d Which site is older?
1 the Great Pyramid **2** the Taj Mahal **3** they are the same age

5 What do the numbers below refer to in the text?

a 1,073 ____________________
b 2 million ____________________
c 100,000 ____________________
d 500 ____________________
e 20,000 ____________________
f 1,000 ____________________

6 Match items a-e with the definitions.

a in common ☐ most beautiful
b slaves ☐ continuing to exist forever
c blocks ☐ the same
d everlasting ☐ large pieces of stone
e loveliest ☐ workers who are not free

7 CLASS VOTE Which of the World Heritage sites in the feature would you like to visit?

GRAMMAR 1

Superlatives

1 Read the sentences and underline the superlative adjectives.

a Two of the most famous cultural sites are the Great Pyramid of Giza and the Taj Mahal in Agra, India.

b The Great Pyramid is the biggest pyramid in the world.

c Some people think the Taj Mahal is the loveliest building in the world.

d The best Roman ruins to visit are Pompeii and Herculaneum.

2 Complete the chart as to the use of superlative adjectives.

superlative adjectives		
	adjective	superlative
Add *-est* to most short adjectives	small	the ______________
Add *most* to long adjectives	famous	the ______________
Irregular forms	good	the ______________

* Use *the* before all superlatives.

3 The chart below presents basic rules for spelling comparatives and superlatives. Use the adjectives in the box to fill in the chart accordingly.

bad big busy famous good interesting old pretty sad smart

comparatives	superlatives
Add *-er* to one syllable adjectives: ______________	Use *the* and add *-est* to one syllable adjectives: ______________
One-syllable adjective with a consonant-vowel-consonant pattern: double the consonant and add *-er*: ______________	One-syllable adjective with a consonant-vowel-consonant pattern: double the consonant and add *-est* (don't forget *the*): ______________
Two-syllable adjectives ending in *-y:* change the *-y* to *-i* and add *-er:* ______________	Two-syllable adjectives ending in *-y:* change the *-y* to *-i* and add *-est* (don't forget *the*): ______________
Adjectives with two or more syllables, use *more* before the adjective: ______________	Adjectives with two or more syllables, use *the most* before the adjective: ______________
Irregular words have no pattern: ______________	Irregular words have no pattern: ______________

4 Underline the correct options in the sentences.

a The Amazon Basin hosts **the most** / **the more** important rainforest in the world.

b I think New York is the **goodest** / **best** city in the world for music.

c The Blue Grotto, on the island of Capri, is one of the **loveliest** / **lovelier** caves in the world.

d The Smithsonian, in the USA, is **the larger** / **the largest** research and museum complex in the world.

e Oymyakon in Russia is said to be one of the **worst** / **bad** travel destinations because it is home to one of **the coldest** / **the most cold** weather in the world.

5 Read about some top rainforests in the world. Complete the statements with the superlative form of the adjectives in parentheses.

Tongass National Forest, Alaska

a Tongass National Forest in the USA is home to ________________ (endangered) species of flora and fauna in the country.

b Ecuador's Cloud forest has more than 1,500 different types of birds; it has some of ________________ (diverse) bird fauna in the world.

c The Amazon rainforest is ________________ (large) rainforest in the world; it provides 20% of the Earth's oxygen.

d Khao Sok National Park in the south of Thailand has an area of untouched rainforest which is one of ________________ (old) evergreen forests in the world.

6 INTERFACE Work in pairs. Talk about places you know using the superlative.

What is the most interesting place you know?

It's the Grand Canyon, and you?

GRAMMAR GUIDE page 138

LISTENING

Amazing Places

1 Look at the pictures and make a guess about the questions below.

a How old is the man?

____

b What kind of building is this?

____

2 Listen and check your answers. 73

3 Listen again and mark the correct options. 73

a When did he start building?

☐ 1961 ☐ 1971

b How big is the building?

☐ $40m^2$ ☐ $8,000m^2$

c Who helps him with the building?

☐ his grandchildren ☐ his nephews

d What materials does he use?

☐ recycled materials ☐ new materials

e What did he advertise on TV?

☐ his building ☐ a sports drink

4 CLASS VOTE What would you prefer to build from recycled materials – a castle or a university?

SPEAKING

A Day Tour

74 Nicholas and Anna are talking about a day tour in Cambridge, Massachusetts, in the USA. Listen and complete the dialogue.

How about going to Cambridge next Saturday?

I think it's a good idea. It's in the Boston area and it has one of **a** ________________ universities, Harvard University. Many famous people were students there!

People say one of **b** ________________ ways to see the sights is by bike. We can book a bike tour or just rent a bike in town.

Great idea! I've also heard they have **c** ________________ Baked Alaskas.

Baked Alaskas? What are they?

They are **d** ________________ sticky treats I've ever tried! They're made of meringue, cake, and ice cream, and they look like a baked glacier. You're seriously missing out!

OK, Baked Alaskas are in ... What else can we see there?

The MIT museum! It is a very popular tourist site and one of **e** ________________ technology museums in the world.

OK! What do you think about buying the train tickets now?

Let's do it!

FUNCTIONAL LANGUAGE

Describing a Place

It's the most famous / interesting / popular place in town.
It's the loveliest / nicest / biggest ...
What can we see there?

The Great Dome of the MIT, Massachusetts

Speaking Task

Join a classmate to plan a day trip together.

Step 1

Fill in the fact file

Where: ________________

To do: ________________

Special treat / food: ________________

Step 2

Think about the questions to ask to your classmate:

What is to do there?
What can we see there?
What places can we visit?
What do you think about ... ?
How about ... ?

Plan possible answers:

It's the best / the most interesting (famous / popular) / the loveliest / biggest / smallest / funniest ...
Great idea!
I'd love to!
Let's go!

Step 3

Change roles asking and answering questions.

CULTURE

Aerial view of the Great Barrier Reef

Traditional Owners of the Great Barrier Reef

The Great Barrier Reef (GBR), located off the coast of Queensland in Australia, is the world's largest coral reef system. It is composed of 2,900 individual reefs and hundreds of breathtaking tropical islands with some of the world's most beautiful golden beaches. It is considered one of the seven wonders of the natural world and the only living thing on Earth which is visible from space as it stretches 2,300 kilometers from Tropical North Queensland in the north, right down to Bundaberg in the south.
Two tribal indigenous groups of Australia have social, economic, and cultural links with the Great Barrier Reef: Aboriginal and Torres Strait Islanders. Around fifty thousand years ago, they established themselves in the area and until now they extract natural resources from the local seacoast. Therefore, the GBR environment is crucial to their cultural values and way of life. These indigenous groups believe they are part of nature: Turtle and fish, for instance, are a principal part of their diet. They are also very important during festivities and ceremonies. Marine animals are totems for some groups. A bird or fish may become a family clan emblem. Combs and shells are carved with images of sea creatures. Traditional dancing sometimes imitates marine creatures.
Local Aboriginal and Torres Strait Islanders help the Marine Park Authority keep the GBR safe as it symbolizes indigenous Australian culture.

Native people during a traditional Aboriginal dance

1 75 **Read and listen to the information above. Then choose the correct alternatives.**

a The Great Barrier Reef is …
- ☐ considered one of the seven wonders of the ancient world.
- ☐ the only living thing on Earth which can be seen from space.

b Aboriginal and Torres Strait Islanders are two …
- ☐ indigenous groups who inhabit the Great Barrier Reef region.
- ☐ indigenous groups who settled in New Zealand not too long ago.

c … are a principal part of their diet.
- ☐ Farm animals
- ☐ Fish and turtle

d The Great Barrier Reef environment …
- ☐ is represented in traditional dances, totems, and objects of locals to this day.
- ☐ was only important for Aboriginal and Torres Strait Islanders 50,000 years ago.

e Local indigenous groups ...
- ☐ see themselves as part of nature.
- ☐ believe to be more evolved than nature.

f Aboriginals and Torres Strait Islanders …
- ☐ refuse any help from the Marine Park Authority.
- ☐ help the Marine Park Authority protect the GBR.

2 **Are there any groups of people historically and culturally representative of your country? Where and how do they live?**

____

____

____

3 INTERFACE **Join a classmate and share your findings.**

VOCABULARY 2

Formation of Adverbs

1 Complete the chart below with the adverb form of the adjectives in the box. Then listen and repeat.

76

~~angry~~ bad ~~careful~~ correct easy ~~fast~~ good happy hard noisy quiet

	adjective	adverb
add *-ly*	careful	carefully
remove *-y*, add *-ily*	angry	angrily
irregular	fast	fast

2 Read the sentences. Which has an adverb and which has an adjective?

a He drove home carefully. ______

b He's a careful driver. ______

3 Look at the sentences in activity 2 and choose the correct words to complete the rule.

Adverbs usually go **at the beginning** / **in the middle** / **at the end** of a sentence.

4 Order the words to make sentences.

a works / My / sister / hard / very

______

b question / student / the / answered / The / correctly

______

c I / homework / carefully / did / my

______

d badly / I / the / play / guitar

______

e drive / very / fast / People / Italy / in

______

f My / speak / can / dad / well / French

______

READING 2

1 Skim the texts and choose the correct option.

The Travel Tips mobile app features …

a a guide for visitors to The Museum of Modern Art.

b user reviews of The Museum of Modern Art.

12:34 100%

TRAVEL TIPS

The Museum of Modern Art (MoMA)

17,996 views

#18 of 1349 things to do in New York City
Art Museums

Isabella_Svensson
Oslo, Sweden
17 contributions

Too crowded
Our expectations were high. Maybe too high because we were disappointed. The line at the entrance was very long and moved slowly because there were few attendants. After waiting almost an hour in line, we finally entered the museum! Too bad it was overcrowded. The famous Van Gogh's *Starry Night* was there, but we could only see it from 20 meters away. There was a big crowd in front of the canvas! The museum urgently needs to limit the number of visitors per day.

Busy_Michael
New York, USA
5 contributions

●●●●●

Amazing collection and friendly staff
Although living in New York, this was my first time at the museum. This was an amazing experience! Van Gogh, Salvador Dalí, Pablo Picasso … All the great masters are there.
Go through all the six floors without hurry and be sure to visit the cafeteria. The dishes are great value for money – my burger was only $4 and was big enough for two people! Also, the staff is friendly: I forgot my cell phone on the table and they quickly came to return it to me.

Just_Harry
London, UK
32 contributions

●●●●○

Modern art is not my thing …
I was at the museum with my mom and dad. They loved it, but I confess I was deadly bored. All those artworks aren't exciting enough for me. What I really liked was a comic book exhibition that was happening on the first floor! While Mom and Dad were looking at modern art, I was reading *Asterix* and *X-Men* comics. For me, this is a great way to enjoy a day at the museum!

2 Read and listen to the texts. Then answer the questions.
77

a What average rating does The Museum of Modern Art have? ________________

b How many New York attractions have a higher rating than the museum? ________

c Of the three reviewers, who is the only one who lives in the United States? ________

d Which reviewer gave the lowest rating?

____

e Which reviewer contributes to the app most often? ____________________

3 Who thinks like that? Write *I* for Isabella, *M* for Michael, and *H* for Harry.

a ☐ The cafeteria has generous portions and attentive staff.

b ☐ The attendants at the entrance are too few.

c ☐ The comic book exhibition is great.

d ☐ Modern art collections are boring.

e ☐ The museum needs to limit the number of visitors.

f ☐ The museum is worth visiting as it has artwork of famous painters.

4 Complete the chart with adverbs from the texts.

adjective	adverb
a dead	
b final	
c friend	
d quick	
e slow	
f urgent	

5 Which adverbs in the chart above are antonyms?

____

TIP
Remember: antonyms are words with opposite meanings.

6 Choose two adverbs from the chart in activity 4 and write sentences with them.

____
____
____
____

7 CLASS VOTE Which of the reviews is the most helpful?

GRAMMAR 2

too, enough, and *not enough*

1 Read the underlined words in sentences a-d. Then number each sentence according to descriptions 1-3.

a ☐ My burger was big enough for two people.

b ☐ We went to the Statue of Liberty, but it was not interesting enough for me.

c ☐ We were too late.

d ☐ We'll have enough time to look carefully at everything.

1 It means that something is more than sufficient or more than necessary.

2 It means that something is sufficient.

3 It means that something is less than sufficient or less than necessary (negative sentence).

2 Look at the position of *too*, *enough*, and *not enough*. Then write which sentence(s) in activity 1 on page 135 exemplifly(ies) each use.

I. *too* + adjective: ___sentence c___

II. *not* (adjective) + *enough*: ______________________

III. *enough* + noun: ______________________

3 Order the words to make sentences.

a money / to take / didn't have / enough / a taxi / I

____

b The / wasn't / cheap / restaurant / enough

____

c hot / It / too / to go sightseeing / was

____

d The / enough / hotel / wasn't / good / so we left

____

4 Complete the sentences with *too* / *enough* / *not ... enough*.

a It was too cold to visit the caves. It was ______________________ (warm).

b We had enough time to visit the castle, but it was ______________________ (crowded).

c Six people wanted to go to the museum. Luckily, Carla's car was ______________________ (big).

d The reef is not safe for children. It's ______________________ (dangerous).

5 Underline the correct options.

Hadrian's wall was built in the north of England by the Roman Emperor Hadrian, and for centuries it was **a big enough / enough big** to stop barbarian invasions. The Romans left Britain at the beginning of the fifth century when the Roman Empire became **b not big enough / too big** and the wall began to become a ruin.

It is the most popular tourist attraction in the area. You can't walk on the wall because it **c is strong enough / isn't strong enough** since it's **d too old / not old enough**. If you have **e too time / enough time**, you can walk along it for 135km, but go in the summer because in winter it's **f too wet / wet enough**!

GRAMMAR GUIDE page 138

CLIL

GEOGRAPHY

THE CREATION OF A WATERFALL

The upper course of a river is usually high above sea level, in hills or mountains. The river travels downwards and cuts through the landscape with vertical erosion. One of the geographical features that are formed by vertical erosion is a **waterfall**. This is typical in the upper course of a river and eventually creates a gorge.
The water travels over the hard rock, also called **cap rock**, and erodes the **softer rock** underneath.
A **plunge pool** forms at the base of the waterfall. The swirling water and rocks erode the soft rock behind it.
Eventually, the front of the cap rock collapses. The waterfall moves backwards and the process is repeated again.

1 Do you know any famous waterfall? If so, write its name below.

____

2 Read and listen. Then match options a-d with their definitions according to the context.

78

a waterfall
b cap rock
c softer rock
d plunge pool

☐ a more resistant rock over a layer of weaker rock
☐ a deep basin excavated underneath a waterfall
☐ a perpendicular descent of the water of a river
☐ a weaker layer of rock that easily erodes with water

3 Look at the picture below and complete the labels with items a-d from activity 2.

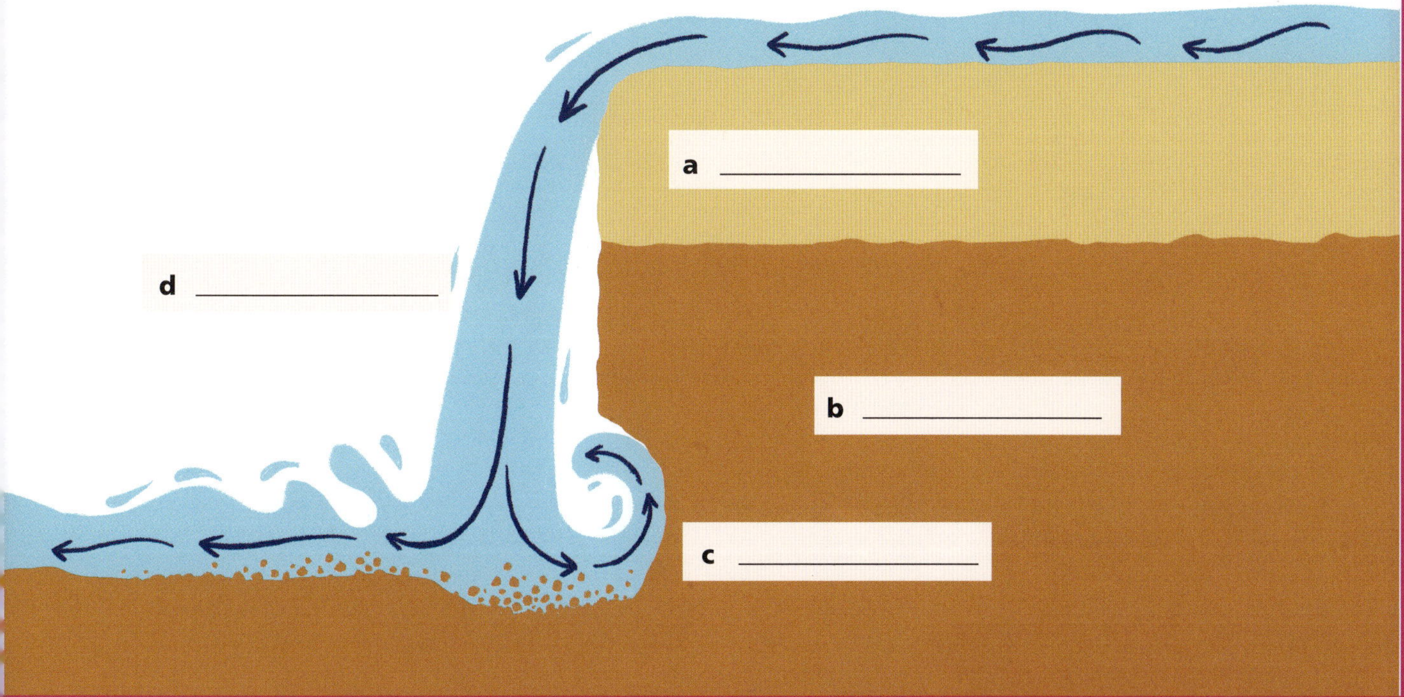

GRAMMAR GUIDE

Superlatives

	adjective	superlative
1 syllable	old large	the old**est** the larg**est**
1 syllable ending in vowel + consonant	big	the big**gest**
2 syllables ending in *-y*	lovely	the lovel**iest**
2 or more syllables	famous	the **most** famous
irregular	good bad	the **best** the **worst**

- we use the superlative to compare more than two things, people, or places or to compare somebody or something with the whole group it belongs to
  It is **the biggest** pyramid in the world.
  The Taj Mahal is **the most famous** monument in India.
  What is **the best** monument in your town?

too, enough, and *not enough*

- we use *too* + adjective to say that something is excessive
  We were **too** late. It was closed.
  We were**n't too** late.
- we use adjective + *enough* to say that something is sufficient
  My tent was big **enough** for two people.
- we use *not* + adjective + *enough* to say that something is insufficient
  My tent was**n't** big **enough** for eight people.
- we use *do* (*not*) + *have enough* to say that something we have is whether sufficient or not
  We **have enough** chocolate for ten people.
  I do**n't have enough** money to buy a car.

6

PROGRESS CHECK

Name: ______________________

Class name / Period: ______________________

Teacher: ______________________

Date: ______________________

Places to Visit 1

1 Complete the sentences below with the words in the box.

cave coastline lighthouse reefs ruins tomb

a The prehistoric paintings in the ______________ were great.

b When people die, they are buried in a ______________.

c The USA has an Atlantic and a Pacific ______________.

d Pollution is killing coral ______________ in many seas.

e When the sailors saw the ______________, they knew they were safe.

Formation of Adverbs

2 Underline the correct words to complete the sentences.

a My mom always drives very **slow** / **slowly**.

b I always do my homework very **careful** / **carefully**.

c Don Justo's work is very **slow** / **slowly**.

d The Taj Mahal is a very **beautiful** / **beautifully** building.

e The museum was very **interesting** / **interestingly**.

Superlatives

3 Complete the sentences using the adjective in parentheses in the superlative form.

a The tomb's ______________ (interesting) attraction.

b Paris is ______________ (beautiful) city in the world.

c Pompeii is ______________ (big) preserved Roman ruin.

d Prague is ______________ (popular) destination in central Europe.

too, *enough*, and *not enough*

4 Complete the sentences with *too*, *enough*, or *not enough*.

a We did __________ have __________ money to go to the castle.

b Are you old __________ to visit the Great Barrier Reef?

c There's __________ time to visit the lighthouse. I'm sorry.

d The caves are __________ small. We can't go in.

Grammar Buildup 7

1 2 3 4 5 6 7 8

5 Underline the correct options.

I **a love / 'm loving** traveling. I think the **b more interesting / most interesting** place in the world is China. The Great Wall of China is amazing. It's **c longer / longest** than the coastline of Spain! The Mogao Caves **d aren't / weren't** as famous as the caves in Lascaux, in France, but the cave paintings are as **e beautiful / more beautiful**. The only problem with China is that it's **f enough / too** big. I **g wasn't having / didn't have** enough time to go everywhere during my vacation.

VOCABULARY IN PICTURES

Places to Visit 1

castle

cave

coastline

lighthouse

opera house

pyramid

rainforest

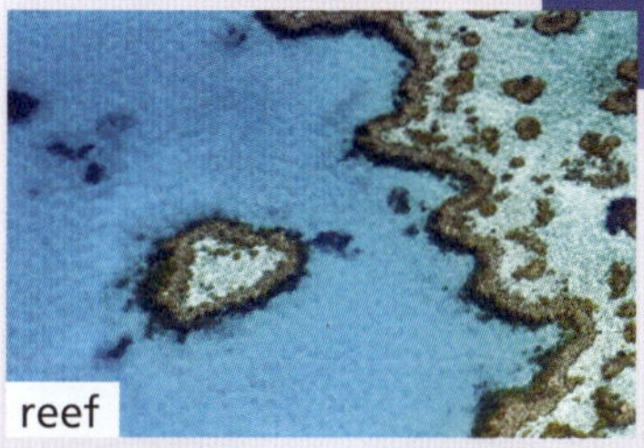
reef

ruin

temple

tomb

Formation of Adverbs

angrily

badly

carefully

correctly

easily

fast

happily

hard

noisily

quietly

well

8

FUN AND GAMES

1

2

3

4

VOCABULARY 1

Playing Games

1 Match pictures 1-7 with the phrases in the box. Mark an X next to the ones that are not in the pictures.

beat ☐ cheat ☐ count ☐ give up ☐ guess ☐ land ☐ lose ☐ miss a turn ☐ move a counter ☐ roll a die ☐

TIP

The plural of *die* is *dice*.
one die – two (or more) *dice*

2 Listen and repeat.

79

3 Complete the sentences with phrases from activity 1.

a He's better in this game than me. Every time I play with him I ______________.

b My brother ______________ at cards. He always looks at the cards of the other players!

c I don't know the answer. I ______________!

d To start the game, ______________ and try to get a six.

Emma Smith Follow
May 29 · 2 min read

A History of Games

Does your family ever sit together and play board games?
This fun activity is, in fact, over 5,000 years old.
Perhaps the first known board game was *Senet*, an ancient Egyptian game which appeared in about 3100 BC!
Archaeologists found many *Senet* boards in Egyptian tombs, but they didn't find the rules anywhere.
A version of backgammon appeared in China about 3,700 years later. *Go* came from China, but it became popular in Japan in the 7th century. They are both games of strategy for two players. In backgammon, the players roll dice to move their pieces. The winner is the first person to take all their pieces off the board. In *Go*, the board is empty at the beginning and the players don't roll dice. The winner is the person who has the most counters on the board at the end.
Playing cards first arrived in Europe in the 1300s from China. Chess appeared about 100 years after that. The modern board game was finally born in 1935 when the company Parker Brothers introduced *Monopoly* to the USA.
Fifty years later, German-style board games began to appear, for example, *The Settlers of Catan* in 1995.
This game is very different from American games like *Monopoly*. In *Settlers*, players build villages and roads across a board, the game moves fast, and players interact with each other when someone rolls the dice. There isn't any direct competition between players and nobody is eliminated.

History Games Board games

READING 1

1 Read and listen to the blog post above. Put the games in the correct chronological order.

80

backgammon ☐ chess ☐ *Go* ☐
Monopoly ☐ playing cards ☐
Senet ☐ *Settlers* ☐

2 Read the text again. Choose the correct options to complete the statements.

a People **played** / **didn't play** board games 4,000 years ago.

b The first board game **comes** / **didn't come** from China.

c Backgammon is **similar to** / **different from** *Go*.

d The modern board game comes from **America** / **Europe**.

3 Match the descriptions with the games.

a Players don't compete against each other. ____________

b Players put counters on an empty board. ____________

c The game has no written instructions. ____________

d Players take their pieces off the board. ____________

4 Make compound nouns using *card* and / or *game* in addition to the words given below.

a ball ____________

b birthday ____________

c board ____________

d computer ____________

e video ____________

TIP
Extend your vocabulary by making a list of compound nouns.

GRAMMAR 1

Review: Simple Present and Present Progressive

1 Read the sentences. Write each of them into the correct chart.

- **a** Does your family ever sit together to play games?
- **b** In the game *Go*, players don't roll dice at the beginning.
- **c** Jack and Jill are playing chess at the moment.
- **d** Jill isn't winning.
- **e** Are you learning how to play *Monopoly*?
- **f** In the game *Settlers*, players build villages and roads across the board.

	simple present
affirmative	
negative	
interrogative	

	present progressive
affirmative	
negative	Jill isn't winning.
interrogative	

2 Complete the rules by writing *simple present* or *present progressive*.

- **a** We use the ______________ to describe habits.
- **b** We use the ______________ to describe activities in progress.

3 Complete the sentences with the correct form of the verbs in parentheses. Use the simple present or the present progressive.

- **a** Every year, our school ______________ (have) a chess competition.
- **b** I never ______________ (take part) because I ______________ (not like) chess.
- **c** At the moment I ______________ (watch) the competition.
- **d** Lou ______________ (not play) right now, but Will ______________ (beat) his opponent.
- **e** Will often ______________ (win) the school competition.
- **f** Look, Will ______________ (stand up) and ______________ (smile). He won!

4 Read the text below and complete the sentences with the correct form of the verbs in parentheses. Use the simple present or the present progressive.

What **a** ___________ these kids ___________ (do) right now? They **b** ___________ (play) a board game called chess. Why do experts always **c** ___________ (say) it is important for children to play chess? For many reasons:

- Playing chess on a regular basis **d** ___________ (teach) the importance of discipline.
- Children who play chess from an early age **e** ___________ (exhibit) extraordinary memory skills.
- Chess also **f** ___________ (help) concentration.

A child who **g** ___________ (not play) chess **h** ___________ (miss) the opportunity to learn a great game! Chess **i** ___________ (make) kids smart!

5 Underline the correct options.

a Board games **help** / **helps** kids interact with each other.

b You **don't** / **doesn't** finish a board game like you do with a video game.

c My friends **are playing** / **play** *Monopoly* now. I **don't like** / **am not liking** it.

d Some people **don't play** / **plays** board games very often because they **assume** / **assumes** all games are long and boring.

6 Order the words to make questions.

you / How often / play / board games / do ?
How often do you play board games?

a your mom / watching / Is / right now / TV ?

b at the moment / you / What / doing / are ?

c celebrate / How / do / your birthday / you ?

d like playing / your family / Does / board games ?

7 Answer the questions in activity 6 so they are true for you.

I sometimes play board games at night.

GRAMMAR GUIDE page 154

LISTENING

Travel Games

1 81 Listen to two children describing three travel games. Do they need a pencil and a piece of paper to play them?

2 81 Listen again and answer the questions.

Game 1

a How many questions can the players ask?

b What are the possible answers to each question?

Game 2

c What do the players describe?

d How many sentences do players have to say?

Game 3

e What is the game called?

f What number do the players count to?

3 Do you know any other travel games? Which one(s)?

SPEAKING

A Chess Competition

82 Rose and Adam are talking about a chess competition at school. Listen and complete the dialogue.

Look, Adam! There is going to be a chess competition at school next month. **a** ___________ you **b** ___________ to take part?

I don't know. I **c** ___________ I'm prepared for it.

How come? You are the best player at school!

Not really … and I **d** ___________ to practice to train my mind for different moves.

So, time to start! What **e** ___________ right now? Just moaning …

Well, I need a partner …

I'm in, but remember, I **f** ___________ some rules, but I **g** ___________ as much as you do.

Like you said, "time to start!" But as long as you **h** ___________ a lot while you play …

OK, I'll have a try; after all, like all other games, it **i** ___________ to be fun!

I can teach you some nice moves too. No worries!

FUNCTIONAL LANGUAGE

Talking about Interests

Do you want to take part?
I don't know. I don't think I'm prepared for …
I'll have a try.

Speaking Task

Talk to a classmate about taking part in a school competition.

Step 1

Decide which competition you and your classmate want to take part in.

WHAT'S ON

- Chess competition: Saturday at 4pm.
- Sports:
  Soccer – Sunday at 9am.
  Basketball – Sunday at 1pm.
  Swimming – Saturday at 9am.

Step 2

Think of what you and your classmate want to say:

What do you think about … ?
Do you want to take part … ?
How about joining … ?

Plan possible answers:

I don't know. I don't think I'm prepared …
OK, I'll have a try.
Great idea!
Let's go!

Step 3

Take turns asking and answering questions.

CULTURE

Canadian Checkers

A regular 10×10 checkers board.

Canadian checkers is a variant of checkers, quite popular in Quebec. Also called Canadian draughts, this game is played on a 12×12 board of 144 squares with 30 pieces on a side, and not a 10×10 checkerboard of 20 pieces per side as in international checkers. Why is this so?

The story goes that a traveler who arrived in Canada from Europe was trying to explain the game to his Canadian friends, but, because he didn't remember the number of squares on the board, he came up with a board with 12 squares per side. However, the rules are the same as for international checkers.

The game is played by two people, on opposite sides of a playing board, alternating moves. One player has dark pieces, and the other has light pieces. Pieces move diagonally and pieces of the opponent are captured by jumping over them. A player wins the game if he or she captures all of the opposing player's pieces or if he or she leaves the opposing player with no legal moves. If neither player can move then, it is a draw or a tie.

A Canadian checkers board, containing 144 squares.

1 83 **Read and listen to the information about Canadian checkers and choose the correct options to complete the sentences.**

a Canadian checkers is popular …
- ☐ all over Canada.
- ☐ mainly in Quebec.

b Canadian checkers is played …
- ☐ on a 10×10 checkerboard.
- ☐ on a 12×12 checkerboard.

c The rules of Canadian checkers are …
- ☐ the same as for international checkers.
- ☐ different from the ones for international checkers.

d … people at a time can play the game.
- ☐ Just two
- ☐ More than two

e A player wins the game …
- ☐ just when he or she captures all of the opposing player's pieces.
- ☐ either when he or she captures all of the opposing player's pieces or when he or she leaves the opposing player with no legal moves.

2 **There are many variants of checkers. Is this board game played in your country? If so, what is the board size? How many pieces per side are there?**

____
____
____

3 **Do you play checkers? What other board games do you play?**

____
____
____

VOCABULARY 2

Places to Visit 2

1 Match the pictures with the words in the box.

art gallery ☐	campground ☐	fishing port ☐	market ☐	monument ☐
safari park ☐	statue ☐	town square ☐	water park ☐	

1

2

3

4

5

6

7

8

9

2 Listen and repeat.

84

3 Choose the correct options.

a Christ the Redeemer is **a statue / an art gallery** in Brazil.

b Plaza Mayor is a famous **market / town square** in Spain.

c The Great Wall of China is **a monument / a market** in China.

4 Write sentences about your vacation preferences. Use the words in activity 1 and your own ideas.

I prefer beaches to water parks.

____

____

____

5 **INTERFACE** Work in pairs. Compare your answers with a classmate's.

READING 2

1 Check the meaning of the words in the box in a dictionary.

dismantle spit tide wander

2 85 Read the thread opened by user Joseph Taylor on an internet forum. What do you think **"in a pickle"** means? Write your answer. Then read and listen to check your guess.

____

READING STRATEGY

Try to deduce the meaning of unfamiliar words from the context.

Joseph Taylor • Follow
Travelling for over 20 years • Updated 1m

Every traveler finds themselves in a pickle sometimes. Tell me about a trouble you had while traveling.

David Simon • September 16, 2022

Once my dad and I went to a campground at the beach. Late at night, we were sleeping when we heard a "splash" very close to us. The tide came in and the waves were crashing into the tent! We had to get up quickly and dismantle the tent so as not to get all our stuff wet.

Upvote Reply

Lea Pérez • August 30, 2022

When I was 8, I went to a safari park with my family. For safety, you are supposed to stay in the car with the windows closed at all times. But I was a disobedient child ... When my parents were distracted taking pictures, I rolled down the backseat window and reached out to touch a llama. Luckily, llamas are not aggressive animals. But I got a big spit on my face!

Upvote Reply

Anne Morris • August 28, 2022

In Madrid, I went to visit Plaza Mayor, the most famous town square in Spain. I was delighted by the historic buildings and charming cafés. When the tour bus driver called the passengers back, I was wandering around. I didn't hear him ... And they left without me! When I realized I was alone, I calmly sat down to have a cup of coffee. But then I spent a lot of money to get back to my hotel by taxi!

Upvote Reply

3 Read the thread again. Match each user's experience to a possible headline.

a David Simon	☐ The distracted traveler
b Lea Pérez	☐ Woken up by the waves
c Anne Morris	☐ The spitting llama

4 Choose the correct options to complete the sentences.

a The "splash" David and his father heard **was** / **wasn't** the wave hitting the tent.

b David and his father **managed** / **didn't manage** to keep their things from getting wet.

c Lea **knew** / **didn't know** that the car windows should remain closed.

d Lea's parents **saw** / **didn't see** her roll down the backseat window.

e Anne **heard** / **didn't hear** the tour bus driver calling passengers back.

f Anne **was** / **wasn't** desperate when she discovered that they had left her behind.

g Anne **spent** / **didn't spend** a lot of money to get back to her hotel in Madrid.

5 INTERFACE Work in pairs. Talk about trouble on trips or outings.

Where were you?

I was at a water park.

What happened?

I accidentally got on the small children's toboggan ...

GRAMMAR 2

Review: Simple Past and Past Progressive

1 Read the sentences in the charts below. Then complete the rules to form the simple past and the past progressive.

	simple past
+	My friends and I **had** a party.
–	We **didn't ride** bikes.
?	**Did** you **go** anywhere last weekend?

	past progressive
+	It **was raining**.
–	We **weren't wearing** comfortable clothes.
?	**Were** you **visiting** the Louvre?

a We use the ______________ to describe finished situations or actions in the past.

b We use the ______________ to describe activities in progress in the past.

c The auxiliaries *did / didn't* are used in questions (or short affirmative answers) and negative sentences in the ______________.

d The verb *be* in the past (*was / were*) + *-ing* form the ______________.

2 Read about Nelson's Column in Trafalgar Square in London. Complete the text with the verbs in parentheses in the simple past or the past progressive form.

Nelson's Column is a monument which commemorates Admiral Horatio Nelson, who **a** ___________ (die) at the Battle of Trafalgar in 1805. The column was built in 1840 and is 52 meters tall.

Admiral Nelson **b** ___________ (spend) most of his life at sea; he **c** ___________ (not like) it very much because he always felt sick while he **d** ___________ (sail). He **e** ___________ (travel) to the Caribbean, Denmark, and Egypt to fight battles and also **f** ___________ (sail) close to the North Pole. However, he **g** ___________ (become) famous during the Battle of Trafalgar while he **h** ___________ (fight) Napoleon, who **i** ___________ (try) to invade Britain. The English **j** ___________ (win) the battle, but Nelson **k** ___________ (die) – he was shot. The soldiers **l** ___________ (capture) the French guns, which were later used around the base of the column.

3 Choose the correct options to complete Keyra's email.

From: keyra.051@supermail.com
To: dermot.936@supermail.com
Subject: Loving Croatia

Hi, Dermot,
We **a left / were leaving** Dubrovnik in Croatia yesterday afternoon. Now I finally have some free time to write this email!
We really **b enjoyed / didn't enjoy** the city. We **c were walking / walked** around the walls that run almost 2 kilometers around the city. Just great! **d Did you know / You knew** that the walls were a popular filming location for the fictional city of King's Landing in the *Game of Thrones* TV series? While we **e were doing / was doing** our walk, we could admire the seaport on the Adriatic Sea! Great view! We **f took / were taking** the cable car to Mount Srd to see the city from above.
Well, we also **g visited / were visiting** some old buildings and churches. The weather was fantastic and the food a must try! We **h were eating / ate** seafood, pasta, vegetables – everything we **i tried / were trying** was spectacular.
Unfortunately, we **j didn't have / weren't having** time to go to the beach! Maybe next time!
Wish you were here.
Keyra

TIP

Different tenses use different time expressions.
Past: *yesterday, last* (*week, month, year, Saturday,* etc.), *ago*
Present: *at the moment, today, now, every day* (*week, month*), *often, sometimes,* etc.

4 Complete the sentences so they are true for you. Use the correct verb tense.

a I ______________ at the moment.

b My best friend often ______________ on the weekend.

c My parents ______________ yesterday.

d I'm going to ______________ this summer.

GRAMMAR GUIDE page 154

WRITING

A Friendly Letter

1 EXPLORING THE CONTEXT

1 Do you know what **snail mail** is? Read a definition.

Snail mail is a slang term for the mail delivered by a postal system, especially when contrasted with email.

2 Think and answer: Why is it called **snail mail**?

____

3 Naomi has a pen pal – a friend who she exchanges letters with. Read and listen. Then number each part of Naomi's letter to her pen pal.
86

1. Greeting **2.** Sender address
3. Date **4.** Sign off **5.** Body

Via Firenze 52 ☐
80016 Marano di Napoli, Naples
ITALY

September 4, 2022 ☐

☐ Dear River,

I hope you're doing well. I'm sitting outside and I'm writing this letter to you on the last day of my vacation. We're all feeling really excited. The vacation is ending!

This wasn't an easy year for me. As I told you in the last letter, we moved here last July and I started my new school in September. But I am lucky – all my classmates are really friendly.

☐ They often invite me to their houses. Once, when we were doing a class project, they all came to my house to write a song together. I made some amazing new friends.

And the vacation? We went to Malta for two weeks. It's an island in the Mediterranean. My dad was born there. I explored the island, visited the museums and monuments, and had a good time.

Did you have a good year? What did you do in the summer? Write soon.

☐ Love from,
Naomi

4 Complete the timeline with Naomi's actions.

Jul 2021	Sep 2021	Jun 2022
Moves to Italy	**a** ______ new school	Vacation starts

(for 2 weeks)	Sep 4, 2022	Sep 5, 2022
b ______ to Malta	**c** ______ to River	Back to school

5 INTERFACE What can be the advantages of keeping a pen pal in English?

2 PLANNING

1 Imagine that you are River (this could be a boy's name or a girl's name!) and you received Naomi's letter. Write a reply to it.

2 Make notes under three headings:
- What did you do this year?
- Where did you go on your last vacation?
- What did you do there?

LANGUAGE FOCUS

Verb Tenses
Make your writing more interesting by using a variety of verb tenses.

1 Find one example of each verb tense in the text.
- **a** simple present ______________________
- **b** present progressive ______________________
- **c** simple past ______________________
- **d** past progressive ______________________

3 WRITING

1 Write a first draft. Use your notes from Step 2 and Naomi's letter to help you.

2 Include a greeting (*Dear / Hi / Hello*) and a sign off: *Love / Yours / Cheers*.

4 CHECKING & EDITING

1 Ask a classmate to read your draft and check his / her draft too.
- Are all parts (sender address, date, greeting, etc.) included?
- Does the letter talk about the past and the present?

2 Use your classmate's suggestions to prepare the final version of your letter.

5 SHARING

1 Let's create pen pal friendships within the class! Place your letter inside an envelope.

2 Place all the envelopes on the teacher's desk and shuffle them.

3 Each student takes an envelope from the pile, read it, and write an answer.

GRAMMAR GUIDE

Review: Simple Present and Present Progressive

	simple present	present progressive
+	I often **beat** him.	**I'm beating** him.
–	He **doesn't cheat**.	She **isn't winning**.
?	**Do** they usually **win**?	**Are** they **losing**?

- we use the simple present for routines and habits
  I **play** cards with my friends on Saturdays.
- we use the present progressive to describe activities that are happening now
  We're **playing** *Monopoly* now. Kyra **is winning**.

Review: Simple Past and Past Progressive

	simple past	past progressive
+	It **appeared** in 1475.	They **were playing**.
–	He **didn't play** *Go*.	She **isn't winning**.
?	**Did** she **win**?	**Were** you **playing**?

- we use the simple past to describe finished actions or situations in the past
  We **played** cards last Saturday and I **won**.
- we use the past progressive to describe activities in progress at a specific time in the past
  We **were playing** cards at 7:30pm.
- we usually use *when* before the simple past and *while* before the past progressive
  When our teacher arrived, we were playing cards.
  While we were playing cards, our teacher arrived.

Time Expressions

- we use different time expressions with different verb tenses
- with the simple present, use words such as: *always*, *usually*, *often*, *sometimes*, *never*
  We **always** study hard.
- with the present progressive, use words such as: *today, at the moment, now*
  You are reading a good book **at the moment**.
- with the simple past, use: *in 1989*, *yesterday*, *5,000 years ago*
  My teacher was born **in 1982**.
  I went to the movies **yesterday**.
  They played soccer **last week**.
- with the past progressive, use: *yesterday at 9pm*, *last night at 3am*
  I wasn't reading a book **yesterday at 9pm**.

Name: ____________________

Class name / Period: ____________________

Teacher: ____________________

Date: ____________________

PROGRESS CHECK

Playing Games

1 Complete the gaming phrases with vowels.

a c h ___ ___ t

b l ___ s e

c m ___ s s ___ t ___ r n

d c ___ ___ n t

Places to Visit 2

2 Identify the places. Write their names.

a ____________________

b ____________________

c ____________________

d ____________________

Review: Simple Present and Present Progressive

3 Write complete sentences. Use the simple present or the present progressive.

a We / play / cards / at the moment

____

b Paula / win / and I / lose / now

____

c We / play cards / often / on Saturday afternoon

____

d We / meet / usually / at Katie's house

____

4 Order the words to make questions.

a cards / your best friend / playing / Is / now ?

____

b your dad / How often / play / does / board games ?

____

c Where / are / today / having / you / dinner ?

____

Review: Simple Past and Past Progressive

5 Complete the sentences with the correct form of the verbs in parentheses.

a She ____________________ (win) the chess competition yesterday.

b I ____________________ (not play) cards at 6pm last night.

c My sister ____________________ (cheat) when we played cards last Friday.

d They ____________________ (lose) the game when I left the stadium.

6 Complete the text with the correct form of the verbs in parentheses. Use the simple past or the past progressive forms.

Last year, we **a** ____________ (go) to Madeira, Portugal, on vacation. We **b** ____________ (see) the whole island. While we **c** ____________ (visit) a museum, I **d** ____________ (meet) a school friend. He **e** ____________ (be) bored so we **f** ____________ (decide) to go to the beach together. We **g** ____________ (play) on the beach when I **h** ____________ (hear) a familiar voice. It **i** ____________ (be) another school friend. We **j** ____________ (spend) the rest of the vacation together. It was the best vacation of my life!

Grammar Buildup 8

1 2 3 4 5 6 7 8

7 Complete the dialogue with the correct form of the verbs in parentheses.

Jane Hooray! We **a** _______________ (finish) the school year!

Mark What **b** _______________ you _______________ (do) tonight? We can **c** _______________ (go) to the movies or we can **d** _______________ (watch) a movie at my house.

Jane I prefer to **e** _______________ (watch) a movie. I **f** _______________ (not have) any money.

Mark Mariah **g** _______________ (not do) anything now.

Jane But she usually **h** _______________ (play) chess on Fridays with her cousin.

Mark She **i** _______________ (not play) now because her cousin **j** _______________ (go) to New York yesterday.

Jane Cool! I'll call Mariah.

VOCABULARY IN PICTURES

Playing Games

beat

cheat

count

give up

guess

land

lose

miss a turn

move a counter

roll a die

Places to Visit 2

art gallery

campground

fishing port

market

monument

safari park

statue

town square

water park

REVIEW 4

VOCABULARY

Start

1

I once went to a __________ in Kenya and took incredible pictures.

2

You can buy fresh fruit and vegetables at the floating __________ in Bangkok, Thailand.

3

If you __________ on a tax space in *Monopoly*, you have to pay taxes.

10

Maua is a famous __________ in Rio de Janeiro, Brazil.

11

They visited this amazing __________ on their trip to the Dominican Republic.

12

Hey! Don't __________, play fair!

13

That __________ is one of the best-known landmarks in northern England.

14

One of Egypt's biggest mysteries is how the __________ at Giza were built.

15

Did you know there are Jesuit __________ in the southern Brazil?

4

She went snorkeling to see the Great Barrier __________ up close.

5

He answered the question __________ and won the prize.

6

You don't play now, you __________!

7

The __________ had the most beautiful view.

8

… And they lived __________ ever after.

9

My little cousin plays his drums very __________!

16

His neighbor __________ complained about the noise.

17

It's very hard to __________ my grandpa in any game.

18

He held the baby __________ and sang a lullaby.

19

OK, so __________ one of my cards.

20

I can't think of an aircraft as __________ as the F-15 Eagle.

Finish

REVIEW 4

GRAMMAR

Superlatives

1 Complete the word sets with the correct words.

adjective: fat
superlative: the fattest

a adjective: easy
superlative: ____________

b adjective: ____________
superlative: the best

c adjective: ____________
superlative: the angriest

2 Complete the sentences with the superlative form of the adjectives in parentheses.

I think history is the most interesting subject. (interesting)

a Paul and Robert are ____________ people in our class. (noisy)

b I'm ____________ soccer player on the team. (bad)

c Climbing up a mountain is ____________ activity. (tiring)

d They live in ____________ house in the village. (large)

3 Rewrite the sentences using the superlative form.

My grandpa / old / member of the family
My grandpa is the oldest member of the family.

a I / big / student of the class
____

b It / exciting / city in the world
____

c David / famous / musician of the city ?
____

d You / happy / person of this group
____

4 Write sentences comparing the hotels in San Francisco in the chart. Use the superlative form.

Hotel	The Vista	The Court	The Beach
luxury	***	****	*****
US$ (night)	$120	$200	$175
distance from sea	500m	250m	100m

luxurious
The Beach is the most luxurious hotel in San Francisco.

a cheap
____

b expensive
____

c close to the sea
____

too, *enough*, and *not enough*

5 Rewrite the sentences using *too*, *enough*, or *not enough* and the adjectives in parentheses.

This town is too small.
(big) This town isn't big enough.

a These exercises aren't easy enough.
(difficult) ____________

b The Formula 1 car isn't fast enough.
(slow) ____________

c Ted is the right height to join the Army.
(tall) ____________

d It wasn't the right temperature to snow.
(cold) ____________

Simple Present and Present Progressive

6 Write sentences with the simple present or the present progressive forms.

We / always / play / cards on vacation
We always play cards on vacation.

a my teacher / use / her laptop in class / twice a week

____

b Sam / listen / to music / at the moment

____

c we / not lose / today

____

d my dad / not work / on Monday mornings

____

e about 26 million people / visit / London / every year

____

Simple Past and Past Progressive

7 Complete the sentences with the simple past or the past progressive forms of the verbs in parentheses.

At 7:30am the sun ___was shining___. (shine)

a I ______________ on the teacher's chair when she came in. (sit)

b My mom's a teacher. She ______________ math at university. (study)

c She was rolling a die when it ______________ on the floor. (fall)

d We ______________ some bottles to the recycling center when we saw my aunt. (take)

e They went to the museum. Then they ______________ the market. (visit)

8 Underline the correct options.

I **won / win** a backgammon competition yesterday.

a Zoe **rides / 's riding** her sister's bike at this moment.

b I was sitting in class when my phone **rang / rings**.

c My parents **get married / got married** in 1997.

d It's lovely today. The sun **is shining / was shining**.

9 Order the words to make questions.

did / you / What / for dinner / yesterday / have ?
What did you have for dinner yesterday?

a listening / at the moment / Are / to me / you ?

____

b carrying / Were / when / saw / you / you / books / I ?

____

c now / you / Why / are / me / following ?

____

d to a theme park / your cousins / did / When / go ?

____

Time Expressions

10 Complete the chart with the time expressions in the box.

~~in 2009~~ often once a month today two weeks ago yesterday

past	present
in 2009	

Respecting Others' Ideas in the Digital World

Don't Do It Online

1 Read, listen, and complete the sentences with the words in the box. Then number the events in the order they occur in the story.

87

behavior ~~classmate~~ forum furious like negative insults question surprised

a ☐ A classmate of the girls joins them and says he didn't ________ *Mad Monkeys 3*.

b ☐ Someone gives a ________ opinion about Lily's favorite movie and she gets ________.

c ☐ Lily ________ the forum user.

d 1 Lily is browsing an internet ________.

e ☐ Grace refer to their classmate's speech to ________ Lily about her online ________.

f ☐ Grace is ________ by Lily's aggressiveness.

2 What is Grace trying to teach Lily?

a Respect the rules of online forums.

b Treat people online the same as you would face to face.

3 Join a classmate and discuss about the questions below. Then share your ideas with the class.

a What are some of the differences between discussing issues in the classroom or at home and doing so in a public space like an internet forum?

b Why are people sometimes more aggressive online than in person?

4 Imagine that you found the following comment about your favorite movie on an internet forum.

(*Movie title*) is not worth watching. The actors are terrible and the script is boring.

Write a comment that **disagrees** with this opinion. Be respectful!

____

____

____

____

5 Work in pairs. Think about your answers to activities 3 and 4. Then write the phrases from the box into the appropriate column. Add other *dos* and *don'ts*. Share your chart with the class.

Acknowledge the other point of view.	Be empathetic.
Make it personal.	Put down the others' ideas.
Treat others how you would like to be treated.	Use CAPITAL LETTERS.

How to be respectful of others' opinions online?	
Do ✓	Don't ✗

Help Make a Difference

What do you do with the things you don't need or don't want anymore?

Many charity organizations collect unwanted clothing and other items. They either recycle, sell, or donate them to help people in need. Can you list such organizations?

Are there any non-profit organizations in your town that take donations?

1 Look at some of the places that accept used but wearable clothing. Match the pictures with the words below.

a Local churches
b Second-hand textile recycling industries
c Community centers
d Thrift stores
e School clothing drives
f Homeless shelters

2 Write the names of the organizations in activity 1 next to their descriptions.

a ______________________:
They are for-profit, but they resell clothing at low prices, which are affordable to low-income families.

b ______________________:
Many educational institutions set a date for students to bring in their unwanted clothes. Others do clothing drives once or twice a year to collect used items.

c ______________________:
They recycle donated second-hand clothing and send them to markets where they are most needed.

d ______________________:
Their mission is to provide people with a safe place to stay or spend the night. They accept all kinds of clothing that will be donated to people who need their services.

e ______________________:
They accept many different types of donations, including clothing items, which are given to other church members or poor people in the neighborhood.

f ______________________:
These public locations in local communities offer their members group activities, meetings, social support, crafts, dances, after-school programs, etc.

3 Search for a non-profit organization in your city which helps improve the life of those in need. Find the following information:

NAME: ______________________

LOCATION: ______________________

SERVICES OFFERED: ______________________

____

____

____

VOLUNTEER HELP (ACCEPTED? HOW?):

____

____

WHAT CAN BE DONATED:

____

____

____

FREE COLLECTION SERVICE: **YES** / **NO**

A Donation Event

You and your classmates will promote a donation day. Choose one or more of the institutions you researched and organize the event.

Doing

1 As a class, decide the following:

a What is the best date for the donation day?

b Will the whole school participate or just your class?

c What items will be accepted for donation (clothing, shoes, linen, blankets, etc.)?

d What is the minimum condition of the items (clean clothing in wearable condition – no stains, rips, or tears)?

2 Form groups of four or five students. Distribute the tasks among the groups:

a Making posters to advertise your donation day.

b Creating a catchy hashtag and using it in posts on social media.

c Decorating the place of the event.

d Selecting and organizing donated items.

e Delivering donations to the chosen institution.

f Filming and photographing the event.

Reflecting

3 After the event, reflect:

a Do you feel more committed to your community? In what ways?

b Do you think you have learned more about social responsibility? How has your thinking changed?

IRREGULAR VERBS

	Infinitive	Simple Past	Past Participle
88	be /bi/	was / were /wɑz/, /wɜr/	been /bin/, /bɪn/
	begin /bɪ'gɪn/	began /bɪ'gæn/	begun /bɪ'gʌn/
	break /breɪk/	broke /broʊk/	broken /'broʊkən/
	bring /brɪŋ/	brought /brɔt/	brought /brɔt/
	build /bɪld/	built /bɪlt/	built /bɪlt/
	buy /baɪ/	bought /bɔt/	bought /bɔt/
	choose /tʃuz/	chose /tʃoʊz/	chosen /'tʃoʊz(ə)n/
	come /kʌm/	came /keɪm/	come /kʌm/
	do /du/	did /dɪd/	done /dʌn/
	drink /drɪŋk/	drank /dræŋk/	drunk /drʌŋk/
	drive /draɪv/	drove /droʊv/	driven /'drɪv(ə)n/
	eat /it/	ate /eɪt/	eaten /'it(ə)n/
	fall /fɔl/	fell /fel/	fallen /'fɔlən/
	find /faɪnd/	found /faʊnd/	found /faʊnd/
	fly /flaɪ/	flew /flu/	flown /floʊn/
	forget /fər'get/	forgot /fər'gɑt/	forgotten /fər'gɑt(ə)n/
	get /get/	got /gɑt/	got /gɑt/, gotten /'gɑt(ə)n/
	give /gɪv/	gave /geɪv/	given /'gɪv(ə)n/
	go /goʊ/	went /went/	gone /gɔn/
	have /hæv/	had /həd/	had /həd/
	hear /hɪr/	heard /hɜrd/	heard /hɜrd/
	know /noʊ/	knew /nu/	known /noʊn/
	learn /lɜrn/	learnt / learned /lɜrnt/, /'lɜrnəd/	learnt / learned /lɜrnt/, /'lɜrnəd/
	leave /liv/	left /left/	left /left/
	lose /luz/	lost /lɔst/	lost /lɔst/
	make /meɪk/	made /meɪd/	made /meɪd/
	meet /mit/	met /met/	met /met/
	pay /peɪ/	paid /peɪd/	paid /peɪd/
	put /pʊt/	put /pʊt/	put /pʊt/
	read /rid/	read /red/	read /red/
	run /rʌn/	ran /ræn/	run /rʌn/
	say /seɪ/	said /sed/	said /sed/
	see /si/	saw /sɔ/	seen /sin/
	sell /sel/	sold /soʊld/	sold /soʊld/
	sing /sɪŋ/	sang /sæŋ/	sung /sʌŋ/
	sit /sɪt/	sat /sæt/	sat /sæt/
	speak /spik/	spoke /spoʊk/	spoken /'spoʊkən/
	take /teɪk/	took /tʊk/	taken /'teɪkən/
	teach /titʃ/	taught /tɔt/	taught /tɔt/
	tell /tel/	told /toʊld/	told /toʊld/
	think /θɪŋk/	thought /θɔt/	thought /θɔt/
	wear /wer/	wore /wɔr/	worn /wɔrn/
	win /wɪn/	won /wʌn/	won /wʌn/
	write /raɪt/	wrote /roʊt/	written /'rɪt(ə)n/

WORKBOOK

CONTENTS

STARTER

Introductions

1 Order the words to make questions. Then match the questions with the answers below.

a name / your / What / is ?

What is your name? ______ [3]

b you / old / How / are ?

______ [ ]

c you / Where / from / are ?

______ [ ]

d hobbies / What / your / are ?

______ [ ]

1 I'm from New York, USA.

2 My hobbies are swimming and surfing.

3 My name's Isabella.

4 I'm 12 years old.

Physical Description

2 Relate the adjectives from the box to the parts of the body they refer to.

blond blue brown curly dark
green long round short
square straight tall wavy

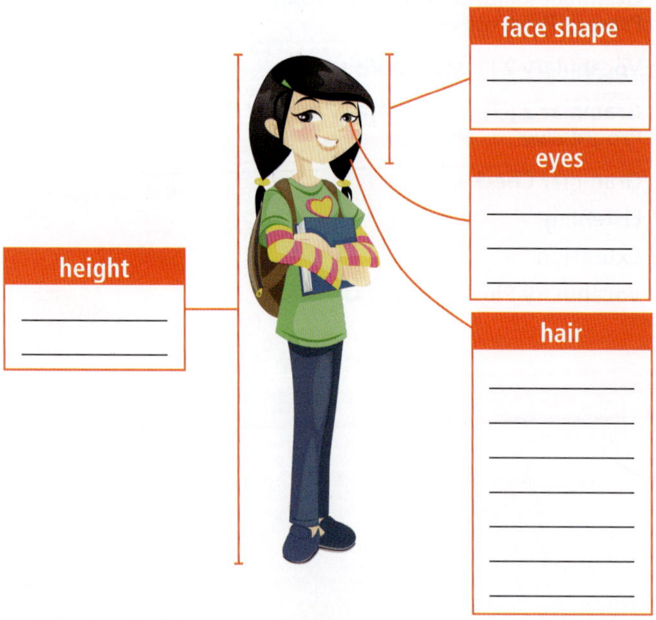

School Subjects and Free-time Activities

3 Complete the timetable using the school subjects so that it's true for you.

art drama English
geography history ICT literature
math music PE science [other]

Mon	Tue	Wed	Thu	Fri
BREAK				

4 Order the letters and name the free-time activities.

a  ylap ctrempuo msgea

______

b  irde ym ekbi

______

c  nelist ot usimc

______

d 

og ot eth seimov

______

e  tchaw vt

______

f  teem ym sendfir

______

g  tetx ym dfnseri

______

Places in Town

5 Order the words to make questions. Then write short answers that are true for you.

often / you / restaurants / go / to / Do?
Do you often go to restaurants?
Yes, I do.

a you / gym / the / Do / go / usually / to ?

b your / house / a / Is / near / supermarket / there ?

c museums / like / you / Do ?

d a / there / Is / in / your / neighborhood / library / public ?

Feelings and Opinions

6 Label the pictures with the feeling words in the box.

angry bored excited scared

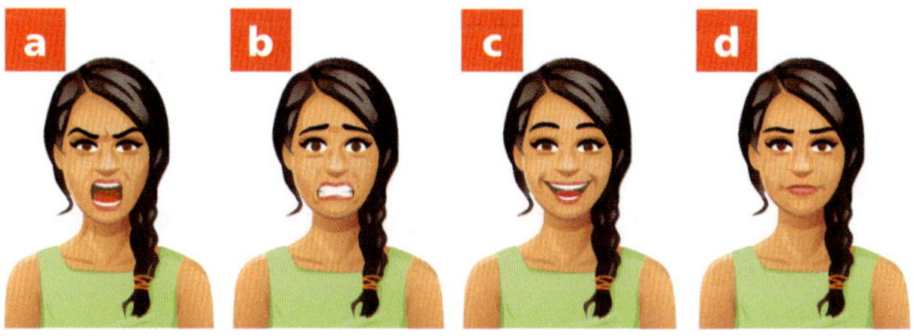

7 Underline the correct words to complete the sentences.

a This movie is making me feel sleepy. It's so **boring / exciting / dangerous**!

b The view in the campground is **easy / amazing / boring**. I feel like staring at it for hours.

c Dancing is very **fun / exciting / difficult**. I feel embarrassed about doing it in public.

d This is a really **boring / dangerous / interesting** book. I can lend it to you when I finish it.

Simple Present: *be* and *have*

8 Complete the text with the correct form of *be* and *have*.

Hi! My name is Luke and I **a** ______ 12 years old. My hobbies **b** ______ listening to music and riding my bike. I **c** ______ one sister. Her name **d** ______ Kelly and she **e** ______ 9. My best friends **f** ______ Jack and Harry. They **g** ______ 12 years old, like me, but they **h** ______ any brothers or sisters. Jack's favorite sport **i** ______ soccer, it **j** ______ tennis. We **k** ______ all from Boston, USA.

9 Circle the correct options to complete the sentences.

My favorite sport **are** / **am** / (**is**) soccer.

a My favorite soccer players **are** / **am** / **is** Cristiano Ronaldo and Messi.

b Cristiano Ronaldo **are** / **am** / **is** from Portugal.

c I think Messi **is** / **has** / **have** about 30 years old.

d Messi **is** / **has** / **have** two brothers, Matias and Rodrigo, and a sister, Maria Sol.

e Neymar and Benzema **are** / **am** / **is** also soccer players.

f Messi, Cristiano Ronaldo, and Benzema **doesn't have** / **don't play** / **aren't** in Brazil.

Subject / Object Pronouns and Possessive Adjectives

10 Circle the correct words.

I'm from Wichita and **I** / (**my**) name is David.

a Lucy is 12 years old and **she / her** is from Chico, California, USA.

b I have two brothers. **His / Their** names are John and Robert.

c Sydney is a beautiful city. **It / She** is in Australia.

d We're from Denver and **our / your** favorite sport is tennis.

e My sister's name is Katy. **Her / His** favorite color is black.

1

FREE TIME

VOCABULARY 1

Free-time Activities

1 Complete the words with vowels.

d_o_ y_o_g_a_

a r___l___x

b d___ ___ m___rt___ ___l ___rt

c h___ng ___ ___t w___th fr___ ___nds

d ch___t ___nl___n___

e g___ t___ th___ m___v___ ___s

f pl___y ___n ___nstr___m___nt

g g___ ___ ___t f___r ___ m___ ___l

2 Match the columns.

a	read	☐	video games
b	do	☐	a book
c	learn	☐	the gym
d	play	☐	a language
e	go to	☐	volunteer work

3 Match phrases from activity 1 with the pictures below.

do yoga

a

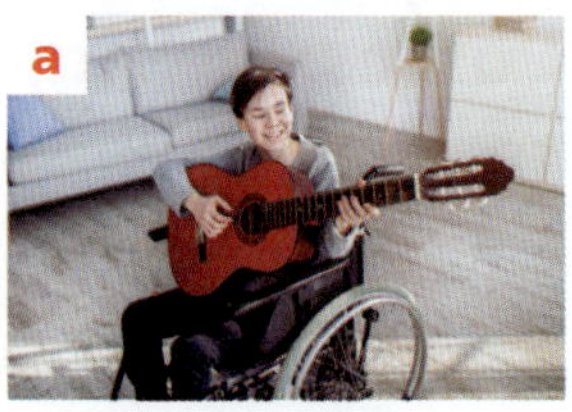

____

b

____

c

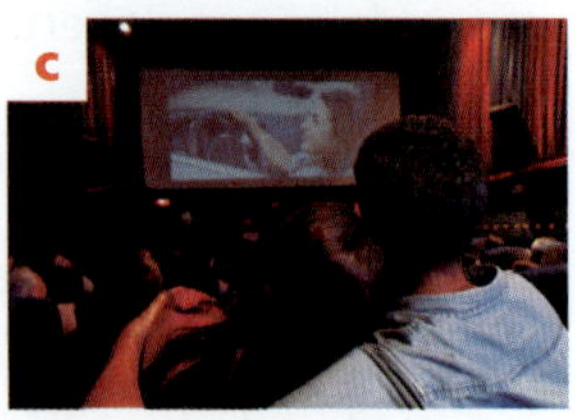

____

4 Match the activities a-h with items 1-8 below.

a [3] draw

b ☐ read a book

c ☐ do a martial art

d ☐ play video games

e ☐ relax

f ☐ learn a language

g ☐ do volunteer work

h ☐ go out for a meal

1 Let's go to the new pizza place on Park Street.

Good idea. I'm really hungry.

2 Are you doing exercises?

Yes, I do karate twice a week.

3 What are you drawing?

He's called Superbaby. I'm going to give him really strong legs and big eyes!

4 You're the blue snake and I'm the red snake. You have to eat all the fruit. Press START when you're ready.

5 This is nice! I love lying on my bed and listening to music.

6 I have audio files and a book. The audio is great because I learn the correct pronunciation. I study for an hour every day.

7 It is the *Murder on the Orient Express*, by Agatha Christie. Fascinating, isn't it?

8 We're cleaning the park today and planting some trees. We don't get any money, but we enjoy it.

GRAMMAR 1

Review: Simple Present and Present Progressive

1 Rewrite the sentences using the adverbs of frequency in parentheses.

My mom is tired after work. (always)
My mom is always tired after work.

a I go to the gym before school. (never)

b Alice gives me guitar lessons. (sometimes)

c Jan is tired on Monday mornings. (often)

d I do volunteer work on Fridays. (usually)

e We're late for school. (hardly ever)

f Caleb plays the cello. (always)

Adverbs of Frequency

2 Write sentences using the information about adverbs of frequency in the chart below.

my life	how often
walk to school	100%
a take taxis	0%
b go to the movies	70%
c go out for a meal	10%
d go to pop concerts	50%
e stay up late on Fridays	80%
f listen to music online	70%

never = 0%
sometimes = 50%
usually = 80%
hardly ever = 10%
often = 70%
always = 100%

I always walk to school.

a

b

c

d

e

f

3 Write sentences about you, your family, and your friends. Use the simple present and the adverbs of frequency in the box.

always hardly ever never often sometimes usually

go to the gym
My parents never go to the gym.

a buy new clothes

b feel stressed

c talk about problems

d get good grades

e play some kind of sport

f chat online

Time Expressions

4 Order the words to make sentences.

is / the evening meal / at / My mom / moment / preparing / the

My mom is preparing the evening meal at the moment.

a twice / goes / guitar classes / a / My brother / week / to

b my friends / weekend / I / every / meet

c this / cartoons / We're / week / in Art class / drawing

d at / wearing / not / moment / my sunglasses / the / I'm

e year / you / concert / Do / every / a / go to ?

f don't / in / I / go / the winter / swimming

5 **Complete the sentences with the simple present or present progressive form of the verbs in parentheses.**

We usually ___have___ lunch in the kitchen, but today we ___are / 're having___ it on the balcony. (have)

a She __________ jeans today. She usually __________ a skirt to work. (wear)

b They usually __________ about movies and music, but they __________ about sports at the moment. (talk)

c They __________ online now, but they usually __________ on the phone. (chat)

d My sister always __________ *Stranger Things*. Today she's sick, so she __________ it in bed. (watch)

e I __________ an email to my cousin right now. I never __________ letters to her. (write)

f Charlie usually __________ happy on weekends, but this weekend he __________ stressed. (feel)

6 **Correct the sentences. Write one negative and one affirmative sentence.**

I'm playing computer games. (✗ chat online)
I'm not playing computer games. I'm chatting online.

a My aunt works in a store. (✗ an office)

____

____

b She goes to her English class on Wednesdays. (✗ the gym)

____

____

c Emily's working at home now. (✗ the library)

____

____

d We're watching a movie at the moment. (✗ play video games)

____

____

e My dad often watches animal shows. (✗ cooking)

____

____

7 **Write questions for the answers.**

Who are you writing to?

I'm writing to my friend in Italy.

a How often ____________________?

I write to her once a week.

b ____________________?

No, she never calls me.

c ____________________ in Italian?

No, I usually write to her in English.

d What ____________________?

I'm telling her about my new hobby – drawing.

e Where ____________________ drawing classes?

I have drawing classes at a place on Selden Street.

f Where ____________________ now?

I'm going to the dentist.

8 **Match a-f with 1-6. Then write sentences using the simple present or present progressive forms of the verbs in parentheses.**

a [5] Chris is using your computer.

b [ ] Cathy isn't eating breakfast.

c [ ] What's that terrible noise?

d [ ] My brother's doing volunteer work today.

e [ ] Look at Andy in this picture.

f [ ] Why are you talking to yourself?

1 I __________ (not talk) to myself.
I __________ (practice) for the school play.

2 She __________ (not eat) in the morning.

3 He often __________ (help) Green Planet to clean the beach.

4 He __________ (stand) on his head!

5 He often ___plays___ (play) computer games.

6 It's my little sister. She__________ (sing) in the shower.

VOCABULARY 2

Character Adjectives

1 Find the opposites of the adjectives in the word search.

absentminded ~~adventurous~~ dishonest friendly funny generous lazy patient quiet shy

E	U	Z	C	A	U	T	I	O	U	S
N	N	X	S	E	L	F	I	S	H	T
E	S	X	T	W	J	C	A	Y	O	O
R	O	A	E	Y	U	O	U	L	B	S
G	C	U	A	Q	N	N	T	G	S	E
E	I	V	C	D	O	F	Q	A	E	R
T	A	L	K	A	T	I	V	E	R	I
I	B	Z	M	H	U	D	K	V	V	O
C	L	E	I	K	Q	E	O	A	A	U
P	E	F	C	A	I	N	D	W	N	S
H	O	N	E	S	T	T	E	O	T	A
X	I	M	P	A	T	I	E	N	T	K

2 Complete the sentences with the adjectives from activity 1.

__Shy__ people are a little frightened of new people.

__Confident__ people feel they can meet people easily.

a ____________ people love chatting. ____________ people don't make a lot of noise.

b ____________ people don't make a lot of friends. ____________ people are kind and helpful to other people.

c ____________ people think a lot. ____________ people make you smile and laugh.

d ____________ people tell the truth and do the right thing. ____________ people tell lies.

e ____________ people are always active and busy. ____________ people don't do any work.

f ____________ people don't like helping others. ____________ people always help others.

3 Match the adjectives in the box with the sentences below.

~~adventurous~~ cautious energetic friendly generous lazy selfish talkative

He's going around the world in a balloon at the moment.
__adventurous__

a I lie on the sofa and watch TV. My dad makes dinner for me and does the washing-up.
____

b Robert doesn't want to come camping because he doesn't like insects and spiders. He wants to stay home and clean up his room this weekend.
____

c Let's go swimming early tomorrow morning. Then we can cook lunch for all your cousins. After that we can go jogging.
____

d Nice to meet you. Would you like to come to the beach with a group of us next weekend?
____

e Put your money away. I'm paying for dinner for everybody.
____

f No, you can't check your email. It's my computer and you can't use it.
____

g I'm always on the phone in the evening.
____

4 Complete the sentences with adjectives. Write a second sentence with an example.

__I am observant. I always notice things that happen around me.__

a I am ____________. I usually ____________
____

b My friend is ____________. He or she
____

c My sister / brother / cousin is ____________. He or she ____________
____

d My teachers are ____________. They
____

e Me and my classmates are ____________. We ____________

f I am ____________
____

GRAMMAR 2

Gerunds

1 Match the sentences with the pictures.

a [1] I'm good at playing guitar.
b [ ] I enjoy relaxing in the garden.
c [ ] He likes playing games on his own.
d [ ] They like swimming classes.
e [ ] They love wearing striped clothes.
f [ ] We aren't into traveling. We like staying home.
g [ ] She's interested in visiting ancient monuments.
h [ ] She's good at drawing portraits.

1

2

3

4

5

6

7

8

2 Order the words to make sentences.

like / early / don't / getting / up / I
I don't like getting up early.

a enjoys / Everyone / presents / getting
____

b learning / Sue / new / is / languages / into
____

c hates / My / karaoke / singing / sister
____

d taking / my / love / pictures / I / friends / of
____

e are / monuments / interested / visiting / My / in / ancient / parents
____

f is / at / playing / friend / My / good / piano
____

g movies / going / the / Saturday / Joan / every / loves / to
____

3 Complete the questions with the gerund form of the verbs in the box.

do ~~go~~ make meet read spend watch

Where do you like going on your holidays?
a Do you enjoy ________ new people?
b What kind of books do you enjoy ________?
c What activities do you like ________ in your free time?
d Do you like ________ cakes?
e What kind of movies do you like ________?
f What do you like ________ your money on?

4 Write questions using the gerund form. Use your own ideas.

a Do you like ________________?
b What do you love ________________?
c Does ________________ enjoy ________________?
d What kind of ________________ does ________________ hate ________________?
e Are you into ________________?
f Is ________________ good at ________________?
g Are you bad at ________________?

GRAMMAR CHECK

1 Read the text and circle the correct options.

From: Danielle
To: Alex
Subject: Sunny California!

Hi, Alex,
I **a** ___ with my cousins in California at the moment. I **b** ___ an amazing time. My cousins are very energetic and we all like **c** ___ outside in the sun. Max **d** ___ us to the beach every day, although he's only sixteen. A lot of kids **e** ___ their driving test at 16 here. Right now, Suze and I **f** ___ on lounge chairs at the beach with our laptops on our laps! Suze **g** ___ an email. She's playing a computer game.
I **h** ___ on this beach! What **i** ___ this summer? **j** ___ still on the school tennis team? Say "hi" to her.
Bye for now,
Danielle

	1	2	3
a	stay	am staying	staying
b	have	has	'm having
c	be	we be	being
d	is driving	drives	drive
e	take	are taking	takes
f	sitting	sit	are sitting
g	not writing	doesn't write	isn't writing
h	loving relax	love relax	love relaxing
i	are you doing	do you do	are you
j	Does Ellie	Ellie is	Is Ellie

2 Listen and check your answers. 1

LISTENING

1 Listen to a radio show for teens. Check off (✓) the things you hear about. 2

- **a** ☐ school subjects
- **b** ☐ the weather
- **c** ☐ movies
- **d** ☐ money
- **e** ☐ friends
- **f** ☐ eating out
- **g** ☐ clothes
- **h** ☐ computer games
- **i** ☐ the internet
- **j** ☐ videos
- **k** ☐ exams
- **l** ☐ sports
- **m** ☐ the beach
- **n** ☐ photography
- **o** ☐ teachers

2 Listen again and write the correct names. 2

- **a** Who likes playing sports? ___________
- **b** Who enjoys art and crafts? ___________
- **c** Who is keen on technology? ___________
- **d** Who is into relaxing activities? ___________

Anna

Adam

Ed

Rosie

EXTENSION

Underline the correct options to complete the dialogue.

Hannah Why **a do you talk / are you talking** to yourself?

Tyler I **b 'm not talking / don't talk** to myself. I **c practice / 'm practicing** for the school play on Saturday.

Hannah Are you enjoying **d to act / acting** in it?

Tyler Yes, I **e do / am**. It's a Shakespearean tragedy.

Hannah What part are you playing?

Tyler I'm Hamlet. I really love **f acting / act**. And I enjoy **g speaking / speak** in front of the whole school.

Hannah You're very confident. I **h hate / am hating** doing that sort of thing. I **i always feel / feel always** stressed when people are watching me.

Tyler All of my family **j is enjoying / enjoys** shows and plays. What about you?

Hannah I **k don't usually like / don't like usually** plays. I **l go hardly ever / hardly ever go** to them because I always **m am falling / fall asleep** in them! But I want to see this one. I want to see you as Hamlet. Hey! What's that noise? **n Does your phone ring / Is your phone ringing**?

Tyler Yes, it **o rings / is**. Who **p calls / is calling** me now?

Hannah Spielberg maybe? Perhaps he wants you in his next movie!

VOCABULARY PLUS

At the Gym

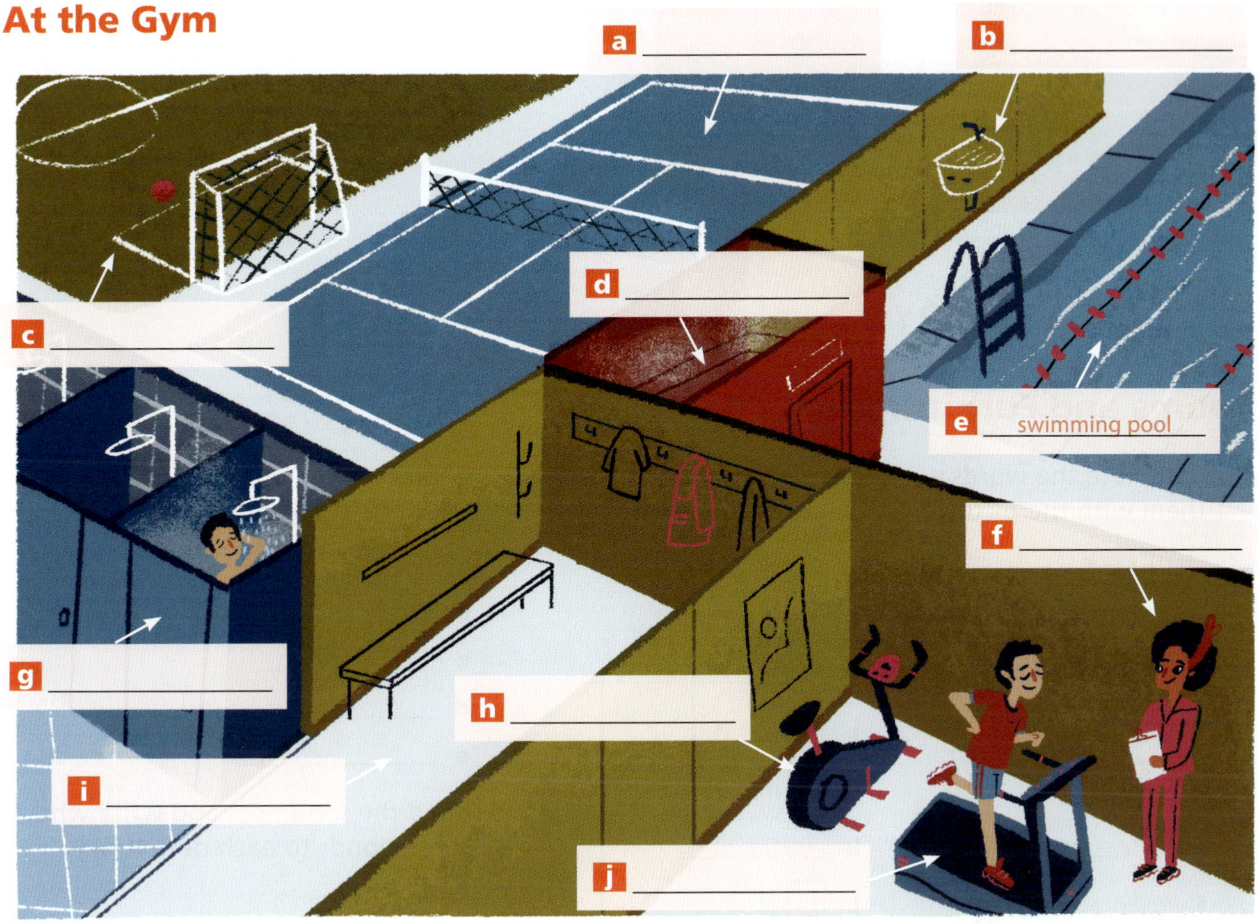

1 Label the picture with the words in the box. Then listen and repeat.

3

drinking fountain	exercise bike	locker room
personal trainer	sauna	showers	soccer field
~~swimming pool~~	tennis court	treadmill

2 Write the corresponding name to each definition below.

a place where you swim. swimming pool

a a place where you wash yourself. ____________

b a thing that you drink from. ____________

c a place that is very hot. ____________

d a place where you get changed. ____________

e a person who trains you. ____________

3 Complete the sentences with the words from activity 1.

Two teams are playing a game on the soccer field.

a I can't stand swimming so I never go in the ____________.

b My brother works in a gym as a ____________.

c Is there a ____________ here? I'm really thirsty.

d How many miles did you cycle on the ____________?

2

HOUSE AND HOME

VOCABULARY 1

Rooms and Furniture

1 Complete the words with vowels. Then match them with the picture.

[3] d_e_s k

a [ ] w__rdr__b__

b [ ] l__mp

c [ ] t____l__t

d [ ] ch____r

e [ ] __rmch____r

f [ ] c__b__n__t

g [ ] st__v__

h [ ] b____kc__s__

i [ ] b__d

j [ ] m__rr__r

k [ ] t__bl__

l [ ] s__f__

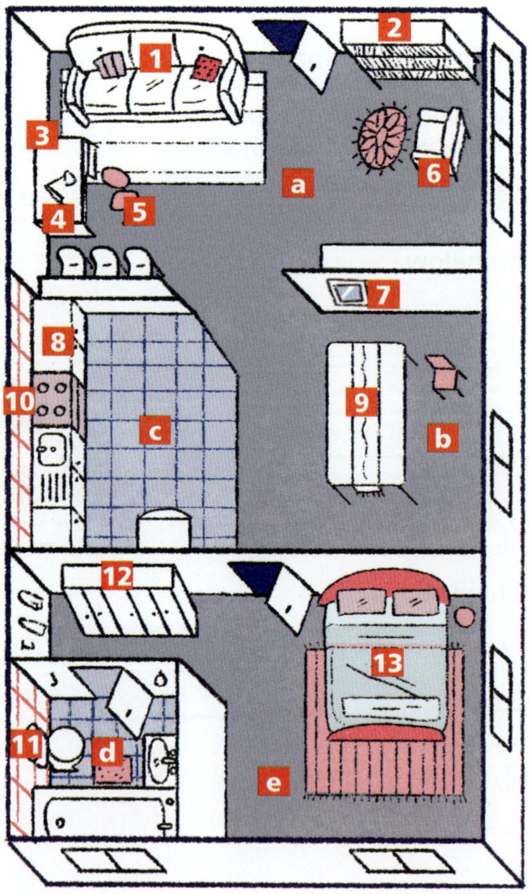

2 Look at the picture in activity 1 and label the rooms.

a living room

b ____________

c ____________

d ____________

e ____________

3 Read the sentences and write what corresponds to each definition.

a You cook on it. ____________

b You put your clothes in it. ____________

c You look at yourself in it. ____________

d You eat your dinner on it. It has four legs. ____________

e You sleep in it. ____________

f You sit on it. It's usually for three people. ____________

g You put books on it. ____________

h You have a shower in here. ____________

i You cook in here. ____________

j There's usually a sofa in here. You watch TV here. ____________

k You usually eat in here, but you don't cook. ____________

l There's usually a bed and a wardrobe in here. ____________

GRAMMAR 1

be: Simple Past

1 Underline the correct words.

This **a** was / **were** my family's beach house. Our summer vacation there **b** **was / were** fantastic. It **c** **wasn't / weren't** a comfortable place to stay. In fact, it **d** **was / wasn't** very basic.

The two bedrooms **e** **wasn't / weren't** big and they **f** **was / were** next to a living room and a small kitchen, and that was all! But it **g** **was / wasn't** a problem – we **h** **was / were** on the beach all day. It **i** **was / were** fun!

2 Rewrite the sentences in the simple past.

The weather isn't bad.
The weather wasn't bad.

a The days in August are long and hot.
____

b The beach is a lot of fun.
____

c The waves aren't very big.
____

d It isn't difficult for us to sleep.
____

3 Rewrite the sentences using the information in parentheses.

The house was near the city. (near the beach)
The house wasn't near the city. It was near the beach.

a It was their permanent home. (vacation home)
____
____

b The house was big. (small)
____
____

c There were five bedrooms. (two bedrooms)
____
____

4 Complete the dialogue with the words in the box.

was ~~was~~ was wasn't were were ~~were~~ weren't

Dad Where ___were___ you last night?
Eva I ___was___ at home.
Dad **a** ____________ Tom and Grace with you?
Eva No, they **b** ____________.
Dad **c** ____________ you in the kitchen?
Eva Yes, I **d** ____________.
Dad **e** ____________ the microwave on?
Eva No, it **f** ____________.

5 Complete the questions a-f with *was* or *were*. Then match the questions with the answer items 1-6 below.

a [2] ___Was___ that your old house, Dad?

b [ ] __________ you born there?

c [ ] Where __________ your bedroom?

d [ ] __________ it small?

e [ ] What color __________ the curtains?

f [ ] __________ you and your family happy there?

1 Next to the bathroom.

~~**2** Yes, it was.~~

3 No, it wasn't. It was big.

4 No, I wasn't.

5 Yes, we were.

6 Blue and white.

6 Write questions with the simple past of *be*. Then write short answers.

the clothes / in the wardrobe? ✗

Were the clothes in the wardrobe?

No, they weren't.

a the lamp / on the desk? ✓

b the books / on the bookcase? ✓

c the bedroom / tidy? ✗

d the cats / on the bed? ✗

e Kieran / in bed? ✓

7 Write questions with the simple past of *be*. Then write short answers for you.

a you / at school / yesterday?

b your birthday / two days ago?

c Where / you / at ten o'clock last night?

VOCABULARY 2

Gadgets

1 Look at the pictures and complete the crossword.

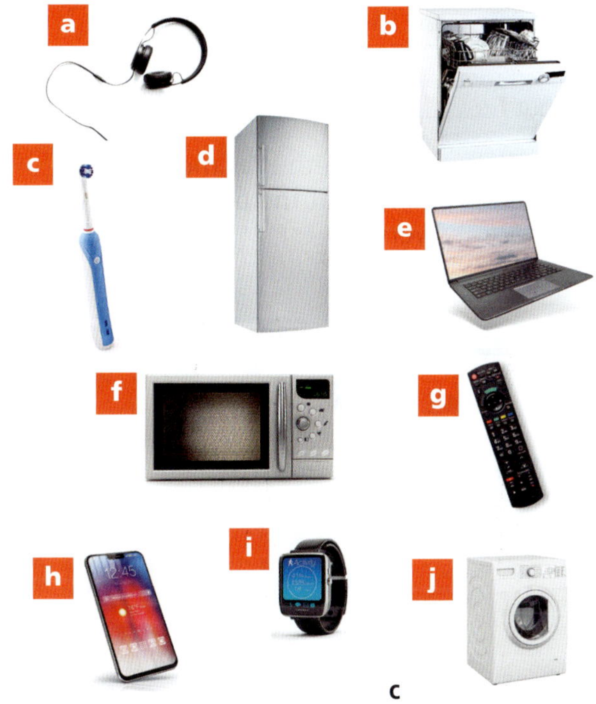

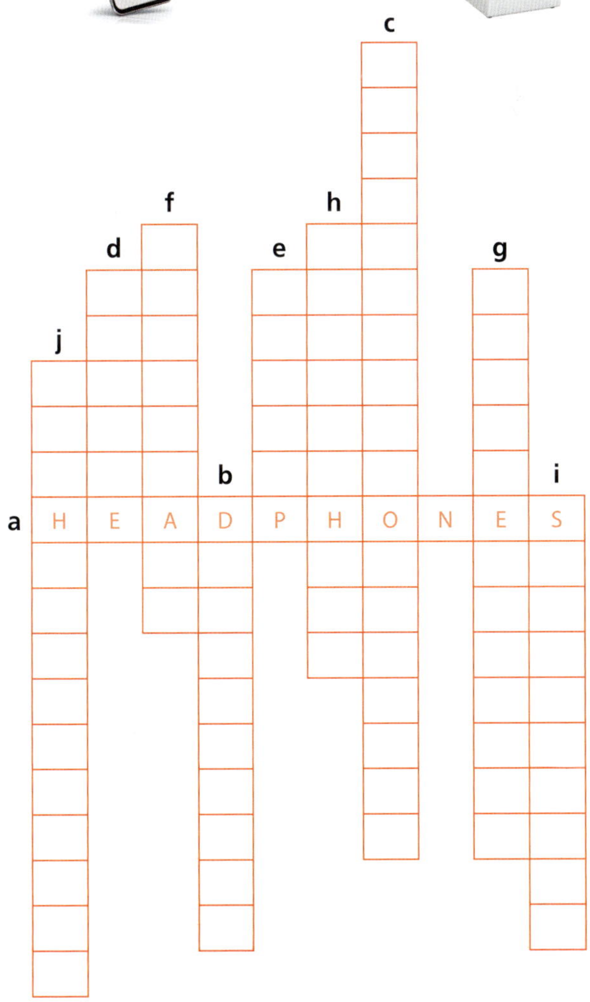

2 Write the name of the corresponding gadgets.

clean clothes ___washing machine___

a take photos ______________

b change channels ______________

c cook food ______________

d surf the internet ______________

e listen to music ______________

3 Complete the missing words with the corresponding gadgets.

What's your favorite gadget? Write and tell us.

Lucy I love the ___smartphone___. I talk on it every day with my friends!

Shakeel The **a** ____________ in the kitchen is my favorite gadget. It washes all the plates and cups for us. I love using it!

Paul My favorite thing is my **b** ____________. I can do my homework on it and surf the internet too!

Kayley I love the **c** ____________ in our kitchen. I can cook food fast in it. It's useful because I'm always very hungry when I get home from school.

Justine I have a new electric **d** ____________. I use it in the bathroom every morning and evening. It's fun!

Morgan I think the **e** ____________ is a really good gadget. I can sit on the sofa and change TV channels with it. It's great!

Olly My set of **f** ____________ is my favorite thing. I listen to music with it all the time.

4 Complete the sentences for you.

a My favorite gadget is ____________.

b I think ____________ is a really useful gadget.

c I also love using ____________ because ____________.

GRAMMAR 2

there was / there were

1 Complete the sentences with *was*, *wasn't*, *were*, or *weren't*.

✓ There ___were___ three bedrooms.

a ✓ There ________ a big bed near the window.

b ✗ There ________ a wardrobe.

c ✓ There ________ a table near my bed.

d ✗ There ________ any chairs.

e ✓ There ________ lots of books.

f ✗ There ________ a lamp.

2 Complete the text with the verb *be* in the simple past and with *there was*, *there wasn't*, *there were*, or *there weren't*.

This is a picture of our living room. It's a beautiful room now, but it **a** ________ a terrible room a month ago. It **b** ________ a very dark room. The walls **c** ________ black and **d** ________ some horrible pictures on them. Now the living room is completely different. The walls are gray and there are some beautiful paintings on them. **e** ________ two old armchairs, but **f** ________ a sofa before. **g** ________ a modern TV, either. Now there's a fantastic sofa and there is a yellow chair. We also have a huge TV now, which doesn't appear in the picture. I love our new living room!

3 Complete the text with *there was*, *there wasn't*, *there were* or *there weren't*.

___There was___ a big kitchen in our house, but **a** ________ a dining room. The kitchen was my favorite room. It was always warm because **b** ________ a very big stove and it was usually on – my mom and dad were really good cooks! **c** ________ some cabinets in front of the stove. **d** ________ any plates in them. **e** ________ some cakes and cookies in them, but **f** ________ any fruit!

4 Write questions with *Was there / Were there*. Then look at the picture and write short answers.

a table
Was there a table?
Yes, there was.

a cabinets
____
____

b a lamp
____
____

c chairs
____
____

d a microwave
____
____

e fridge
____
____

GRAMMAR CHECK

1 Read the text and circle the correct answers.

I **a** ___ a TV show **b** ___ night called *Help My House*. It was about a couple, Sally and Chris, and their kitchen. A team of people **c** ___ at Sally and Chris's house early in the morning. Sally **d** ___ there, but Chris was. He showed them the kitchen. It **e** ___ terrible. There wasn't a stove and there **f** ___ any cabinets. Then the team got to work. Some of them installed cabinets and a new stove, and others **g** ___. Exactly an hour later, everyone **h** ___. Not surprisingly, Sally **i** ___ when she walked into her new kitchen later that day!

	1	2	3
a	(watched)	'm watching	watch
b	at	last	in
c	arrive	arrived	arrives
d	isn't	weren't	wasn't
e	was	were	is
f	wasn't	aren't	weren't
g	decorate	decorated	are decorating
h	stopped	stops	stoped
i	cries	is crying	cried

2 Listen and check your answers.
4

LISTENING

1 Listen to the dialogue and answer the questions.
5

a How many bedrooms were there?

____

b How many bathrooms were there?

____

c Where was the kitchen?

____

d What room was at the top of the house?

____

2 Listen again and check off (✓) the furniture and gadgets that the speakers mention.
5

- **a** ☐ armchair
- **b** ☐ cabinet
- **c** ☐ dishwasher
- **d** ☐ lamp
- **e** ☐ microwave
- **f** ☐ mirror
- **g** ☐ stove
- **h** ☐ headphones
- **i** ☐ table-tennis table
- **j** ☐ washing machine

3 Listen again and write the adjectives used to describe the objects you checked off in activity 2.
5

____

____

____

____

____

____

____

____

EXTENSION

Circle the correct options to complete the text.

Thorpeness is a small village in the east of England and we **a was / were** there on our vacation last month. We usually stay in a hotel when we're on holiday, but this time we **b was / were** in a house for two weeks. It's called the "House in the Clouds" because it's about 21 meters high! It's an interesting house. About ninety years ago it **c was / were** a water tower. Do you know what a water tower is? **d There were / Were** a lot of them before.

They **e was / were** tall buildings and they contained water for the houses around them. Anyway, water towers **f were / was** ugly so the architect designed this one to look like a house. There **g was / were** a house under the water tower at that time. Then, in 1977, they converted the building into a house. It isn't a water tower now. My bedroom **h were** / **was** on the fourth floor so I could see Thorpeness beach and the sea. The sand on the beach **i was / were** lovely. **j There was / There were** an artificial lake in the village. You can't swim in it, but you can go boating. It **k was / were** fun!

See you soon,

Lily

VOCABULARY PLUS

Houses

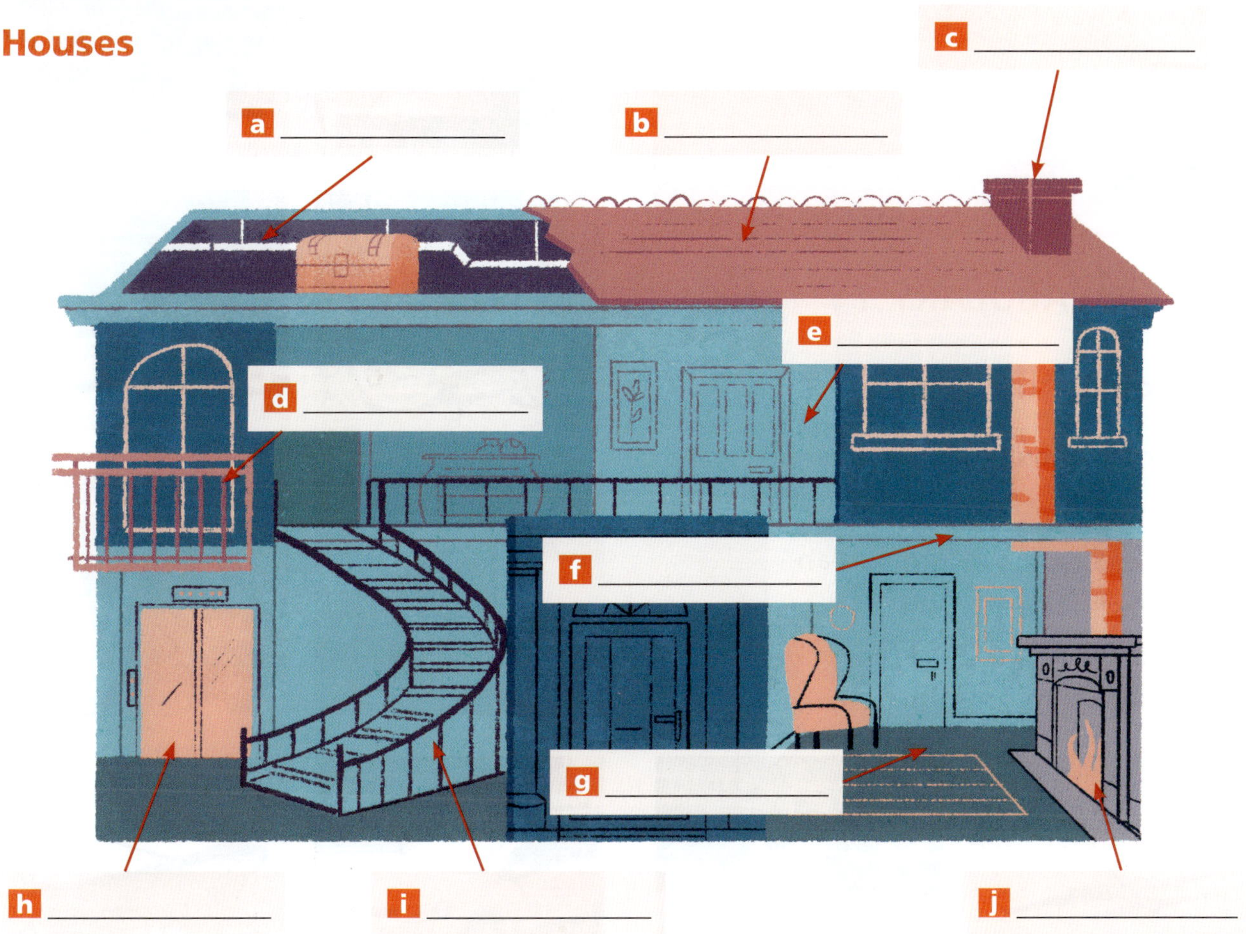

1 Read the words in the box below. Then listen and repeat.
6

balcony	ceiling	chimney	elevator
fireplace	floor	loft	roof	stairs	wall

2 Label the picture with the words in activity 1.

3 Order the letters and write the words.

abclnoy ___balcony___

a cegiiln ______

b airsst ______

c allw ______

d aceefilpr ______

e foor ______

f yeimcnh ______

g tflo ______

h oaveterl ______

4 Complete the chart with the words in activity 1.

inside	outside
ceiling	

5 Circle the correct words.

I'm tired so I'm using the (**elevator**) / **stairs**.

a People say that Santa Claus comes down the **chimney / fireplace**.

b Our cat is very good at climbing. It often sits on our **roof / ceiling**.

c At the top of our house, there's the **loft / fireplace** with all our old toys and clothes.

d In the summer, my mom sits on the **balcony / elevator** in the sun.

e In my bedroom, three **walls / floors** are white and one is orange.

3

TRAVEL

VOCABULARY 1

Transportation

1 Match the words with the pictures.

a	[1] plane	**f**	[ ] bus
b	[ ] truck	**g**	[ ] train
c	[ ] bike	**h**	[ ] motorcycle
d	[ ] streetcar	**i**	[ ] car
e	[ ] boat	**j**	[ ] taxi

3

4

5

6

7

8

1

2

9

10

2 Write the words in activity 1 in the correct group.

no wheels ___boat___

a 2 wheels ______________

b 3-4 wheels ______________

c 4+ wheels ______________

3 Read the clues and write the corresponding words.

I go on water. I don't have any wheels.
What am I? ___a boat___

a You can ride me on land. I have two wheels. You move your feet when you're riding me. I don't have a motor.
What am I? ______________

b I'm big and sometimes very long. I transport things on land. I have more than four wheels and you often see me on highways.
What am I? ______________

c Many people can travel on me at the same time. I take them all over the world. My tickets are often expensive. I fly in the air.
What am I? ______________

d I have two wheels and a motor, but you don't drive me. You ride me.
What am I? ______________

e You often see me in towns and cities. I have four wheels and someone drives me. A lot of different people travel in me every day. It costs money. I can carry a maximum of five people, including the driver.
What am I? ______________

f I can carry a lot of people at the same time. I'm quite long. I usually travel in towns and cities as well as between them. I have four or more wheels.
What am I? ______________

GRAMMAR 1

Simple Past (Affirmative Regular Verbs)

1 Complete the sentences with the simple past form of the verbs in parentheses.

Louis Blériot designed a plane in 1909. (design)

a He __________ it Blériot XI. (call)

b It __________ two wheels and an Anzani engine. (contain)

c On July 25th, 1909, Blériot __________ to fly across the English Channel in it. (try)

d After 37 minutes, he __________ in England. (arrive)

e He was the first pilot to do this and he __________ a £1,000 prize for it. (receive)

f Lots of people __________ to see this historic event. (gather)

g The Los Llanos museum in Spain __________ the Blériot XI. (exhibit)

h Louis Blériot also __________ the first practical headlamps for trucks. (develop)

2 Look at the pictures of Lucy's dad's trip. Match the verbs to the phrases.

a	travel	☐	a bed
b	decide	☐	to travel first class
c	use	☐	his eyes
d	order	☐	his credit card
e	turn into	☐	to New York in economy class
f	close	a	to London last week
g	dream	☐	orange juice and caviar
h	return	☐	like a child

3 Write sentences about Lucy's dad in the simple past. Use the verbs and phrases in activity 2.

a Lucy's dad traveled to London last week.

b ____________________

c ____________________

d ____________________

e ____________________

f ____________________

g ____________________

h ____________________

4 Complete the text with the simple past form of the verbs in the box.

arrive decide pick realize start travel wait watch

Last summer my family and I **a** ____________ to Singapore on an A380. I was really excited. We **b** ____________ at the airport at seven o'clock and **c** ____________ there for four hours. I **d** ____________ a seat by the window and there were lots of movies to watch. I **e** ____________ to watch one called *Snakes on a Plane* starring Samuel L. Jackson. I usually like him! Anyway, I **f** ____________ the movie for half an hour and then I **g** ____________ to think there were snakes under my seat. It was terrible. I **h** ____________ it was a bad idea to watch a movie like that on a plane!

5 Underline the correct verbs to complete the story.

Last summer my friends and I were at an amusement park. They **a decided / arrived** to go on the roller coaster. At first I **b wanted / refused** to go on it because I hate traveling fast, but I **c decided / started** to give it a try anyway!

Suddenly the train **d started / decided** to move. It was really fast and I **e hated / loved** it – it was horrible! I **f wanted / refused** to get off, but it was impossible. Five minutes later, the train **g stopped / continued**. I was very happy then! Obviously I only **h followed / watched** my friends go on the roller coaster the second time. I'm never stepping on it again!

6 Complete the sentences using the simple past form of the verbs in parentheses. Then check (✓) the sentences that are true for you.

a ☐ I ________ a taxi last week. (call)

b ☐ I ________ to a nearby town by bus this year. (travel)

c ☐ My parents ________ a bike last year. (rent)

d ☐ My parents ________ a car at the crosswalk once. (stop)

VOCABULARY 2

Travel

1 Underline the correct verbs.

try / **visit** museums

a **make** / **take** pictures

b **climb** / **take** mountains

c **have** / **visit** a good time

d **go** / **explore** new places

e **lay out** / **take** in the sun

f **explore** / **make** new friends

g **relax** / **have** in a café

h **taste** / **experiment** local food

2 Match the pictures with the phrases from activity 1.

visit museums

a

____

b

____

c

____

d

____

e

____

f

____

g

____

h

____

3 Complete the sentences with the simple present form of the verbs in the box.

explore	lay out	make	relax	take	~~visit~~

I'm interested in history so I often __visit__ museums.

a The sun is very strong between twelve and three o'clock. It isn't a good idea to __________ then.

b My parents are very friendly. They always __________ friends when they're on vacation.

c It's the weekend. Let's __________ and do nothing!

d I love my new camera. I __________ pictures all the time.

e It's fun to __________ new places. You just need a good map!

4 Complete the text with travel verbs.

TRANQUILITY TROPICAL RESORT

Leave the city and come to TRANQUILITY TROPICAL RESORT. It's the perfect place to **a** __________ for a week or two. There are eight hours of sunshine every day, so you can **b** __________ in the sun all day. TRANQUILITY TROPICAL RESORT is located at the foot of the coast range, so we also have equipment for you to use if you want to **c** __________ a mountain. Lots of young people like to come here during school holidays to enjoy the beach and meet new people. It's very easy to **d** __________ friends here! TRANQUILITY TROPICAL RESORT is near the historic town of Capitola, in California. Every Saturday morning there's a huge market in Capitola. It's a fantastic place to go shopping and **e** __________ local food. Don't forget your digital camera! You can **f** __________ pictures of all the beautiful things at TRANQUILITY TROPICAL RESORT.

Come to TRANQUILITY TROPICAL RESORT and have a great time!

GRAMMAR 2

Simple Past: Regular Verbs (Spelling)

1 Write the missing words.

	verb	simple past
	call	called
a	________	liked
b	play	________
c	________	stopped
d	use	________
e	________	wanted
f	try	________
g	________	lived
h	look	________

2 Complete the sentences with the simple past form of the verbs in activity 1.

Mr. Brown stopped to talk to me.

a They ________ the baby Eva.

b Lots of people ________ to see the city's attractions.

c I ________ to get up early, but it was impossible.

d She ________ a life full of adventures.

e He ________ basketball last summer.

f I ________ the movie. It was really good.

g He ________ around, but there was nobody there.

h In the past, people ________ horses in agriculture.

3 Write the verbs from activity 1 in the chart according to their spelling rules.

add *-ed*

add *-d*

omit the *-y* and add *-ied*

double the final consonant and add *-ed*

4 Complete the sentences with the simple past form of the verbs in parentheses.

Thomas Davenport invented the direct current electric motor in 1834. (invent)

a He ________ in the USA. (live)

b He ________ as a blacksmith, forging iron. (work)

c He ________ a battery-powered electric motor. (develop)

d In 1833 he ________ a workshop where an electromagnet was operating. (visit)

e He ________ electromagnetism to develop his invention. (study)

f After that, he ________ an electric motor. (design)

g He ________ the first patent for an electric machine in the USA. (receive)

5 Write sentences that are true for you.

a watch (TV show) last night

____

b talk to (person) yesterday

____

c play (sport) three days ago

____

d study (subject) last year

____

GRAMMAR CHECK

1 Read the text and circle the correct answers.

I **a** ________ something very strange in Boston last week. At first I **b** ________ and it was just an unusual green bus. I **c** ________ it driving towards the River Charles. But it never **d** ________ when it **e** ________ the river! It actually **f** ________ driving!

It **g** ________ the water and suddenly the bus was a boat! Later, a friend **h** ________ to me that an American **i** ________ this type of vehicle during World War II. It was a DUKW, but people **j** ________ it the "duck" or the "duck boat". They're still used worldwide, but mainly for tourism purposes!

	1	2	3
a	did witness	witnessed (circled)	'm witnessing
b	look	did look	looked
c	watched	did watch	watch
d	stopped	did stop	's stopping
e	reaches	reached	's reaching
f	's continuing	continues	continued
g	did enter	enters	entered
h	explained	explains	did explain
i	designs	designed	's designing
j	calls	called	did call

2 Listen and check your answers.

7

LISTENING

1 Listen to the dialogue and answer the questions.

8

a Where does Kate live?

____

b Where is Larry from?

____

c Where are they?

____

2 Listen again and underline the correct answers.

8

Kate and Larry get **on / off** the Tube.

a Larry **likes / hates** traveling on the Tube.

b You **can / can't** see the city when you're on the Tube and that's a problem for him.

c Kate and Larry **waited / didn't wait** a long time for a train.

d The trains usually come every **six / seven** minutes.

e They sit at the **back / front** of the train.

f There isn't a **driver / computer** on the train.

g There **are some / aren't any** automated trains in Larry's home town in the USA.

EXTENSION

<u>Underline</u> the correct words to complete the text.

- The London Underground or "the Tube" first **a starts / started** operating in 1863. It was the world's first underground system.
- People **b call / called** it "the Tube" in 1890. In 1908 they developed the London Underground's logo – a red circle and a blue rectangle. The rectangle contains the word UNDERGROUND or the name of the underground station.
- There **c is / are** eleven lines and 270 stations today.
- Early maps of the London Underground were geographic, but they **d wasn't / weren't** simple and people **e dislikes / disliked** them.
- Harry Beck **f designs / designed** a schematic map in 1931. He received the equivalent of around US$15 for his work! The map was very popular when people **g used / use** it for the first time in 1933.
- Today's map **h is / was** a modern version of Beck's map. It's a design icon and we **i often see / see often** it on souvenirs of London.
- People who live in London or tourists who **j is / are** visiting for a short time can buy an Oyster Card. It's an electronic ticket you **k use / 're using** to travel on any public transportation in the city.
- Around half a million **l mouses / mice** live in the London Underground. You sometimes see them on the line when you're waiting at a station!

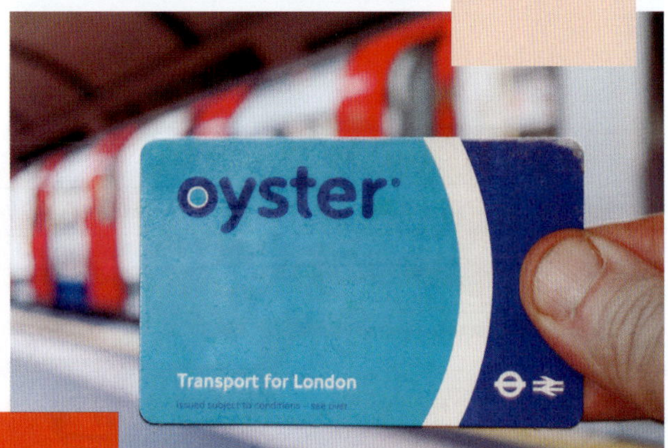

VOCABULARY PLUS

Things You Take on Vacation

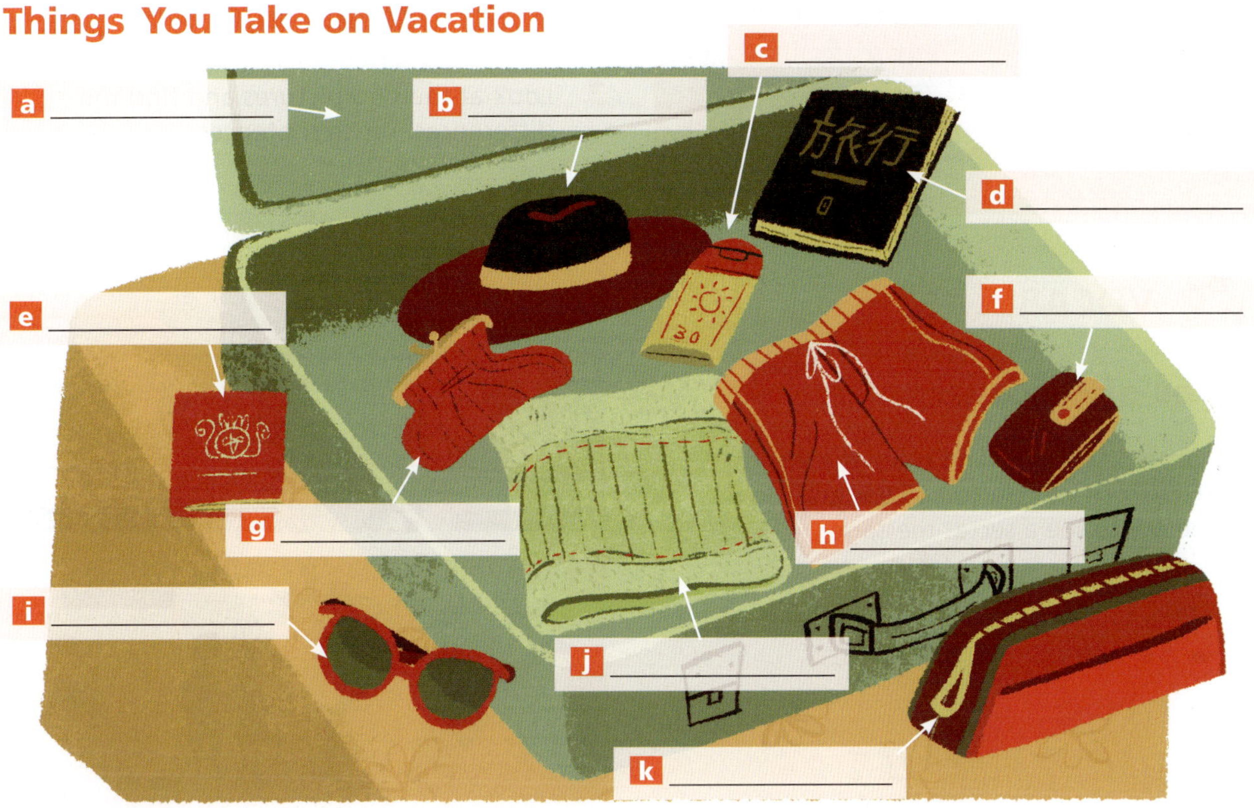

1 Check the meaning of these words. Then listen and repeat.

9

coin purse	sunscreen
hat	towel
passport	swimming trunks
phrase book	wallet
suitcase	toiletry bag
sunglasses	

2 Label the picture with the words in activity 1.

3 Match the columns to form words or phrases.

a phrase ☐ glasses
b suit ☐ screen
c sun ☐ bag
d sun ☐ case
e toiletry ☐ port
f pass [a] book

4 Write the correct words for the definitions.

Men wear these shorts for swimming. swimming trunks

a You need this official document to travel to another country. ____________

b You put coins in it. ____________

c You use this to dry yourself. ____________

d A small book with useful words and expressions in another language.
____

e You put your toothbrush, toothpaste, and shampoo in this bag. ____________

5 Complete the sentences for you. Try to use words from activity 1.

a When I go to school, I sometimes take my ____________.

b When I was very little, I didn't have ____________.

c On my last vacation, I took a ____________ ____________. It was very useful!

d For my next trip, I'm planning to buy ____________.

4

HISTORY

VOCABULARY 1

Verbs of Discovery

1 Order the letters and write the words. Then write the letters in the gray boxes below to see a secret message.

leeva — l e a v e

a redvi

b fyl

c eidr

d nadl

e og

f eatkffo

g vosdirce

h ratlev

i reariv

j sial

k pexrole

H _ _ _   _   _ _ o _   _ _ _ _ !

2 Complete the headlines with the words in the box.

drive	fly	land	ride	~~sail~~	take off

1580 – Francis Drake is the first English to ___sail___ around the world.

a 1886 – Thomas Stevens is the first person to ________ a bicycle around the world.

b 1919 – The first passenger planes ________ from Paris and ________ in London.

c 1978 – At last! Three Americans become the first people to ________ over the Atlantic Ocean by hot air balloon.

d 1996 – Two British journalists are the first people to ________ a car to the North Pole.

3 Look at the two pictures and find the differences. Write sentences.

1

2

Picture 1: A girl is riding a **bicycle**.
Picture 2: A girl is riding a **horse**.

a ________________________________

b ________________________________

c ________________________________

d ________________________________

4 Complete the sentences for you.

a My favorite way of traveling is by ____________ because ____________.

b I hate traveling by ____________ because ____________.

c A country I would love to explore is ____________ because ____________.

d My favorite trip was to ____________ because ____________.

e My least favorite trip was to ____________ because ____________.

GRAMMAR 1

Simple Past (Affirmative and Negative)

1 Write the simple past form of the verbs.

verb	simple past
discover	discovered
a cook	________
b love	________
c take	________
d cry	________
e sell	________
f watch	________
g begin	________
h eat	________

2 Complete the text with the simple past form of the verbs in parentheses.

The Ancient Greeks ___ate___ (eat) flat bread with herbs, onions, or garlic, but they **a** ________ (not eat) pizza with tomatoes like we do today. In 1522, European explorers **b** ________ (find) tomatoes in Peru and they **c** ________ (sail) with them back to Europe. Poor people in Naples, Italy, **d** ________ (cook) tomatoes with bread and they **e** ________ (invent) pizza. In the second half of the 19th century, many Italians **f** ________ (not want) to stay in Italy. They **g** ________ (travel) to live in America. But they **h** ________ (not forget) Italian food! They **i** ________ (take) pizzas with them. The first pizzeria that **j** ________ (sell) pizzas in the USA was in New York City, in 1905. And the rest is history!

3 Complete the sentences with the simple past form of the verbs in the box.

cry die discover
grow have leave watch

a I ________ home early at 7am.
b My grandfather ________ potatoes in his garden.
c My friends and I ________. The movie was really sad.
d I ________ a lot of homework yesterday.
e We ________ four movies on TV last night.
f My cat ________ last year.
g Barbara and I ________ a new Thai restaurant.

4 Rewrite the sentences in activity 3 with the negative form.

a ________
b ________
c ________
d ________
e ________
f ________
g ________

5 Match the past time expressions in the box with the letters on the time line.

four days ago ~~in 2020~~ last year
on Tuesday three months ago ~~yesterday~~

2020 → **TODAY – Thursday**
a b c d e f

a in 2020
b ________
c ________
d ________
e ________
f yesterday

6 Look at the headlines from yesterday's news and write sentences with the simple past.

a Scientists Discover New Planet

Scientists discovered a new planet.

____

b Young Sailor Arrives Home

____

____

c Lost Children Come Home

____

____

d 90-Year-Old Man Walks 20km To Find His Dog

____

____

e 700 Million People Watch World Cup Final

____

____

f New Ship Sails Into Barcelona

____

____

7 Look at the pictures of Martha's week. Complete the text with the affirmative or negative simple past form of the verbs in the box.

arrive	be (×2)	eat	get	like
play	rain	stay	study	think	want

Martha **a** ____________ an A on her English test on Monday. The teacher **b** ____________ very happy about it! On Tuesday, Martha **c** ____________ for a math test. The test was on Wednesday and it was very difficult. But her friends **d** ____________ it was easy. On the same day, Martha's cousin **e** ____________. He **f** ____________ to read. He **g** ____________ soccer with Martha. It **h** ____________ fun. On Thursday, it **i** ____________ all day. Martha **j** ____________ at home and watched TV. On Friday, the family **k** ____________ fish for dinner. Martha **l** ____________ it. The week started well, but ended up terribly!

VOCABULARY 2

Natural Disasters

1 Find nine natural disasters in the word search.

E	I	T	S	U	N	A	M	I	E
D	A	O	H	G	B	R	K	F	L
O	D	R	O	U	G	H	T	L	A
F	W	N	T	F	U	U	M	O	N
A	F	A	D	H	Q	O	K	O	D
M	Q	D	F	H	Q	M	R	D	S
I	O	O	T	I	U	U	E	X	L
N	U	R	R	I	R	A	A	E	I
E	A	T	O	R	N	E	D	K	D
E	H	U	R	R	I	C	A	N	E

2 Match the words in the box with the pictures.

~~fire~~ flood landslide tornado tsunami volcanic eruption

fire

a

____

b

____

c

____

d

____

e

____

3 Complete the news reports with words from activity 1.

World News

The **a** __________ continues in Central Africa. It last rained here two years ago and everything is very dry. Some people don't have any food at all. **b** __________ in this part of the continent is very serious indeed.

People are talking about the **c** __________ in California on Tuesday. Jolene McKlusky said, "The kitchen floor moved and then plates, cups, and food fell onto the floor. We all ran under the table." The incident caused a **d** __________ which hit the coast. One witness said, "I was on the beach and I saw very big waves in the sea. It was really scary."

A report is coming in from the National Weather Center about the **e** __________ that is affecting Florida. It is very windy and rainy at the moment, so stay inside.

In Mexico, the rain continues and the water is rising. There are **f** __________ all over the country. Many people are sleeping in shelters tonight. The heavy rain caused a **g** __________ which cut off many villages in the mountains yesterday. Large rocks fell onto the road.

The **h** __________ in Greece is continuing in the forest. It is destroying the trees and killing the wildlife. It began with a cigarette. Emergency service personnel are working in the area.

GRAMMAR 2

Simple Past (Questions and Short Answers)

1 Match the questions with the answers.

a Did your dad drive to work?
b Did you ride your bike?
c Did your sister watch TV?
d Did your friends go out?

[ ] No, she didn't.
[ ] Yes, they did.
[a] Yes, he did.
[ ] No, I didn't.

2 Write questions in the simple past. Then write short answers.

[✗] Marco Polo / go / to America?
Did Marco Polo go to America?
No, he didn't.

a [✗] Sally Ride / land / on the Moon?
____
____

b [✓] The Chinese / invent / tomato ketchup?
____
____

c [✗] Jacques Cousteau / explore / the mountains?
____
____

d [✓] You / see / the news last night?
____
____

3 Write questions using the simple past. Then write answers for you.

a Where / you / be / on Saturday at two o'clock?
____
____

b What / you / watch / on TV yesterday?
____
____

c What time / you / arrive / home on Saturday?
____
____

could / couldn't

4 Complete the sentences with *could* or *couldn't*.

[✗] The people couldn't stop the fire.
a [✗] I __________ play tennis when I was 10.
b [✓] My cousin __________ draw well when he was three.
c [✓] My sister __________ speak English really well when she lived in Canada.
d [✗] My friends __________ cook a year ago.
e [✗] We __________ watch TV last night.
f [✗] My aunt __________ visit me because she was traveling.
g [✓] I __________ swim really well when I was in high school.

5 Complete the sentences with *could* or *couldn't* and the verbs in parentheses.

Beethoven couldn't hear. (not hear)

a Albert Einstein __________ until he was nearly three years old. (not speak)
b When Messi was five, he __________ soccer very well. (play)
c Pablo Picasso __________ well when he was very young. (draw)
d Thomas Edison __________ quietly at school so his mother taught him at home. (not sit)
e Lady Gaga __________ the piano when she was four years old. (play)
f Billie Eilish __________ music since she was twelve years old. (write)
g Michael B. Jordan __________ basketball very young. (play)

6 Complete the text with *could* or *couldn't*.

Dylan's parents think he is very intelligent and talented. When he was two years old, he **a** __________ speak. He talked all the time. One year later, he **b** __________ read and write. In fact, he read a book every day at bedtime! But he **c** __________ ride a bike. At the age of four, he **d** __________ finally ride a bike, but he **e** __________ play basketball. He **f** __________ cook when he was five years old. He made a pizza and spaghetti for his mom and dad. He **g** __________ play basketball before he was seven years old.

GRAMMAR CHECK

1 Read the text and circle the correct answers.

When he **a** ___ 17, the English archaeologist Howard Carter **b** ___ to Egypt to find out more about ancient Egypt. Lord Carnarvon, a rich Englishman, **c** ___ also interested in ancient Egypt, and, in 1907, Carter **d** ___ to work for him. On November 4, 1922, Carter's team **e** ___ a door. They **f** ___ all very excited. Did **g** ___ the door? No, they **h** ___ open the door because Lord Carnarvon **i** ___ there. Three weeks later, he arrived in Egypt with his daughter. What **j** ___ find when they opened the door? **k** ___ a room full of objects. They **l** ___ see boxes, chairs, sofas, and even flowers. It was Tutankhamun's tomb.

	1	2	3
a	(was)	were	had
b	did travel	traveled	was travel
c	was	were	be
d	begin	began	begun
e	discover	discovered	did discover
f	are	was	were
g	they opened	they open	open they
h	didn't	wasn't	not
i	didn't	wasn't	not
j	they did	did they	do they
k	There was	There were	There is
l	can	did can	could

2 Listen and check your answers.
10

LISTENING

1 Listen to three news reports. Match each report with the correct image.
11

San Francisco

London

Bristol

2 Listen again and complete the chart with information about each report.
11

	report 1	report 2	report 3
What was the disaster?			
When did it happen?			
What did it destroy?			
How many people did it kill?			

EXTENSION

Circle the correct words to complete the text.

Frank Lobos **a plays / played** for the national Chilean soccer team in the 1980s and 1990s. Today he **b don't / doesn't** play professional soccer, he works as a miner. Carlos Barrios **c drive / drives** a taxi and he also works as a miner. Carlos Mamani is from Bolivia, but he **d move / moved** to Chile 10 years ago.

What do these men have in common? Well, they **e work usually / usually work** in the San José mine, but **f his / their** lives changed on August 5, 2010. There **g was / were** a landslide inside the mine. Thirty-three miners were 700m under the ground and they **h could / couldn't** leave. How did they **i survive / survived**? They had air and it was warm under the ground. They ate fish and cookies and drank milk. On Day 17, the men sent a note to the surface. It said, "The 33 of us are well."

Now, I'm outside the San José mine in Chile, 69 days after the landslide. **j There is / There are** many people here, including relatives, journalists, and the president of Chile. **k When / Why** are they screaming and shouting? Because the last miner **l comes / is coming** out right now. It's 10pm on Wednesday, October 13, 2010. The rescue operation is finished and the 33 miners are safe!

VOCABULARY PLUS

Other Means of Transportation

a

b

c

d

e

f

g

h

i

1 Read the transportation words. Then listen and repeat.

12

barge cable car ferry helicopter
high-speed train hot-air balloon
rowboat trailer yacht

2 Label the pictures with the words in activity 1.

3 Complete the chart with the words in activity 1.

air	land	water
hot-air balloon,		

4 Write the correct words for the definitions.

We use this long flat boat on canals.
barge

a A small boat that needs oars to move.

b It flies and has long metal blades on top.

c A large boat that can carry cars.

d A car pulls this mobile home.

e This train travels very fast.

5 Complete these sentences for you. Try to use words from activity 1.

a In my town, we don't have any ______ or any ______.

b I would like to travel by ______ because ______.

c I wouldn't like to travel by ______ because ______.

5

MYTHS AND LEGENDS

VOCABULARY 1

Character Adjectives

1 Complete the words with vowels and with the letter *y* when necessary.

br_a_v_e_

a cr____ ____l

b w____s____

c st____bb____rn

d l____ ____ ____l

e l____z____

f ch____ ____rf____l

g sh____

h f____nn____

i k____nd

j s____lf____sh

k fr____ ____ndl____

2 Write the words in activity 1 in the correct group.

positive brave, ____________________

negative cruel, ____________________

3 Underline the correct words.

How many of these legends do you know?

Beowulf was a **a shy / brave** man. He sailed to Denmark and killed a terrible monster called Grendel.

Minos was a **b cheerful / cruel** king who had a monster called the Minotaur. He fed children to his "pet."

Maud was **c kind / selfish**. When she found a baby dragon, she wanted to help it, but her father said no. But Maud was **d stubborn / funny**. She asked him again and again, and in the end he agreed. The dragon was always **e cruel / loyal** to Maud because of her kindness.

Rip Van Winkle was a **f lazy / wise** farmer who never did any work. One day he drank a magic potion and fell asleep for many years.

4 Complete the sentences with words from activity 1.

a Alice always thinks about others and treats everyone very well. She's __________.

b My brother is always singing and smiling. He's very __________.

c Josh would never say anything bad about his friends because he's very __________.

d My grandma knows a lot about the world and she always has good ideas. She's __________.

e Our uncle never lets the dog in the house, even when it's really cold outside. He's __________.

f I don't like giving in to other people's opinions. As I'm __________, I never change my mind.

GRAMMAR 1

Past Progressive

1 Write the missing words.

verb	*-ing* form
fight	fighting
a rule	___________
b ___________	invading
c swim	___________
d ___________	attacking
e listen	___________
f ___________	winning
g play	___________
h ___________	smiling

2 Complete the text with the past progressive form of the verbs in parentheses. Then answer the question.

It was raining (rain) when the art thief took another painting. When Sherlock Holmes arrived at the museum, the museum director **a** ___________ (explain) everything to the police. Holmes asked several workers, "What were you doing at 4pm?" The museum guard answered, "I **b** ___________ (have) a cup of tea in my office." The woman in the ticket office said, "I was with my friend. We **c** ___________ (walk) around the museum." Her friend replied, "We **d** ___________ (talk) about the weather." The museum director said, "I **e** ___________ (sit) outside in the museum garden." Dr. Watson **f** ___________ (listen) to these interviews. Sherlock Holmes suddenly looked up and said, "It was the director!" How did he know?

____

____

3 Write sentences using the past progressive form.

it / rain
It was raining.

a Grandpa / play / soccer
____

b Joe / walk / the dog
____

c Tom and Bud / play / frisbee
____

d Mom and Grandma / have / a picnic
____

e Dad / take / a picture
____

f the birds / fly / in the sky
____

4 Look at the picture below and correct the sentences in activity 3.

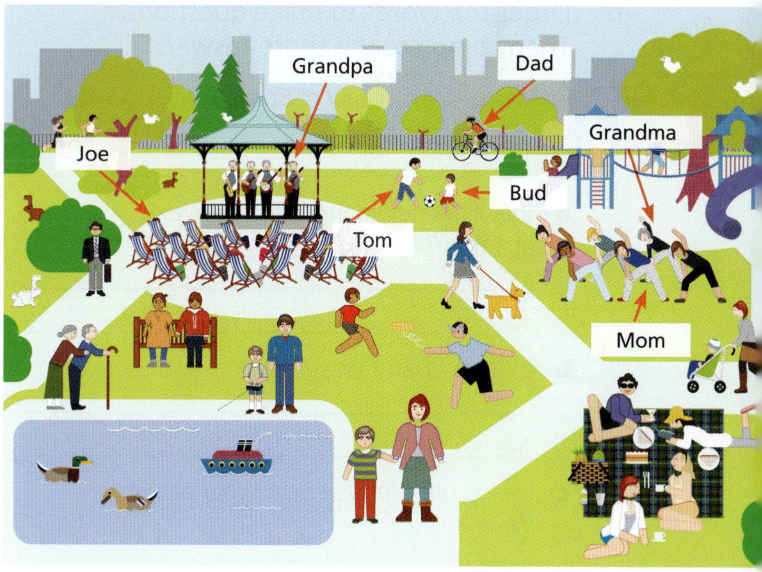

It wasn't raining.
The sun was shining.

a ____
____

b ____
____

c ____
____

d ____
____

e ____
____

f ____
____

5 Complete the questions with *Was* or *Were*. Then match the questions with the short answers below.

[1] Were you watching TV at 8pm last night?

a [ ] ________ your dad sitting on the sofa?

b [ ] ________ your friends chatting on the phone?

c [ ] ________ your dog sleeping in the kitchen?

d [ ] ________ I talking too much?

e [ ] ________ we having a good time?

1 Yes, I was.

2 No, they weren't.

3 Yes, we were.

4 No, he wasn't.

5 Yes, it was.

6 Yes, you were.

6 Order the words to make questions. Then complete the short answers.

watching / Was / Paul / at 8pm / TV ?
Was Paul watching TV at 8pm?
Yes, he was.

a they / talking / to their friends / Were / at 11pm ?

____

No, ________________________.

b at 2am / Dan / Was / reading ?

____

Yes, ________________________.

c having breakfast / at 8am / your parents / Were ?

____

Yes, ________________________.

d Were / at 8pm / you / having dinner ?

____

Yes, ________________________.

e Nicole / playing / at 11am / soccer / Was ?

____

No, ________________________.

f speaking / during vacation / Were / English / you ?

____

Yes, ________________________.

7 Write questions using the past progressive form. Then look at the picture below and write short answers.

Evie / chat / with Lola ?
Was Evie chatting with Lola?
Yes, she was.

a Robert / listen / to the teacher ?

____

____

b Juliet and Sophie / work / hard ?

____

____

c the teacher / look / at the students ?

____

____

d the cat / eat / a fish ?

____

____

8 Write questions using *you* in the past progressive form.

a dance / at 2am on Saturday night ?

____

____

____

b play basketball / at 8am on Sunday morning ?

____

____

____

c have breakfast / at 8am yesterday ?

____

____

____

VOCABULARY 2

Movement Verbs

1 Find thirteen movement verbs in the word search.

C	R	O	S	S	S	T	A	N	D	N	S
L	M	I	T	D	C	K	U	L	I	F	T
H	L	D	O	O	G	H	L	G	E	O	E
F	D	O	R	N	F	N	A	P	U	L	L
A	E	T	H	O	E	A	E	H	Y	L	U
L	U	J	U	M	P	P	U	S	H	O	E
L	E	P	O	O	E	T	A	Y	R	W	A
T	E	V	I	A	O	L	C	S	R	M	A
O	E	A	D	N	P	N	A	I	O	D	L
E	S	C	D	R	H	H	R	T	A	A	T
M	O	S	E	O	A	D	R	E	E	G	T
E	L	L	B	E	M	G	Y	T	O	H	O

2 Complete the sentences with the words in the box.

~~carry~~ cross follow jump move pull sit

I often carry a lot of books in my school bag.

a I always ________ that road very carefully. It's dangerous.

b I can't see the screen. Can you ________, please?

c Elephants can't ________ because they are very big and heavy.

d I don't like standing at basketball games so I usually ________ at the front.

e The door didn't open when I pushed it so I decided to ________ it.

f When I hike with my family, my mom leads and we ________ her.

3 Underline the correct words.

Weird Events
Wife-carrying

In this event from Finland, the men need to **a carry / follow** their wives for 253.5m. They can't **b fall / drop** their wives. And of course, the wives can't **c fall / lead**.

Mob Football

This isn't a normal football match because any number of people can play and there are no rules. The players **d follow / jump** a ball as it **e pulls / crosses** the town. Players throw or **f carry / stand** the ball, but they hardly ever kick it.

4 Rewrite the sentences for you.

a I always stand at sports games.

____

b I drop my cell phone every day.

____

c I fell and broke my leg when I was young.

____

d I usually play sports on the weekend.

____

GRAMMAR 2

Simple Past and Past Progressive

1 Match the columns.

a While I was having breakfast	☐ they were buying popcorn.
b Laura was crossing the road	a my phone rang.
c When we arrived home	☐ while I was jumping over the wall.
d When I saw my friends	☐ he fell and broke his arm.
e While James was climbing a tree	☐ the dog was eating our lunch.
f I dropped my keys	☐ when she found $50.

2 Complete the sentences with the simple past or the past progressive form of the verbs in parentheses.

I was __doing__ (do) my homework when my mom __arrived__ (arrive) home.

a My sister ________ (carry) the groceries when she ________ (drop) the eggs.

b I ________ (stand) outside the movie theater when I ________ (see) Brad Pitt.

c When my teacher ________ (walk) into the classroom we ________ (listen) to music.

d My friends ________ (play) soccer when a dog ________ (take) their ball.

e We ________ (look) for wood to build a fire when we ________ (discover) a secret cave.

f When I ________ (get) the text message I ________ (sit) at the dinner table.

3 Rewrite the sentences in activity 2 using *While*.

While I was doing my homework, my mom arrived home.

a While ____________________

____

b While ____________________

____

c While ____________________

____

d While ____________________

____

e While ____________________

____

f While ____________________

____

4 Complete the text with the simple past or the past progressive forms of the verbs in the box.

call chat do have listen sleep not watch win

www.coollife.com/interview/aliciagarcia

As part of our Ordinary Lives series, *Cool Life* magazine is interviewing Alicia Garcia. Alicia's from Spain, but she lives in Miami with her family.

Cool Life Hi, Alicia. What **a** ________ you ________ last night at 8pm? **b** ________ you ________ dinner?

Alicia No, I wasn't. I **c** ________ with my friends on the internet. We had dinner at 9pm.

Cool Life **d** ________ you ________ in your bed at 11pm?

Alicia No, I wasn't. I **e** ________ to music in my bedroom. While I was doing that, my friend Katia **f** ________ me on her new cell phone.

Cool Life You're from Spain. When Spain **g** ________ the World Cup, what were you doing?

Alicia I **h** ________ the game because I was camping with some friends.

GRAMMAR CHECK

1 Read the text and circle the correct options.

How Did It Happen?

There are many stories about inventions and discoveries, and most of them are probably not true!

Q How did Sir Isaac Newton discover gravity?

A He **a** ___ under a tree **b** ___ an apple fell onto his head.

Q Where does the word "Eureka" come from?

A One day, Archimedes **c** ___ a bath when he **d** ___ that the water level rose when he got into the bathtub. He exclaimed *Eureka!*, which means "I've found it!"

Q Who invented bubble gum?

A It was Thomas Adams in 1869. He was using the gum to make toys when he **e** ___ it into his mouth and he liked it. In 1900, people all over the USA **f** ___ chewing gum.

Q When did Levi Strauss invent jeans?

A People **g** ___ for gold in California **h** ___ a young man called Levi Strauss moved to San Francisco. They were working hard and they needed stronger pants. Levi Strauss used a material from France called denim and he invented "blue jeans."

	1	2	3
a	was sit	(was sitting)	is sitting
b	when	while	what
c	take	were taking	was taking
d	notice	noticing	noticed
e	put	puts	putting
f	was	were	are
g	were looking	was looking	looked
h	while	what	when

2 Listen and check your answers.

13

LISTENING

1 Listen to a radio interview. Order the words you hear.

14

☐ hunter

☐ sewer

☐ farms

☐ toilet

☐ alligator

2 Listen again and circle T for *true* or F for *false*.

14

a Amber Martin is in Florida. T / F

b In the 1930s, rich families went to Florida on vacation. T / F

c People brought their alligators to New York. T / F

d Legend says that the people threw their alligators into the trash can. T / F

e Nobody saw the alligators in the sewers. T / F

f People hunted these animals in the sewers. T / F

EXTENSION

Circle the correct words to complete the text.

a **What / When** is your favorite story about your city?

I'm Gaspard from Paris, France. About 14 million people **b visit / are visiting** Paris every year and definitely the most popular monument is the Eiffel Tower. This Tower was built in 1889 for the Paris Exposition, but by 1925 it **c was / were** in a terrible condition. A very intelligent man, Victor Lustig, was living in Paris at this time. Lustig told Andre Poisson, a rich businessman, that he was working for the city. He said the city **d didn't have / not have** any money and **e couldn't / didn't can** repair the Tower so they **f sell / were selling** it. This wasn't true, of course; Lustig was playing a cruel joke. Poisson gave a lot of money to Lustig to buy the Tower. Lustig took the money and escaped from France. Poisson **g not went / didn't go** to the police because he was very embarrassed.

VOCABULARY PLUS

Fictional Characters

1 Read the words in the box. Then listen.

15

dragon ☐	fairy ☐	ghost ☐
hero ☐	heroine ☐	monster ☐
unicorn ☐	witch ☐	

2 Match the pictures above with the words in activity 1.

3 Complete the words with consonants.

wi_t_c_h_

a ____a__o__

b __e__o

c u__i__o____

d ____o____

e __ai____

f __e__oi__e

4 Complete the sentences with words from activity 1.

A _unicorn_ has a white horn.

a A _______ is a woman with magical powers.

b A _______ is an animal that can breathe fire.

c A _______ is a small creature with large insect-like wings.

d A _______ is a large scary creature.

e A _______ is a woman who is good and brave.

5 Which word is the odd one out? Why? Use the words in the box to help you.

animal	fly	good	magic	~~man~~	real

witch <u>hero</u> heroine _A hero is a man._

a witch dragon unicorn __________

b hero ghost heroine __________

c monster witch fairy __________

d witch fairy heroine __________

e dragon monster fairy __________

6

WISE SPENDING

VOCABULARY 1

Money

1 Find ten verbs in the wordsnake.

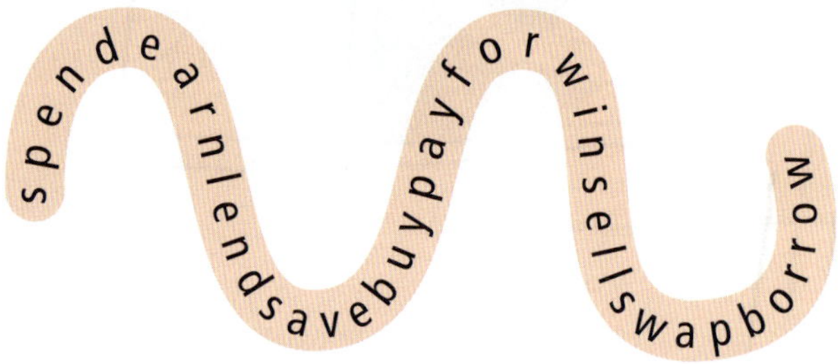

2 Look at the pictures below and complete the sentences with the verbs in the box.

buy	lend	save	sell	~~spend~~	win

Jane went shopping, but she didn't __spend__ any money.

a Tom didn't ________ any money on the game show.

b Could you ________ me your book for a moment, please?

c Do you ________ your allowance or spend it?

d Where did you ________ your dress? It's great!

e They want to ________ their old DVDs.

3 Complete the dialogue with the correct form of verbs in activity 1.

Erick Mom, can you **a** ________ me a new bike?

Mom You can **b** ________ your sister's bike. She doesn't use it anymore.

Erick I know, but she doesn't want to **c** ________ it to me. She says it's special because she **d** ________ it in that competition last year.

Mom I can't **e** ________ a bike at the moment, I **f** ________ a lot of money on a new TV last week. Maybe you can have a new bike for your birthday.

Erick But it's not until October!

4 Answer the questions for you. Write full sentences.

a What do you spend your money on?

____

b What was the last thing you bought?

____

c Do you swap things? What?

____

d What do you never lend?

____

GRAMMAR 1

Comparatives

1 Write the missing words.

adjective	comparative
rich	richer
a ______	fatter
b large	______
c heavy	______
d ______	worse
e far	______
f expensive	______
g ______	older
h intelligent	______

2 Complete the sentences with the comparative form of the adjectives in parentheses.

A $1 coin is heavier than a half-dollar coin. (heavy)

a My feet are ______ than my dad's feet. (small)

b Are video games ______ than DVDs? (cheap)

c Is math ______ than history? (difficult)

d Modern bicycles are ______ than old bicycles. (fast)

e A £50 bill is ______ than a £5 bill. (big)

f People say dogs are ______ friends than people. (good)

3 Look at the picture below and complete the text with the comparative form of the adjectives in the box.

expensive good intelligent long ~~old~~ rich small young

Hi! I'm James and this is my family. My dad is Alan and my mom is Clare. I have two brothers, Harry and Nathan. Harry is 18 and Nathan is 16. Harry is older than Nathan, but Nathan is tall for his age. Harry is **a** ______ than him, but he has a **b** ______ hair! I'm only 12, so I'm **c** ______ than all of them. I think they're very intelligent, but I'm **d** ______ than them when it comes to some activities. For example, I'm **e** ______ at the piano than my brothers. My dad's brother, uncle John, has a lot of money – he's **f** ______ than my dad. His car was **g** ______ than our car. It's very fast!

4 Complete the sentences with the comparative form of the adjectives in parentheses.

Vilaflor, in Spain, is <u>higher</u> than Madrid. (high)

a My cat is ____________ than Mary's cat. (old)

b Rafael Nadal is ____________ than Andy Murray at playing tennis. (good)

c These shoes are ____________ than this purse. (expensive)

d The Bank of China in Hong Kong is ____________ than the other banks. (tall)

5 Underline the correct options.

My brother is incredibly **a tall / taller**. In fact he's **b tall / taller** than most of our school's basketball players. One day I want to be **c tall / taller** than him – and **d good / better** than him at basketball too! I have four cats. Rosie is only two weeks old. She's black with **e big / bigger** blue eyes. I love her. I think she's **f beautiful / more beautiful** than any other cat!

6 Complete the sentences for you. Use comparative adjectives + *than*.

a Soccer is ______________________ basketball.

b Being an actor is ______________________ being a teacher.

c A speaker is ______________________ earbuds.

d My best friend is ______________________ me.

(not) as ... as

7 Underline the correct words.

I'm going to eat now. **<u>I'm as</u> / 'm not as** hungry as a horse.

a I can't see the board, but you can. My eyes **are as / aren't as** good as yours.

b The Pyrenees **are as / are not as** high as the Alps.

c Are you OK? You're very pale. You**'re as / aren't as** white as a sheet!

d Rome isn't **as old as / as older as** Athens.

e This exercise is simple! It**'s as / isn't as** easy as ABC.

f The Atlantic Ocean isn't **as bigger as / as big as** the Pacific Ocean.

8 Rewrite the sentences using *not as ... as*.

The Eiffel Tower is higher than the London Eye. ✗
<u>The London Eye is not as high as the Eiffel Tower.</u>

a The Parthenon is older than the Colosseum. ✗

____

b Egypt is hotter than Spain. ✗

____

c Tenerife is bigger than La Gomera. ✗

____

d Castles are more interesting than caves. ✗

____

e Delhi is noisier than London. ✗

____

f Norway is colder than England. ✗

____

VOCABULARY 2

Technology Devices

1 Complete the words with vowels. Then match them with the picture.

[4] scr_e_ _e_n
a [ ] l___pt___p
b [ ] pr___nt___r
c [ ] d___skt___p
d [ ] w___bc___m
e [ ] m___ ___s___
f [ ] sp___ ___k___r
g [ ] k___yb___ ___rd
h [ ] sc___nn___r

2 Read the sentences and write the corresponding words.

You use this to click on something. _mouse_
a This can put images onto paper. ___________
b You use this to type on a computer. ___________
c You use these to listen to music or sound. ___________
d This is a small computer that you can use anywhere. ___________
e You can use this to send live images to your friends when you're on the computer. ___________
f You can use this to copy paper documents or pictures onto your computer. ___________

3 Complete the phone messages with the words in the box.

earbuds	laptop	tablet	USB hub

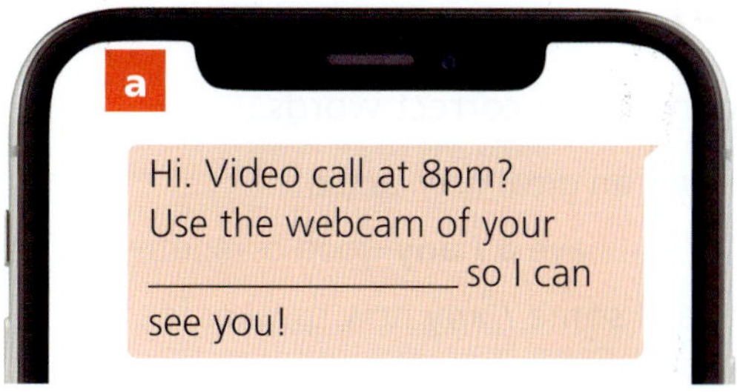

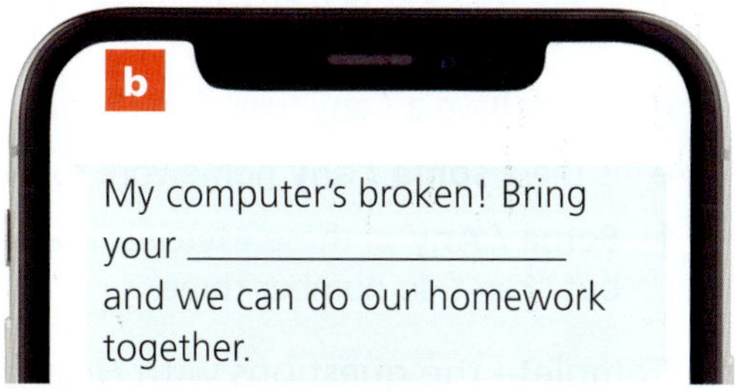

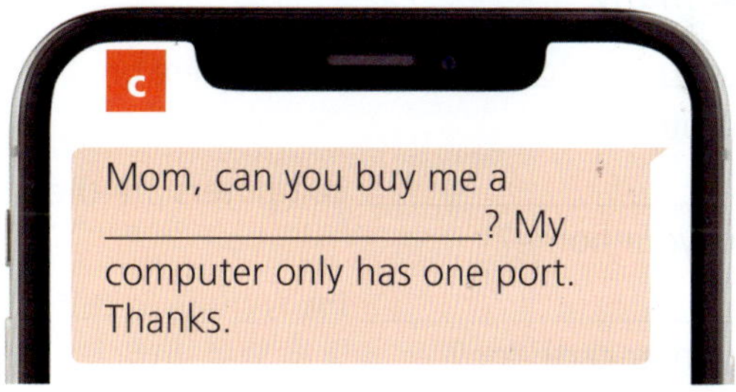

4 Answer the questions for you. Write full sentences.

a What is your favorite piece of technology?
____
____

b Which websites do you use?
____
____

c What do you use a computer for?
____
____

d What technology does your school have?
____
____

GRAMMAR 2

a / an, some, any, much, many, a lot of

1 Underline the correct words.

I have a / an great new laptop.

a Do you have **a / any** good computer games?

b I need **some / any** new speaker for my desktop.

c There isn't **some / any** fruit. Can you go to the store?

d I don't have **a / any** ruler. Can I borrow yours?

e Is there **some / any** homework for Monday?

f **Some / Any** of these exercises are very easy, but I can't do number three.

2 Complete the questions with *How much* or *How many.*

___How much___ memory is there on the laptop?

a ____________ computers are there in your home?

b ____________ ink is there in this printer cartridge?

c ____________ money does that tablet cost?

d ____________ homework do you have this weekend?

e ____________ teachers are there in your school?

f ____________ people use this website?

3 Complete the sentences with *a, an, some,* or *any.*

Do you have ___an___ English dictionary?

a I have ____________ amazing new computer.

b Do you have ____________ video games?

c There are ____________ new students in my class.

d I have my bag, but I don't have ____________ money.

e You need ____________ speaker for your computer.

f This computer has ____________ lot of memory.

4 Circle the correct options.

We don't have **much / many** computers at school.

a This cartridge doesn't have **much / many** ink left.

b I write **much / a lot of** my blog on the school computers.

c How **much / many** pictures do you have on your laptop?

d My computer is old and it doesn't have **much / many** memory.

e **Much / A lot of** my friends use earbuds.

f How **much / many** time do you spend writing on your blog?

5 Complete the dialogue with *a, an, some, any, much, many,* or *a lot of.*

Briony That's **a** ________ amazing laptop!
Emma It's my mom's.
Briony How **b** ________ did it cost?
Emma A lot!
Briony Wow! There are **c** ________ movies on it. How **d** ________ movies do you have?
Emma I don't know. About thirty, I think. My mom downloaded **e** ________ new movies last weekend. Are there **f** ________ movies you want to watch?
Briony Yes, please! Those comedies look good.
Emma OK. We could watch **g** ________ this afternoon.

6 Complete the sentences for you.

a I never lend my friends any ____________.

b Some ____________ are ____________ than others.

c I don't have a lot of ____________.

d A lot of ____________ are very expensive.

e I'd like an ____________ or a ____________.

GRAMMAR CHECK

1 Read the dialogue and circle the correct answers.

Laura Look! There's a fun poetry competition on this web page. We can win **a** ______ great things. The first prize is a new laptop with **b** ______ special printer and a speaker.

Sam Let's see. Oh, there are **c** ______ good poems. Which do you think is **d** ______ than the others?

Laura Well, this one is more romantic than the others, and this one's good, but our poem can be more original. **e** ______ long are the poems? Is there a limit?

Sam Yes, look! The poems can't be longer **f** ______ 140 letters. That isn't a lot of words! How **g** ______ time do we have?

Laura The competition ends tomorrow. Come on! Do we have **h** ______ paper? It's easier to write it on paper first. Now we just need two pens and **i** ______ idea!

	1	2	3
a	a	(some)	any
b	a	any	an
c	much	many	a lot of
d	worse	better	good
e	Are	What	How
f	that	than	of
g	much	many	a lot of
h	an	some	any
i	an	some	any

2 Listen and check your answers.
16

LISTENING

1 Listen to two interviews. Check (✓) the things they mention.
17

a ☐ laptop
b ☐ video console
c ☐ trophy
d ☐ pet
e ☐ cell phone
f ☐ ring
g ☐ picture
h ☐ sports shoes

2 Listen again and underline the correct options.
17

a Lara and William are doing the survey for a school **magazine / project**.

b The boy uses his first possession with his **brother / brother and mother**.

c The boy's **uncle / mom** gave him his second possession.

d The boy and his uncle have the same **name / sports hobby**.

e The girl keeps **messages / pictures** in her important possession.

f The girl has an old picture of **her friend / herself**.

g The girl keeps the picture **at home / with her** all the time.

EXTENSION

Underline the correct options to complete the text.

How **a** **often / many** do you read a book? **b** **Much / A lot of** people love reading, but we **c** **aren't often / don't often** read books more than once. Nowadays, people are **d** **beginning / begin** to buy e-books and read them on special screens like iPads or Kindles, but **e** **some / any** people prefer paper books. However, paper books are becoming **f** **expensiver / more expensive**. What can you do if you like real books, but you don't have **g** **much / many** money? Is there a **h** **cheaper / cheap** option? Yes! You can join bookcrossing.com. It's a free book club, and there **i** **is / are** nearly a million members around the world. It's also a book club with a difference. When you finish a book, you go to the web page and you write a message, for example, **j** "**I leave / I'm leaving** *Hamlet* in the park, next to some red roses, at 5pm on Friday." Then you take the book to that place and leave it with a message for another person. It's **k** **an / any** original idea for swapping books and you can sometimes make new friends. There are also a lot of official bookcrossing zones in cafés around the world, from Denmark to United Arab Emirates, and Singapore to Spain. The free book club bookcrossing.com **l** **did start / started** in 2001. It grew slowly, but now more than six million books are moving around. Why not try it?

VOCABULARY PLUS

Using the Computer

1 Read the computer words in the box. Then listen and repeat. 18

click download log in log off print receive scan search send shut down

2 Label the picture above with the words in activity 1.

3 Find six computer verbs in the word search.

X	F	C	V	K	S	X	S	S	P
R	E	C	E	I	V	E	C	E	R
L	O	G	O	F	F	K	A	N	I
B	B	A	F	N	I	M	N	D	N
D	O	W	N	L	O	A	D	C	T

4 Complete the sentences with words from activity 1.

Can you _scan_ the newspaper article and email it to me, please?

a Before you can look at this web page, you need to ________.

b When you finish, can you ________ the computer, please?

c I sometimes ________ the internet for information for my homework.

d I love this picture. I'm going to ________ it.

5 Answer the questions for you. Write full sentences.

a How often do you download music?

____

b What kinds of things do you print?

____

c Who do you send messages to?

____

7 AMAZING PLACES

VOCABULARY 1

Places to Visit 1

1 Match the items a-e with the pictures of the places.

a [5] castle
b [ ] opera house
c [ ] pyramid
d [ ] rainforest
e [ ] temple

1

Sydney, Australia

2

Amazon, Brazil

3

Giza, Egypt

4

Parthenon, Greece

5

Windsor, England

2 Complete the words with vowels. Then match them with the numbers on the map.

a [4] c_a_v_e_
b [ ] c__stl_n_
c [ ] l_ghth__s_
d [ ] r__f
e [ ] r__n
f [ ] t_mb

3 Match the places in the box with the sentences below.

castle	cave	lighthouse	opera house
~~rainforest~~	reef	ruins	tomb

The trees were really high. We saw monkeys, parrots, and capybaras. rainforest

a Look at the fish. They are such beautiful colors. I love exploring underwater. ______

b These buildings were stores and houses. They don't have roofs now and some walls are missing, but you can still imagine the rooms. ______

c They built it in a very strong position on this mountain. Nobody could attack it. ______

d I heard Plácido Domingo sing here once. It was a Mozart opera. ______

e It says, "Here lies Agnes Maitland, who died August 19, 1906." ______

f It has huge lamps that go round. Ships know they are near a dangerous coastline when they see it. ______

g I don't want to go into it. It's very dark. I'm sure it's full of spiders and bats. ______

GRAMMAR 1

Superlatives

1 Write the comparative and superlative forms.

adjective	comparative	superlative
short	shorter	the shortest
a new	______	______
b hot	______	______
c sad	______	______
d funny	______	______
e interesting	______	______
f beautiful	______	______
g good	______	______
h bad	______	______

2 Classify the adjectives in activity 1 according to their comparative and superlative form.

1 syllable	1 syllable ending in vowel + consonant

2 syllables ending in *-y*

2 or more syllables

irregular

3 Complete the sentences with the superlative form of the adjectives in parentheses.

Picasso is ___the most famous___ Spanish painter in history. (famous)

a ______________ pyramid in Egypt is the Pyramid of Djoser. (old)

b Chamomile tea is ______________ tea to help relax. (good)

c Soccer is ______________ sport worldwide. (popular)

d English is one of ______________ languages to learn. (easy)

e Love is ______________ value to many people. (important)

f Sweets are ______________ kind of food for a bad tooth. (bad)

4 Complete the sentences with the superlative form of the adjectives in the box.

big	dangerous	heavy	high
long	old	~~popular~~	pretty

The British Museum is ___the most popular___ tourist attraction in London. It gets more than five million visitors a year.

a ______________ cave passage in the world is in Vietnam. It's 4.5 kilometers long.

b Loarre Castle is one of ______________ castles in Spain. It's nearly 1,000 years old.

c ______________ pyramid in the world is the Great Pyramid at Giza, Egypt. It's 138.8 meters high.

d North Yungas Road in the Bolivian Andes is ______________ road in the world. Around 150 people die on it every year.

e ______________ snake in the Amazon rainforest is the anaconda. It can weigh nearly 180 kilos.

f Alaska is ______________ state in the USA.

g Many people think that Formentera has ______________ coastline in the Balearic Islands because it has white sandy beaches and clear blue water.

5 Rewrite the sentences using the superlative form.

The Eiffel Tower observation deck is higher than any other in Europe.
The Eiffel Tower observation deck is the highest in Europe.

a Sechin Bajo in Peru is older than any other ruin in the Americas.

____

b Ethiopia is hotter than all other African countries.

____

c Great Britain is bigger than any other island in Europe.

____

d Brazil is more populated than any other South American country.

____

e Karachi, in Pakistan, is noisier than all other cities in the world.

____

f Mongolia is colder than all other countries in Asia.

____

6 Write questions with *Which* and a superlative adjective. Then write answers for you.

old building / your town
Which is the oldest building in your town?
The library is the oldest building in my town.

a good café / near your house

____

____

b hot month / your country

____

____

c expensive clothes store / you know

____

____

d noisy street / your town

____

____

7 Complete the text with the superlative form of the adjectives in parentheses.

From: Georgia
To: Mary
Subject: Sicily :)

Hi, Georgia,
I'm on vacation in Sicily, Italy. It's the biggest (big) island in the Mediterranean. It isn't **a** ______________ (quiet) of them all, and the beaches here aren't **b** ______________ (beautiful), for example, like some of the beaches on the Greek islands. But the ancient sites and the Greek temples are just **c** ______________ (good) to see! In ancient times, from about 800 BC, Greeks lived in Sicily.
Agrigento, a World Heritage site in the south of Sicily, has **d** ______________ (large) Greek temples outside of Greece. Sicily isn't **e** ______________ (popular) tourist destination in Italy, but the towns here are **f** ______________ (interesting) when you think of a combination of beaches and historical sites. There are some 11th-century buildings in the city of Palermo that have some of **g** ______________ (wonderful) Byzantine mosaics in the world. In fact, I think Sicily is one of **h** ______________ (fascinating) places in the world. Even if you are not as interested in architecture as me, there are lots of other great things about Sicily. It's one of **i** ______________ (warm) and **j** ______________ (sunny) places in Italy. The fruit and vegetables are **k** ______________ (delicious) in Europe. The shoe stores are among **l** ______________ (cheap) in Italy. And the ice-cream stores have **m** ______________ (unusual) flavors in the world. I found a store selling onion-flavored ice cream! Don't worry – I didn't try it! I got the gianduia one (hazelnut and chocolate) instead.
See you soon!
Mary

VOCABULARY 2

Formation of Adverbs

1 Write the adverbs.

adjective	adverb
correct	correctly
a noisy	
b bad	
c quiet	
d easy	
e careful	
f angry	
g happy	
h hard	
i fast	
j good	

2 Underline the correct words.

And they all lived **happy / happily** ever after. That's the end of the story.

- **a** You really are a **good / well** singer. Why don't you join a band?
- **b** He always drives very **careful / carefully**.
- **c** She's a very **bad / badly** loser. If she doesn't win, she doesn't speak to you for hours.
- **d** He guessed my age **correctly / correct**.
- **e** They played **bad / badly** in the semifinal, but Uruguay played **good / well**.
- **f** You look **happy / happily**. Are you in love or something?
- **g** My ears are hurting. That trumpet is too **noisy / noisily**!
- **h** If I remember **correct / correctly**, they are visiting Mexico.

3 Order the words to make sentences.

drives / fast / grandmother / My / never
My grandmother never drives fast.

- **a** always / hard / very / work / You ____________________
- **b** cycled / very / up the hill / She / easily ____________________
- **c** was / quietly / so / shut / Grandpa / the door / I / asleep ____________________
- **d** friends / happily / her / new / She's / talking / to ____________________
- **e** table / carefully / put / He / the / it / on ____________________
- **f** eight questions / the students / correctly / answered / Most of / on the test ____________________

4 Complete the sentences with adjectives or adverbs from activity 1.

You're only 16 and you want to buy a car this year. Please think about this very carefully.

- **a** She does her exercises ____________ at the gym.
- **b** Her English is very ____________. She doesn't make many mistakes.
- **c** She doesn't like spending a lot. She's always ____________ with her money.
- **d** You cook really ____________. Can I come to dinner at your house again?
- **e** She's smiling. I think she's feeling ____________.
- **f** The doorbell was ringing ____________ this morning.

GRAMMAR 2

too, enough, and *not enough*

1 Complete the sentences with *too* and the adjectives in the box.

crowded	dangerous	difficult	expensive	short	~~tired~~

I can't play with you now.
I'm ______too tired______.

a Dan can't do the math homework.
It's ________________.

b We can't swim in that fast river.
It's ________________.

c I got those jeans when I was 12. I can't wear them now.
They're ________________.

d Don't pay 50 dollars for those sunglasses.
That's ________________.

e Let's leave this café. There aren't any seats.
It's ________________.

2 Match the sentence beginnings with the endings.

a [6] I can't finish this email now. I don't have ...
b [ ] She didn't buy the laptop. She didn't have ...
c [ ] We couldn't see anything in the caves. There wasn't ...
d [ ] I couldn't make a cheesecake because I didn't have ...
e [ ] I couldn't get my shoes into the suitcase. There wasn't ...
f [ ] The party wasn't much fun because there weren't ...
g [ ] The trees didn't grow in that area because there wasn't ...
h [ ] We can't go skiing. There isn't ...

1 enough snow.
2 enough light.
3 enough money.
4 enough people.
5 enough space.
6 enough time.
7 enough water.
8 enough eggs.

3 Complete the text with *isn't / aren't / wasn't ... enough* and the adjectives in the box.

big	deep	light	~~near~~	old	warm	windy

From: Paul
To: Ryan
Subject: Holiday

Hi, Ryan,

I'm not having a very good holiday! The campground is terrible. It **a** ______isn't near enough______ to the town to walk there, so we have to spend every evening here. The weather is awful. It **b** ________________ to swim. And, anyway, the swimming pool is just for babies. It **c** ________________ to swim in. There are four of us in one tent, but it **d** ________________ even for two people. So I can't get to sleep at night, but there **e** ________________ to read. We tried to rent some motorized bikes yesterday, but we **f** ________________. You have to be 16. So we went to the beach and tried to rent windsurf boards. Guess what! It **g** ________________ to go windsurfing.

Send me an email!
Paul

4 Complete the answers to the questions. Use *too* or *enough* and the words in parentheses.

"Are they going to get married?"
"No, they aren't ______old enough______." (old)

a "Can you drive me to the station?"
"Sorry, I'm ________________ at the moment." (busy)

b "Are you going to make soup tonight?"
"No, we don't have ________________." (vegetables)

c "Let's run to the lake and back."
"No. I'm not very good at running and that's ________________ for me." (far)

d "Is this coffee OK?"
"Put some more sugar in it. It isn't ________________." (sweet)

e "Let's build a fire on the beach."
"How can we? We don't have ________________." (wood)

GRAMMAR CHECK

1 Read the text and circle the correct options.

I think the **a** ___ coastline in Rhode Island is in Newport. The water there is **b** ___ than in most places. Of course, the water isn't as **c** ___ as in Florida, but it's not too cold **d** ___. Easton's Beach (1st Beach to the locals) is probably **e** ___ popular beach in the state. All the teenagers go there. But it's **f** ___ crowded for me. I prefer Sachuest (2nd Beach). If you go there and it isn't **g** ___ to swim one day, go and visit the Norman Bird Sanctuary. It has one of **h** ___ beautiful views in Newport. Block Island also has some wonderful coastlines. It's wilder than Newport and you get fewer people around, so the beaches are quiet **i** ___ to relax and read a book. Still in Newport there is one of **j** ___ beautiful lighthouses around, called Castle Hill Lighthouse. If you are **k** ___, you can swim around the rocks nearby.

	1	2	3
a	good	best (circled)	better
b	clean	cleanest	cleaner
c	warm	warmer	warmest
d	to swimming	for swim	to swim
e	more	the most	as
f	too	most	more
g	warmest	too warm	warm enough
h	most	more	the most
i	enough	as	more
j	the most	more	as
k	more energetic	too energetic	energetic enough

2 Listen and check your answers.

19

LISTENING

1 Listen and write T for *true*, F for *false*, or DK for *don't know*.

20

- **a** Emperor Shah Jahan only married once. ☐
- **b** He didn't have many children. ☐
- **c** He died in 1666. ☐
- **d** There is Chinese writing on the Taj Mahal as decoration. ☐
- **e** Very early morning is a good time to visit the Taj Mahal. ☐
- **f** The best month to visit the Taj Mahal by moonlight is December. ☐

2 Listen again and write the missing words.

20

The Taj Mahal

Emperor Shah Jahan built the Taj Mahal in memory of his **a** ______________ wife, Mumtaz Mahal.

She died when she was having their **b** ______________. He started building it in **c** ______________ and finished it in **d** ______________.

They buried Shah Jahan next to Mumtaz when he died in **e** ______________.

Big groups of tourists arrive at **f** ______________ in the morning.

The light is perfect for pictures in the **g** ______________.

You can visit the Taj Mahal by moonlight, but you can only stay for **h** ______________ minutes. They only allow **i** ______________ people in each group at night.

EXTENSION

Underline the correct options to complete the text.

www.blogspot.com/vacationtime

Jonathan Colins Follow

May 29 3 min read

I really enjoy **a to look / looking** at maps. When I look at maps, I **b start / am starting** to think about all the places I would like to visit. Last year, I **c went / was** to Kerala in the south of India. I **d flew / was flying** to Cochin. The drive from the airport to my hotel was the **e most / more** frightening half-hour of my life! There were animals and bicycles on the road! I was almost too scared **f for looking / to look** out of the window.

Once, while we **g drove / were driving** along in Kerala, I saw elephants working in the fields. The Keralans are also into **h put / putting** colorful decorations on elephants and then they **i ride / rode** them in festivals. I **j rode / was riding** an elephant there and I also helped people wash elephants in a sanctuary.

Indian food in Los Angeles is nice, but it isn't **k very / as** good as the food in Kerala. The food there was **l better / more good** than any Indian food in California.

At the moment, I **m am thinking / think** about a trip to Brazil, but I only have a week's vacation. Unfortunately, I don't think that's **n long enough / too long** to visit that huge country.

Trip New places Culture

Kerala, India

Kerala, India

Indian food in Cochin, India

VOCABULARY PLUS

On the Beach

1 Label the picture above with the words in the box. Then listen and repeat.
21

beach chair	lifeguard
beach towel	pebbles
beach umbrella	sand
cliff	sandcastle
jellyfish	waves

2 Read the definitions and write the correct words.

Someone who works on the beach. lifeguard

a A geographical feature. ______

b Something to protect you from the sun. ______

c A sea creature. ______

d Something you use after swimming. ______

e Something you build using sand. ______

3 Underline the correct option. Then write.

We aren't going swimming. There are jellyfish in the water.

1 towels **2** jellyfish **3** waves

a The ______ says it isn't safe to swim today.

1 cliff **2** lifeguard **3** jellyfish

b The ______ is so hot that you can't walk on it.

1 waves **2** beach chair **3** sand

c There are ______ on that beach, but there isn't any sand.

1 jellyfish **2** sand **3** pebbles

d There weren't any ______ so they sat on their beach towels.

1 beach chairs **2** lifeguards **3** sandcastles

e You need good ______ to go surfing.

1 cliffs **2** beach umbrellas **3** waves

8

FUN AND GAMES

VOCABULARY 1

Playing Games

1 Look at the pictures and complete the words with vowels.

b__e__ __a__t

a ch___ ___t

b c___ ___nt

c g___v___ ___p

d g___ ___ss

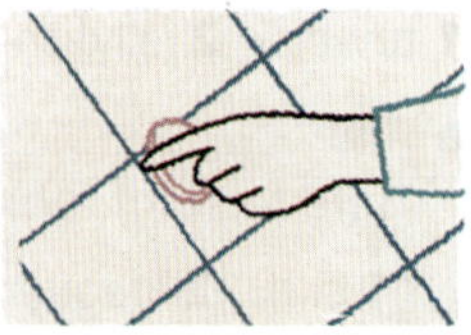

e l___nd

f l___s___

g m___ss ___ t___rn

h m___v___ c___ ___nt___r

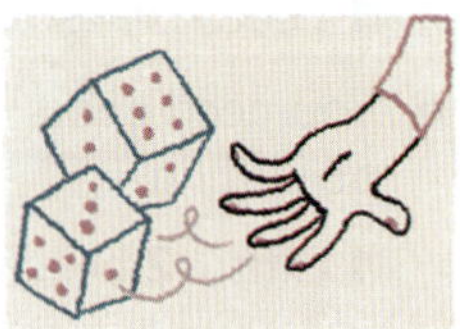

i r___ll th___ d___c___

2 Complete the sentences with the words in the box.

beat ~~cheat~~ give up guess miss move

It's not fair! You shouldn't ___cheat___ when you play.

a To play, you must __________ your counter on the board.

b I don't want to play anymore. I __________!

c You're going to __________ me again. You always win.

d The red squares mean you must __________ a turn. You have to wait.

e If you don't know the answer, you can always __________.

3 Complete the sentences with the correct form of verbs in activity 1.

a You really shouldn't __________ when you play games; it isn't honest.

b Let's __________. The person with the highest number starts.

c I always __________ when we play this game. I can't play it at all!

d Hey! You didn't __________ to twenty!

e I have a great word, you'll never __________ it! Come on, ask me a question.

f If you __________ on that square first, you win the game.

4 Answer the questions for you. Write full sentences.

a What's your favorite game?

____

b Do you cheat when you play games?

____

c What was the last game you played?

____

d Do you usually win when you play games?

____

GRAMMAR 1

Review: Simple Present and Present Progressive

1 Match the sentences with the correct tenses.

1 He often plays chess with his brother.
2 They're winning! Fantastic!

a ☐ simple present
b ☐ present progressive

2 Read the sentences and think if the actions are in progress or if they describe habits. Write *P* (in progress) or *H* (habit).

H I go to school.

a ☐ I watch really boring card games on TV.
b ☐ He is running to the bus stop.
c ☐ She is losing the match.
d ☐ You cheat every time you play with me!
e ☐ They are trying to guess her age.
f ☐ He lands on a pink square.

3 Underline the correct options.

I go / **'m going** to school every day.

a I **play / 'm playing** a computer game at the moment.
b My uncle **plays / is playing** chess professionally, but he doesn't earn much money.
c He **has / 's having** breakfast at the moment. Can you call back later?
d My mom **always cheats / is always cheating** when we play tennis.
e She **only goes / 's only going** out on weekends.
f Please be quiet! I **count / 'm counting**!

4 Complete the text with the simple present or the present progressive form of the verbs in parentheses.

My old sister often **a** ____________ (play) card games like *UNO* with her friends. She **b** ____________ (go) to her friend's house every Saturday, and they sometimes **c** ____________ (have) tournaments. I **d** ____________ (like) those games, too, and my sister **e** ____________ (become) good at them, but these days she **f** ____________ (spend) a lot of time playing cards. My parents are worried – they say that she **g** ____________ (grow) up at the moment, and she has to change. I hope so – she never **h** ____________ (want) to play with me these days!

5 Match the beginnings a-e with the endings 1-5 to make questions.

a Are	1 is not waiting for the bus.
b He	2 he counting to ten?
c Do	3 she often cheat?
d Does	4 they enjoying the game at the moment?
e Is	5 you always win when I play with you?

6 Complete the questions with *do* or *does*.

__Does__ she sleep eight hours a night?

a ________ you swim in this lake?

b ________ he talk to you very often?

c How often ________ he usually win?

d What ________ you usually do on weekends?

e ________ they listen to the radio every day?

f How often ________ it rain in your area?

7 Complete the questions with the correct form of the verbs in the box.

ask do play (×2) need want write

Lily Why **a** ________ Mom that question?

Jake Because she wants me to guess the name of a famous person.

Lily Ah! **b** ________ a game?

Jake Yes, *Twenty Questions*.

Lily How **c** ________ it?

Jake It's easy. One person thinks of a famous person, and the other person asks questions to guess.

Lily Why **d** ________ the answers in a notebook?

Jake Because she doesn't want to forget them.

Lily **e** ________ a notebook and a pen to play?

Jake No, you don't. **f** ________ to play?

Lily OK. It sounds fun. But you ask the questions.

Jake OK. What **g** ________ now?

Lily I'm looking for a famous person on the internet.

8 Underline the correct options.

From: Aisha
To: Ella
Subject: I miss you <3

Hi, Ella,

It's Friday afternoon and it **a 's raining / rains**. I **b sit / 'm sitting** inside and writing an email to you because my cell phone is broken, it crashed yesterday!

I **c am thinking / think** of you today. I know you **d are / being** very busy because you **e prepare / are preparing** for your exams.

I **f am having / have** a difficult week at school because we **g have / are having** exams all week long – two every day. We **h don't have / are not having** the results yet. But I **i am thinking / think** they are OK. We also **j playing / play** basketball on Wednesdays – teachers against students! It is great. The students always win, of course. :-) I am taking some pictures. I **k send / am sending** you some with this email.

What are your plans for the weekend? Can you come to the park tomorrow?

Write soon! Love,

Aisha

9 Complete the questions a-c with your own ideas. Then write answers for you.

a When do you ________? ________

b How often do you ________? ________

c At the moment, are you ________? ________

VOCABULARY 2

Places to Visit 2

1 Look at the pictures and complete the crossword.

1

6

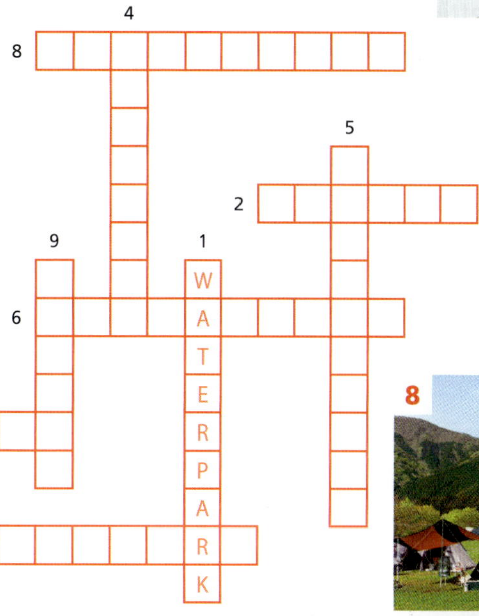

2

3

7

8

4

5

9

2 Write the words in activity 1 in the correct group.

Indoors	Outdoors
____________	water park, ____________
____________	____________
____________	____________
____________	____________
____________	____________

3 Complete the sentences with words from activity 1.

a My best day out with my family was at the ____________. We love looking at paintings.

b We went to a great ____________ by a lake. It was fun sleeping in a tent.

c We visited a ____________, we got very wet on some of the rides.

d We went to a big ____________ and we bought some souvenirs and lots of food.

e We saw elephants and lions at the ____________. It was great.

4 Answer the questions for you.

a Where is your favorite market?

____

b Is there a statue in your town? What is it?

____

c What is the best monument in your town?

____

d Which do you like best, water parks or art galleries? Why?

____

GRAMMAR 2

Review: Simple Past and Past Progressive

1 Underline the correct options.

I **a played / was playing** a game on my mom's tablet when she came into the living room. She **b saw / was seeing** me with her tablet and she **c got / was getting** angry. I **d told / was telling** her I **e didn't do / wasn't doing** anything bad. My mom **f started / was starting** to watch, and then she **g began / was beginning** to play! We **h played / were playing** when Dad **i came / was coming** in. He **j wanted / was wanting** to know what we **k did / were doing**. Then he **l wanted / was wanting** to play too. These days, I can't play the game because Mom and Dad are always playing it!

2 Complete the sentences with the simple past or the past progressive form of the verbs in parentheses.

While he ___was watching TV___ (watch TV), his mom ___arrived___ (arrive).

a The cat ________ (sleep) when the bird ________ (sit) on its head.

b While they ________ (cheat), the teacher ________ (see) them.

c While he ________ (play), he ________ (cut) his leg.

d While she ________ (look) at the cell phone, someone ________ (take) her wallet.

e He ________ (listen) to the teacher when he ________ (fall asleep).

3 Match the beginnings a-d with the endings 1-4 to make questions.

a Did	**1** Ellen playing chess with you?
b Were	**2** played dominoes with you?
c Was	**3** you beat the other players last night?
d Who	**4** you sleeping when I called last night?

4 Complete the questions with *did*, *was*, or *were*.

___Was___ she sleeping when he arrived?

a ________ you see him yesterday?

b Who ________ he talking to?

c ________ they looking at us?

d How often ________ it rain in your area last year?

e ________ your family at the water park last weekend?

GRAMMAR CHECK

1 Read the dialogue and circle the correct options.

Emily What **a** ___ playing?

Oliver We're playing checkers. It's really fun!

Emily How do you play?

Zoe You **b** ___ your checkers on the board, and you must capture your opponent's checkers. Look, now I'm **c** ___ one of my checkers here and capture one of my opponent's.

Oliver Ouch! You keep **d** ___ my checkers. How **e** ___ that?

Zoe I was **f** ___ about taking control of the center of the board when I **g** ___ the checker.

Emily And where **h** ___ this game?

Oliver My uncle **i** ___ it in a toy store.

Emily Maybe I can ask my mom to buy it for me too.

Oliver Don't worry! I can ask my uncle **j** ___ one for you.

Emily Oh, really? That would be awesome, thanks!

	1	2	3
a	you're	you are	(are you)
b	to move	move	moves
c	going land	land	going to land
d	capturing	capture	captures
e	you did	did you	did you do
f	think	to think	thinking
g	moves	to move	moved
h	did you get	you got	do you got
i	buyed	did buy	bought
j	buying	buy	to buy

2 Listen and check your answers.
22

LISTENING

1 Listen to a tour guide and circle the places mentioned.
23

London Eye	China	Beijing
Eiffel Tower	Paris	Big Ben

2 Listen again and circle the correct options.
23

a The London Eye also has another name: The Millennium **Wheel** / **Eye**.

b The London Eye was built in **1999** / **2000**.

c There are taller ferris wheels in Singapore and **China** / **the USA**.

d More than **3.5 million** / **3.9 million** tourists visit it every year.

e In the past, the symbols of London included red **taxis** / **buses**.

f The eggs or capsules can hold **75** / **25** people in each one.

g The London Eye closed the first day it opened because **it was too fast** / **it didn't work**.

h If you go on the London Eye, you stay inside the egg for **13** / **30** minutes.

EXTENSION

Circle the correct options to complete the text.

Windsor Castle in England is the world's **a older and bigger / oldest and biggest** inhabited castle, but **b does anybody live / somebody lives** there? Yes: Queen Elizabeth lives there on weekends and during some holidays. In fact, in one of the photographs, the Queen is at the castle. How do we know? Because her special flag **c is flying / flies**. When she has important visitors, she **d usually meets / meets usually** them at Windsor. But tourists can also **e to visit / visit** Windsor Castle, and it's a very interesting place.

William the Conqueror, who **f was / were** king in the 11th century, **g did build / built** the first part of the castle in 1070, and, with the help of **h a lot / many** of different kings and queens, the castle **i became / become** bigger and bigger. It also has an enormous park. If you go to Windsor, visit the castle to see the rooms and the big Doll's House.

VOCABULARY PLUS

Types of Games

a ______________

b ______________

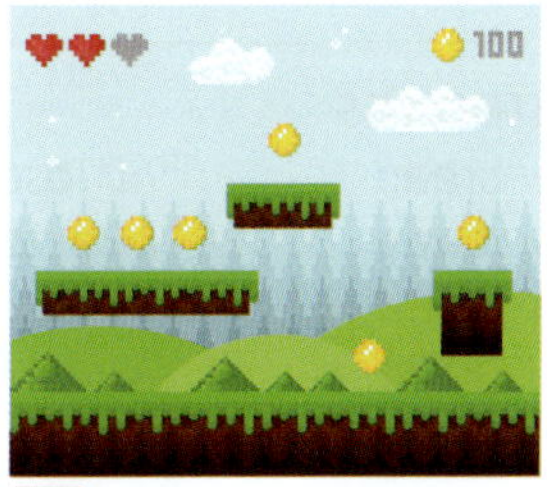

c ______________

d ______________

e ______________

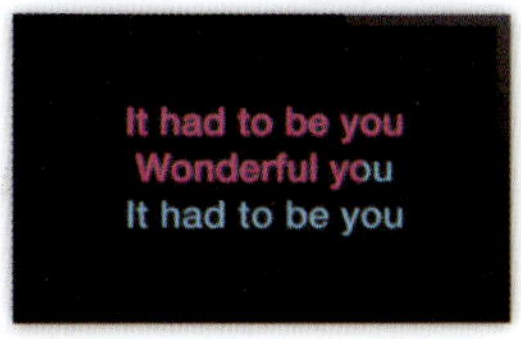

f ______________

g ______________

h ______________

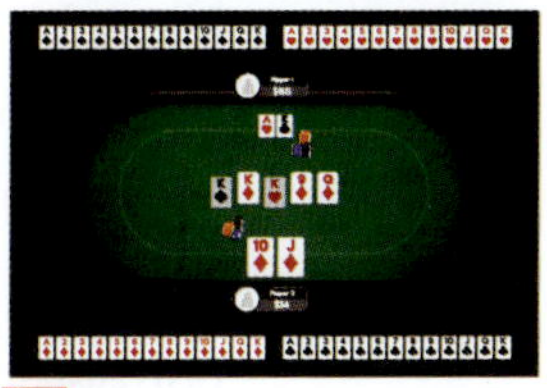

i ______________

j ______________

1 Read the words in the box. Then listen and repeat. 24

action	brain game	karaoke
life simulation	platform	racing
role-playing game	sports	strategy	war

2 Label the pictures with the words in activity 1.

3 Match the person a-e with the type of game 1-5.

- **a** I like creating new towns and places.
- **b** I like fast cars.
- **c** Tennis is my favorite sport.
- **d** I like improving my IQ.
- **e** I love singing.

1. karaoke
2. racing
3. brain game
4. sports
5. life simulation

4 Complete the sentences with the words in the box.

action	karaoke	life simulation
~~role-playing~~	sports	strategy

In a(n) __role-playing__ game, you become a different person.

- **a** In a(n) ______________ game, you can try things like skiing or rugby.
- **b** In a(n) ______________ game like chess, you need to think carefully before you move.
- **c** In a(n) ______________ game, you need to create your own town, zoo, amusement park, etc.
- **d** A(n) ______________ game is very exciting and you often go on an adventure.
- **e** In a(n) ______________ game you read the words and sing a song.

5 Answer these questions for you. Write full sentences. Try to use words from activity 1.

- **a** What is your favorite game?

____
____
____

- **b** What types of games do you never play?

____
____
____

- **c** What types of games do your friends like?

____
____
____

WORDLIST

PHONETIC CHART

25 **VOWELS AND DIPHTHONGS**

/ɪ/ pig	/e/ bread	/u/ lose	/aɪ/ I
/i/ she	/ɜr/ curly	/ə/ actor	/ɔɪ/ toy
/æ/ cat	/ɔ/ ball	/ʌ/ sunny	/aʊ/ mountain
/ɑ/ arm	/ʊ/ good	/eɪ/ USA	/oʊ/ boat

26 **CONSONANTS**

/p/ potato	/tʃ/ chair	/s/ Spain	/n/ newsstand
/b/ blue	/dʒ/ fridge	/z/ easy	/ŋ/ spring
/t/ taxi	/f/ finish	/ʃ/ shower	/l/ lake
/d/ drama	/v/ verb	/ʒ/ television	/r/ read
/k/ carrot	/θ/ bathroom	/h/ hi	/j/ yesterday
/g/ grandpa	/ð/ there	/m/ mouth	/w/ water

27 A

aboriginal housing (n) /ˌæbəˈrɪdʒən(ə)l ˈhaʊzɪŋ/

achieve (v) /əˈtʃiv/

admit (v) /əd'mɪt/

adventurer (n) /əd'ventʃərər/

adventurous (adj) /əd'ventʃərəs/

along (adv / prep) /əˈlɔŋ/

always (adv) /ˈɔlˌweɪz/

Ancient Greece (n) /ˈeɪntʃənt gris/

angrily (adv) /ˈæŋgrɪli/

animation movie (n) /ˌænɪˈmeɪʃ(ə)n ˈmuvi/

apply a discount (v) /əˈplaɪ ə ˈdɪsˌkaʊnt/

Arctic area (n) /ˈɑrktɪk ˈeriə/

armchair (n) /ˈɑrmˌtʃer/

army (n) /ˈɑrmi/

arrive (v) /əˈraɪv/

art gallery (n) /ɑrt ˈgæl(ə)ri/

at the moment (adv) /ət ðə ˈmoʊmənt/

attempt (n) /əˈtempt/

award-winning (adj) /əˈwɔrd ˈwɪnɪŋ/

28 B

backwards (adj / adv) /ˈbækwərdz/

badly (adv) /ˈbædli/

barge (n) /bɑrdʒ/

battle (n) /ˈbæt(ə)l/

beach umbrella (n) /bitʃ ʌmˈbrelə/

beat (v) /bit/

bed (n) /bed/

bike (n) /baɪk/

boat (n) /boʊt/

bone (n) /boʊn/

bookcase (n) /ˈbʊkˌkeɪs/

borrow (v) /ˈbɔroʊ/

brain game (n) /breɪn geɪm/

brave (adj) /breɪv/

bus operator (n) /bʌs ˈɑpəˌreɪtər/

busy (adj) /ˈbɪzi/

buy (v) /baɪ/

29 C

cable car (n) /ˈkeɪb(ə)l kɑr/

cabinet (n) /ˈkæbɪnət/

camera (n) /ˈkæm(ə)rə/

cap rock (n) /kæp rɑk/

car (n) /kɑr/

carefully (adv) /ˈkerf(ə)li/

carry (v) /ˈkeri/

castle (n) /ˈkæs(ə)l/

cautious (adj) /ˈkɔʃəs/

cave (n) /keɪv/

centimeter (n) /ˈsentɪˌmitər/

chair (n) /tʃer/

chat online (v) /tʃæt ˈɑnˌlaɪn/

cheap (adj) /tʃip/

cheat (v) /tʃit/

cheerful (adj) /ˈtʃɪrf(ə)l/

chemist (n) /ˈkemɪst/

circumnavigate (v) /ˌsɜrkəmˈnævɪˌgeɪt/
click (v) /klɪk/
cliff (n) /klɪf/
coastline (n) /ˈkoʊstˌlaɪn/
coin purse (n) /ˈkɔɪn ˈpɜrs/
collapse (n) /kəˈlæps/
combustion engine (n) /kəmˈbʌstʃ(ə)n ˈendʒɪn/
communication system (n) /kəˌmjunɪˈkeɪʃ(ə)n ˈsɪstəm/
confident (adj) /ˈkɑnfɪdənt/
contemplate (v) /ˈkɑntəmˌpleɪt/
count (v) /kaʊnt/
course (n) /kɔrs/
cross (v) /krɔs/
cruel (adj) /ˈkruəl/

30)) **D**

decide (v) /dɪˈsaɪd/
desert (n) /ˈdezərt/
design (n) /dɪˈzaɪn/
desktop (n) /ˈdeskˌtɑp/
discover (v) /dɪˈskʌvər/
dishonest (adj) /dɪsˈɑnəst/
dishwasher (n) /ˈdɪʃˌwɑʃər/
dome (n) /doʊm/
double-decker (adj) /ˌdʌb(ə)l ˈdekər/
download (v) /ˈdaʊnˌloʊd/
downwards (adv) /ˈdaʊnwərdz/
dragon (n) /ˈdrægən/
draw (v) /drɔ/
drinking fountain (n) /ˈdrɪŋkɪŋ ˈfaʊnt(ə)n/
drive away (v) /draɪv əˈweɪ/
drop (v) /drɑp/
drought (n) /draʊt/
durable (adj) /ˈdʊrəb(ə)l/

31)) **E**

earn (v) /ɜrn/
earthquake (n) /ˈɜrθˌkweɪk/
easily (adv) /ˈizəli/
electric toothbrush (n) /ɪˈlektrɪk ˈtuθˌbrʌʃ/
energetic (adj) /ˌenərˈdʒetɪk/
equipment (n) /ɪˈkwɪpmənt/
eventually (adv) /ɪˈventʃuəli/
every day (adv) /ˈevri deɪ/
exercise bike (n) /ˈeksərˌsaɪz baɪk/
expensive (adj) /ɪkˈspensɪv/
explore (v) /ɪkˈsplɔr/

32)) **F**

fairy (n) /ˈferi/
fall (v) /fɔl/
famine (n) /ˈfæmɪn/
fee (n) /fi/
ferry (n) /ˈferi/
fire (n) /faɪr/
fishing port (n) /ˈfɪʃɪŋ pɔrt/
flood (n) /flʌd/
fly (v) /flaɪ/
follow (v) /ˈfɑloʊ/
fracture (n) /ˈfræktʃər/
frame (n) /freɪm/
fridge (n) /frɪdʒ/
friendly (adj) /ˈfren(d)li/
full-length (adj) /fʊl leŋθ/
funny (adj) /ˈfʌni/

33)) **G**

gadget (n) /ˈgædʒət/
gather (v) /ˈgæðər/
generous (adj) /ˈdʒen(ə)rəs/
ghost (n) /goʊst/
giant (n) /ˈdʒaɪənt/
give up (v) /gɪv ʌp/
gorge (n) /gɔrdʒ/
guess (v) /ges/

34)) **H**

happily (adv) /ˈhæpɪli/
hard (adj) /hɑrd/
hardly ever (adv) /ˈhɑrdli ˈevər/
hat (n) /hæt/
have a good time (v) /hæv ə gʊd taɪm/
heading (n) /ˈhedɪŋ/
height (n) /haɪt/
helicopter (n) /ˈhelɪˌkɑptər/
hero (n) /ˈhɪroʊ/
heroine (n) /ˈheroʊɪn/
high-speed train (n) /haɪ spid treɪn/
hill (n) /hɪl/
honest (adj) /ˈɑnəst/

horse-drawn (adj) /hɔrs drɔn/

hot-air balloon (n) /hɑt er bə'lun/

hurricane (n) /'hʌrɪˌkeɪn/

35 I

iceberg (n) /'aɪsˌbɜrg/

igloo (n) /'ɪglu/

inch (n) /ɪntʃ/

indoors (adv) /ɪn'dɔrz/

inflatable boat (n) /ɪn'fleɪtəb(ə)l boʊt/

Inuit (n / adj) /'ɪnuɪt/

invent (v) /ɪn'vent/

36 J

jellyfish (n) /'dʒeliˌfɪʃ/

judo (n) /'dʒudoʊ/

37 K

kangaroo (n) /ˌkæŋgə'ru/

karaoke (n) /ˌkeri'oʊki/

keyboard (n) /'kiˌbɔrd/

kilometer (n) /kɪ'lɑmətər/

kind (adj) /kaɪnd/

knit (v) /nɪt/

38 L

ladder (n) /'lædər/

lamp (n) /læmp/

landscape (n) /'lændˌskeɪp/

landslide (n) /'lændˌslaɪd/

laptop (n) /'læpˌtɑp/

layer (n) /'leɪr/

lazy (adj) /'leɪzi/

lead (v) /lid/

leaning branch (n) /'linɪŋ bræntʃ/

leave (v) /liv/

legend (n) /'ledʒənd/

lend (v) /lend/

life simulation (n) /laɪf ˌsɪmjə'leɪʃ(ə)n/

lifeboat (n) /'laɪfˌboʊt/

lifeguard (n) /'laɪfˌgɑrd/

lift (v) /lɪft/

lighthouse (n) /'laɪtˌhaʊs/

locker room (n) /'lɑkər rum/

log in (v) /lɔg ɪn/

log off (v) /lɔg ɑf/

loyal (adj) /'lɔɪəl/

39 M

maintenance cost (n) /'meɪntənəns kɔst/

marathon (n) /'merəˌθɑn/

maritime tragedy (n) /'merəˌtaɪm 'trædʒədi/

market (n) /'mɑrkət/

meal (n) /mil/

measurement (n) /'meʒərmənt/

memory card (n) /'mem(ə)ri kɑrd/

meter (n) /'mitər/

microwave (n) /'maɪkrəˌweɪv/

miraculously (adv) /mə'rækjələsli/

mirror (n) /'mɪrər/

miss a turn (v) /mɪs ə tɜrn/

monster (n) /'mɑnstər/

monument (n) /'mɑnjəmənt/

motorcycle (n) /'moʊtərˌsaɪk(ə)l/

mouse (n) /maʊs/

move a counter (v) /muv ə 'kaʊntər/

40 N

never (adv) /'nevər/

nickname (n) /'nɪkˌneɪm/

noisily (adv) /'nɔɪzəli/

nomadic tribe (n) /noʊ'mædɪk traɪb/

now (adv) /naʊ/

nylon (n) /'naɪˌlɑn/

41 O

often (adv) /'ɔf(ə)n/

opera house (n) /'ɑp(ə)rə haʊs/

optical illusion (n) /'ɑptɪk(ə)l ɪ'luʒ(ə)n/

outdoors (adv) /aʊt'dɔrz/

42 P

parachuting accident (n) /'perəˌʃutɪŋ 'æksɪdənt/

passenger ship (n) /'pæsɪndʒər ʃɪp/

passport (n) /'pæspɔrt/

pay (for) (v) /peɪ fɔr/

pebble (n) /'peb(ə)l/

personal trainer (n) /'pɜrsən(ə)l 'treɪnər/

phrase book (n) /freɪz bʊk/

plane (n) /pleɪn/

plastic (n) /ˈplæstɪk/
platform (n) /ˈplætˌfɔrm/
plunge pool (n) /plʌndʒ pul/
prestigious (adj) /preˈstidʒəs/
print (v) /prɪnt/
printer (n) /ˈprɪntər/
pull (v) /pʊl/
push (v) /pʊʃ/
pyramid (n) /ˈpɪrəmɪd/

43 Q

quickly (adv) /ˈkwɪkli/
quiet (adj) /ˈkwaɪət/
quietly (adv) /ˈkwaɪətli/
quite the opposite (adj) /kwaɪt ðə ˈɑpəzɪt/

44 R

rainforest (n) /reɪn ˈfɔrəst/
receive (v) /rɪˈsiv/
reef (n) /rif/
relax (v) /rɪˈlæks/
release (v) /rɪˈlis/
roll the dice (v) /roʊl ðə daɪs/
route (n) /rut, raʊt/
row (n) /roʊ/
rowboat (n) /ˈroʊˌboʊt/
royal family (n) /ˈrɔɪəl ˈfæm(ə)li/
ruin (n) /ˈruɪn/
running race (n) /ˈrʌnɪŋ reɪs/

45 S

sail (v) /seɪl/
sandcastle (n) /ˈsæn(d)ˌkæs(ə)l/
sandstone (n) /ˈsæn(d)ˌstoʊn/
sauna (n) /ˈsɔnə/
save (v) /seɪv/
scan (v) /skæn/
scanner (n) /ˈskænər/
screen (n) /skrin/
sea level (n) /si ˈlev(ə)l/
search (v) /sɜrtʃ/
selfish (adj) /ˈselfɪʃ/
sell (v) /sel/
send (v) /send/
serious (adj) /ˈsɪriəs/
shawl (n) /ʃɔl/
shelter (n) /ˈʃeltər/
shower (n) /ˈʃaʊər/
shy (adj) /ʃaɪ/
sit (v) /sɪt/
soccer field (n) /ˈsɑkər fild/
sofa (n) /ˈsoʊfə/
soldier (n) /ˈsoʊldʒər/
sometimes (adv) /ˈsʌmtaɪmz/
spare time (n) /sper taɪm/
speaker (n) /ˈspikər/
spend (v) /spend/
stadium (n) /ˈsteɪdiəm/
stand (v) /stænd/
statue (n) /ˈstætʃu/
stick figure (n) /stɪk ˈfɪgjər/
stove (n) /stoʊv/
strategy (n) /ˈstrætədʒi/
streetcar (n) /ˈstritˌkɑr/
stubborn (adj) /ˈstʌbərn/
suitcase (n) /ˈsutˌkeɪs/
sum up (v) /sʌm ʌp/
sunbathe (v) /ˈsʌnˌbeɪð/
sunglasses (n) /ˈsʌnˌglæsəz/
sunscreen (n) /ˈsʌnˌskrin/
swap (v) /swɑp/
swimming trunks (n) /ˈswɪmɪŋ trʌŋks/
symbol (n) /ˈsɪmb(ə)l/

46 T

table (n) /ˈteɪb(ə)l/
take off (v) /teɪk ɑf/
talkative (adj) /ˈtɔkətɪv/
taxi (n) /ˈtæksi/
telegraph (n) /ˈteləˌgræf/
telephone (n) /ˈteləˌfoʊn/
temple (n) /ˈtemp(ə)l/
tennis court (n) /ˈtenɪs kɔrt/
tepee (n) /ˈtiˌpi/
therapeutic (adj) /ˌθerəˈpjutɪk/
through (prep) /θru/
tomb (n) /tum/
tornado (n) /tərˈneɪdoʊ/
towel (n) /ˈtaʊəl/
town square (n) /taʊn skwer/

trailer (n) /ˈtreɪlər/

transmit (v) /trænzˈmɪt/

travel (v) /ˈtræv(ə)l/

treadmill (n) /ˈtredˌmɪl/

truck (n) /trʌk/

tsunami (n) /tsuˈnɑmi/

TV presenter (n) /ˌti ˈvi prɪˈzentər/

twice a week (adv) /twaɪs ə wik/

47 U

uncountable (adj) /ʌnˌkaʊntəb(ə)l/

underneath (adj / adv) /ˌʌndərˈniθ/

unicorn (n) /ˈjunɪˌkɔrn/

unsociable (adj) /ʌnˈsoʊʃəb(ə)l/

upper (adj) /ˈʌpər/

usually (adv) /ˈjuʒuəli/

48 V

vertical erosion (n) /ˈvɜrtɪk(ə)l ɪˈroʊʒ(ə)n/

Victorian Era (n) /vɪkˈtɔriən ˈerə/

victory (n) /ˈvɪkt(ə)ri/

video call (n) /ˈvɪdioʊ kɔl/

visit museums (v) /ˈvɪzɪt mjuˈziəmz/

volunteer work (n) /ˈvɑlənˌtɪr wɜrk/

voyage (n) /ˈvɔɪɪdʒ/

49 W

wallet (n) /ˈwɑlət/

war (n) /wɔr/

wardrobe (n) /ˈwɔrdˌroʊb/

washing machine (n) /ˈwɑʃɪŋ məˈʃin/

water park (n) /ˈwɔtər pɑrk/

waterfall (n) /ˈwɔtərˌfɔl/

webcam (n) /ˈwebˌkæm/

well (adv) /wel/

wire (n) /waɪr/

wise (adj) /waɪz/

witch (n) /wɪtʃ/

wizard (n) /ˈwɪzərd/

Based on *InstaEnglish* and *Motivate*
© Macmillan Education Brasil 2019 and Macmillan Education Limited 2013
Written by Emma Heyderman, Fiona Mauchline, Patrick Howarth, Patricia Reilly and Olivia Johnston
Grammar, Speaking, and *Culture* pages adapted by Gisele Marçon Bastos Périgo
Vocabulary, Reading, and *Writing* pages adapted by Thelma de Carvalho Guimarães
Digital Literacy and *Global Citizenship* pages created by Thelma de Carvalho Guimarães

Director of Languages Brazil: Patricia Souza De Luccia
Publishing Manager and Field Researcher: Patricia Muradas
Content Creation Coordinator: Cristina do Vale
Art Coordinator: Jean Aranha
Lead Editors: Gabriel França, Roberta Somera
Content Editors: Ana Beatriz da Costa Moreira, Gabriel França, Roberta Somera, Tatiana Martins Santana
Digital Editors: Deborah Stafussi, Elaine Lins
Editorial Assistant: Daniela Alves
Editorial Intern: Pedro Improta
Art Assistant: Jacqueline Alves
Art Intern: Victor Augusto Amorim
Editorial Apprentice: Beatriz Jacinto
Graphic Production: Alexandra L. S. de Carvalho, Thais Mendes P. Galvão
Proofreaders: Ana Lúcia Mendes Reis, Cátia de Almeida, Edward Willson, Rhiannon Ball, Tony O'Sullivan
Design Concept: Martha Tadaieski
Page Makeup: Figurattiva Editorial
Photo Research: Marcia Sato
Illustrations: Eber Helom, Hiro Kawahara, Suryara Bernardi
Image Processing: Jacqueline Alves, Jean Aranha, Victor Augusto Amorim
Extra Interactive Activities Content Development: Daniela Alves
Cover Concept: Jean Aranha
Cover photography: soleg/iStockphoto/Getty Images
Audio: Argila
Video: Desenredo

We would like to dedicate this book to teachers all over Brazil. We would also like to thank our clients and teachers who have helped us make this book better with their many rich contributions and feedback straight from the classroom!

The authors, adaptor and publishers would like to thank the following for permission to reproduce the photographic material:
p. 8: FatCamera/iStockphoto/Getty Images. P. 9 Photo Italia LLC/iStockphoto/Getty Images. P. 10: Rowan Jordan/iStockphoto/Getty Images. p. 12: South_agency/iStockphoto/Getty Images; AaronAmat/iStockphoto/Getty Images; RyanKing999/iStockphoto/Getty Images; Imgorthand/iStockphoto/Getty Images. P.13: piola666/iStockphoto/Getty Images; Mima88/iStockphoto/Getty Images. p. 15: Chris Young/The Canadian Press/AP Photo/Imageplus; Igor Alecsander/iStockphoto/Getty Images; Bobex-73/iStockphoto/Getty Images; PeopleImages/iStockphoto/Getty Images. p. 16: insta_photos/iStockphoto/Getty Images; uzhursky/iStockphoto/Getty Images; RgStudio/iStockphoto/Getty Images. p. 17: Jennifer Dudley-Nicholson/iStockphoto/Getty Images; jmurraywd/iStockphoto/Getty Images; BraunS/iStockphoto/Getty Images; lindsay_imagery/iStockphoto/Getty Images. p. 18: bubaone/iStockphoto/Getty Images; 4x6/iStockphoto/Getty Images; Oksana Sazhnieva/iStockphoto/Getty Images; skdesigns/iStockphoto/Getty Images; Aaltazar/iStockphoto/Getty Images; HOCH ZWEI/picture alliance/dpa/Imageplus; PA Wire/ZUMA Press Imageplus; Clemens Niehaus/Geisler-Fotopress/picture alliance/dpa/Imageplus; John Nacion/Future-Image/ZUMA Press/Imageplus; zz/Galaxy/STAR MAX/IPx 2022/AP Photo/Imageplus. p. 20: Drazen_/iStockphoto/Getty Images; Prostock-Studio/iStockphoto/Getty Images; Ljupco/iStockphoto/Getty Images. p. 21: Jose Martinez Calderon/iStockphoto/Getty Images; Chaosamran_Studio/iStockphoto/Getty Images; sarah5/iStockphoto/Getty Images; 3Dmask/iStockphoto/Getty Images. p. 23: Fly View Productions/iStockphoto/Getty Images; Prostock-Studio/iStockphoto/Getty Images; PeopleImages/iStockphoto/Getty Images. p. 24: adamkaz/iStockphoto/Getty Images; torwai/iStockphoto/Getty Images; eclipse_images/iStockphoto/Getty Images. p. 25: FG Trade/iStockphoto/Getty Images; master1305/iStockphoto/Getty Images; SDI Productions/iStockphoto/Getty Images; Margaryta Basarab/iStockphoto/Getty Images; Oleksandr Todorov/iStockphoto/Getty Images; Jovanmandic/iStockphoto/Getty Images; nd3000/iStockphoto/Getty Images; andresr/iStockphoto/Getty Images; Geber86/iStockphoto/Getty Images; undrey/iStockphoto/Getty Images; LightFieldStudios/iStockphoto/Getty Images; Jovan Doncic/iStockphoto/Getty Images; BraunS/iStockphoto/Getty Images; Adene Sanchez/iStockphoto/Getty Images; p. 26: Whatafoto/iStockphoto/Getty Images; p. 28: urfinguss/iStockphoto/Getty Images; talevr/iStockphoto/Getty Images; Sjo/iStockphoto/Getty Images; Firmafotografen/iStockphoto/Getty Images; Clu/iStockphoto/Getty Images. p. 29: JazzIRT/iStockphoto/Getty Images; del-mar/iStockphoto/Getty Images; Matike/iStockphoto/Getty Images; monkeybusinessimages/iStockphoto/Getty Images; Akabei/iStockphoto/Getty Images; Deberarr/iStockphoto/Getty Images; p.30: wolv/iStockphoto/Getty Images. p. 31: canicula1/iStockphoto/Getty Images. p. 32: Capuski/iStockphoto/Getty Images. p. 33: lucentius/iStockphoto/Getty Images; 13threephotography/iStockphoto/Getty Images. p. 34: KariHoglund/iStockphoto/Getty Images; JazzIRT/iStockphoto/Getty Images; bonetta/iStockphoto/Getty Images; denisk0/iStockphoto/Getty Images; onurdongel/iStockphoto/Getty Images; xxmmxx/iStockphoto/Getty Images; eyewave/iStockphoto/Getty Images. P. 36: Library of Congress; FatCamera/iStockphoto/Getty Images. 9. 39: deepblue4you/iStockphoto/Getty Images; natatravel/iStockphoto/Getty Images; bonetta/iStockphoto/Getty Images; adventtr/iStockphoto/Getty Images. P. 40: interling/iStockphoto/Getty Images; ajt/iStockphoto/Getty Images. P. 41: del-mar/iStockphoto/Getty Images; Rouzes/iStockphoto/Getty Images; Firmafotografen/iStockphoto/Getty Images; Matike/iStockphoto/Getty Images; Emevil/iStockphoto/Getty Images; urfinguss/iStockphoto/Getty Images; Henvry/iStockphoto/Getty Images; JazzIRT/iStockphoto/Getty Images; talevr/iStockphoto/Getty Images; clu/iStockphoto/Getty Images; Liudmila Chernetska/iStockphoto/Getty Images; Sjo/iStockphoto/Getty Images; Anthony Paz - Photographer/iStockphoto/Getty Images; mKariHoglund/iStockphoto/Getty Images; bonetta/iStockphoto/Getty Images; denisk0/iStockphoto/Getty Images; JazzIRT/iStockphoto/Getty Images; xxmmxx/iStockphoto/Getty Images; adventtr/iStockphoto/Getty Images; deepblue4you/iStockphoto/Getty Images; scanrail/iStockphoto/Getty Images; onurdongel/iStockphoto/Getty Images; natatravel/iStockphoto/Getty Images. p. 47: 221A/iStockphoto/Getty Images; JackF/iStockphoto/Getty Images. p. 48: carmengabriela/iStockphoto/Getty Images. p. 50: Library of Congress, Washington DC; benedek/iStockphoto/Getty Images; arlutz73/iStockphoto/Getty Images; noor hossain/iStockphoto/Getty Images. p. 51: Meinzahn/iStockphoto/Getty Images; fdastudillo/iStockphoto/Getty Images; Contra Costa Times/Karl Mondon/ZUMA Press/Imageplus; Courtesy Rinspeed/ZUMA Press/Imageplus; Bike Forest/iStockphoto/Getty Images. p. 52: Trygve Finkelsen/iStockphoto/Getty Images. p. 53: Ipinchuk/iStockphoto/Getty Images. p. 54: moomusician/iStockphoto/Getty Images. AFZALKHAN M/iStockphoto/Getty Images. AndresGarciaM/iStockphoto/Getty Images. p. 55: bloodua/iStockphoto/Getty Images; David Crespo/iStockphoto/Getty Images; Grafissimo/iStockphoto/Getty Images. p. 56: AlenaPaulus/iStockphoto/Getty Images; nd3000/iStockphoto/Getty Images; itsskin/iStockphoto/Getty Images; FG Trade/iStockphoto/Getty Images; AleksandarNakic/iStockphoto/Getty Images; monkeybusinessimages/iStockphoto/Getty Images. p. 57: Casey Rodgers for Dos Equis/AP Photo/Imageplus; Jovana Stojanovic/iStockphoto/Getty Images. p. 58: hadynyah/iStockphoto/Getty Images; SHansche/iStockphoto/Getty Images. p. 59: no_limit_pictures/iStockphoto/Getty Images; MR1805/iStockphoto/Getty Images; Dimitrios Karamitros/iStockphoto/Getty Images. p. 61: frankpeters/iStockphoto/Getty Images; drnadig/iStockphoto/Getty Images; Rawpixel/iStockphoto/Getty Images; _ultraforma_/iStockphoto/Getty Images; kadmy/iStockphoto/Getty Images; Denis_prof/iStockphoto/Getty Images. p. 62: Halfpoint/iStockphoto/Getty Images. p. 63: Zolga_F/iStockphoto/Getty Images; Calin Stan/iStockphoto/Getty Images; DarthArt/iStockphoto/Getty Images; jaminwell/iStockphoto/Getty Images; Nikkolia/iStockphoto/Getty Images; Peter_Horvath/iStockphoto/Getty Images; THEPALMER/iStockphoto/Getty Images; frankpeters/iStockphoto/Getty Images; Beeldbewerking/iStockphoto/Getty Images; Andyqwe/iStockphoto/Getty Images; wildart/iStockphoto/Getty Images; PeopleImages/iStockphoto/Getty Images; Liderina/iStockphoto/Getty Images; fizkes/iStockphoto/Getty Images; MesquitaFMS/iStockphoto/Getty Images; Drazen_/iStockphoto/Getty Images; pixdeluxe/iStockphoto/Getty Images; Pollyana Ventura/iStockphoto/Getty Images; FilippoBacci/iStockphoto/Getty Images; monkeybusinessimages/iStockphoto/Getty Images; SolStock/iStockphoto/Getty Images. p. 66: Library of Congress, Washington DC; British Library, London; Private Collection. p. 67: National Gallery of Victoria, Melbourne, Australia; NASA Images; Eduardo Di Baia/AP Photo/Imageplus; badmanproduction/iStockphoto/Getty Images; Shaiith/iStockphoto/Getty Images; Moncherie/iStockphoto/Getty Images. p. 68: Avalon_Studio/iStockphoto/Getty Images. p. 69: Macmillan. p. 70: SrdjanPav/iStockphoto/Getty Images. p. 71: New York Library; Justin Hobson/iStockphoto/Getty Images; Johann K Johannsson/iStockphoto/Getty Images; Josephine Jullian/iStockphoto/Getty Images; Sarah J Lee/iStockphoto/Getty Images; Joa_Souza/iStockphoto/Getty Images; Andrew McArthur/iStockphoto/Getty Images. p. 73: Xantana/iStockphoto/Getty Images; Biblioteca Nacional de Portugal, Lisboa. p. 74: Myper/iStockphoto/Getty Images. p. 77: Stas_V/iStockphoto/Getty Images; Justin Hobson/iStockphoto/Getty Images; Dimple Bhati/iStockphoto/Getty Images; Joa_Souza/iStockphoto/Getty Images; Bulgac/iStockphoto/Getty Images; Cheryl Ramalho/iStockphoto/Getty Images. p. 78: RgStudio/iStockphoto/Getty Images. p. 79: NickyLloyd/iStockphoto/Getty Images; CandyRetriever/iStockphoto/Getty Images; FG Trade/iStockphoto/Getty Images; Imgorthand/iStockphoto/Getty Images; spooh/iStockphoto/Getty Images; Mihail Mihaylov/iStockphoto/Getty Images; guvendemir/iStockphoto/Getty Images; kali9/iStockphoto/Getty Images; PeopleImages/iStockphoto/Getty Images; Boogich/iStockphoto/Getty Images; aapsky/iStockphoto/Getty Images; MesquitaFMS/iStockphoto/Getty Images; Joa_Souza/iStockphoto/Getty Images; Bulgac/iStockphoto/Getty Images; Stas_V/iStockphoto/Getty Images; Dimple Bhati/iStockphoto/Getty Images; Cheryl Ramalho/iStockphoto/Getty Images; Andrew McArthur/iStockphoto/Getty Images; Josephine Jullian/iStockphoto/Getty Images; dwryan/iStockphoto/Getty Images; Johann K Johannssonv/iStockphoto/Getty Images; Justin Hobson/iStockphoto/Getty Images. p. 80: Alessandro Rizzo/iStockphoto/Getty Images; BlackSnake/iStockphoto/Getty Images; SolStock/iStockphoto/Getty Images. p. 81: beavera/iStockphoto/Getty Images; champpixs/iStockphoto/Getty Images; Cesar Okada/iStockphoto/Getty Images; Bulgac/iStockphoto/Getty Images. p. 85: FatCamera/iStockphoto/Getty Images. p. 86: baona/iStockphoto/Getty Images; Yuliya Baranychv/iStockphoto/Getty Images. p. 88: serts/iStockphoto/Getty Images. p. 90: Walt Disney Pictures/Photo12/Imageplus; NEW LINE CINEMA/LORD ZWEITE PRODUCTIONS DEUTSCHLAND FILMPR/Ronald Grant Archive/Mary Evans/Imageplus; UNIVERSAL PICTURES/Ronald Grant Archive/Mary Evans/Imageplus; Everett Collection/asypix Brasil; Hartswood Films/Entertainment Pictures/ZUMA Press/Imageplus; Hallmark/Entertainment Pictures/ZUMA Press/Imageplus. p. 92: Елена Бабенкова/iStockphoto/Getty Images. p. 94: Prostock-Studio/iStockphoto/Getty Images; LightFieldStudios/iStockphoto/Getty Images; gbh007/iStockphoto/Getty Images; cokada/iStockphoto/Getty Images. p. 95: NoemiC/iStockphoto/Getty Images; chrisdorney/iStockphoto/Getty Images; LeoMercon/iStockphoto/Getty Images. p. 96: GummyBone/iStockphoto/Getty Images. p. 97: Derick Hudson/iStockphoto/Getty Images; Panuwat Dangsungnoen/iStockphoto/Getty Images; Anna Fedorova/iStockphoto/Getty Images; Vershinin/iStockphoto/Getty Images; Mark Kostich/iStockphoto/Getty Images; Rainer Lesniewski/iStockphoto/Getty Images. p. 99: Pavel1964/iStockphoto/Getty Images; FotoGablitz/iStockphoto/Getty Images. p. 102: bpperry/iStockphoto/Getty Images. p. 103: Everett Collection/Easypix Brasil; LaylaBird/iStockphoto/Getty Images; Walt Disney Pictures/Photo12/Imageplus; xavierarnau/iStockphoto/Getty Images; Giulio Fornasar/iStockphoto/Getty Images; FG Trade/iStockphoto/Getty Images; fizkes/iStockphoto/Getty Images; PeopleImages/iStockphoto/Getty Images; Ranta Images/iStockphoto/Getty Images; NEW LINE CINEMA/LORD ZWEITE PRODUCTIONS DEUTSCHLAND FILMPR/Ronald Grant Archive/Mary Evans/Imageplus; Doucefleur/iStockphoto/Getty Images; Hartswood Films/Entertainment Pictures/ZUMA Press/Imageplus. P. 104: Rawpixel/iStockphoto/Getty Images. P. 106: mphillips007/iStockphoto/Getty Images; Prostock-Studio/iStockphoto/Getty Images; JackF/iStockphoto/Getty Images; Ridofranz/iStockphoto/Getty Images; FG Trade/iStockphoto/Getty Images. P. 107: acilo/iStockphoto/Getty Images. P. 109: IKvyatkovskaya/iStockphoto/Getty Images; Ksenia Shestakova/iStockphoto/Getty Images; Marcus Lindstrom/iStockphoto/Getty Images; digitalskillet/iStockphoto/Getty Images; Thais Ceneviva/iStockphoto/Getty Images; GibsonPictures/iStockphoto/Getty Images; 1205467353/iStockphoto/Getty Images. P. 110: Chris Ryan/iStockphoto/Getty Images. P. 111: ArtMarie/iStockphoto/Getty Images; Igor-Kardasov/iStockphoto/Getty Images; rapeImages/iStockphoto/Getty Images; CatLane/iStockphoto/Getty Images. p. 112: xxmmxx/iStockphoto/Getty Images; mauro_grigollo/iStockphoto/Getty Images; popovaphoto/iStockphoto/Getty Images; jordanchez/iStockphoto/Getty Images; turk_stock_photographer/iStockphoto/Getty Images; goir/iStockphoto/Getty Images; Anthony Boulton/iStockphoto/Getty Images; imaginima/iStockphoto/Getty Images; Yazgi Bayramv/iStockphoto/Getty Images; Loradov/iStockphoto/Getty Images. p. 113: Rost-9D/iStockphoto/Getty Images; eriksvoboda/iStockphoto/Getty

Images; t_kimura/iStockphoto/Getty Images; endlessxv/iStockphoto/Getty Images; Olga Strelnikova/iStockphoto/Getty Images. p. 115: sorrapong/iStockphoto/Getty Images; rusm/ iStockphoto/Getty Images. p. 117: Anthony Boulton/iStockphoto/Getty Images; popovaphoto/iStockphoto/Getty Images; Rodrusoleg/iStockphoto/Getty Images; mauro_ grigollo/iStockphoto/Getty Images; -slav-/iStockphoto/Getty Images; goir/iStockphoto/ Getty Images. p. 118: Tarzhanova/iStockphoto/Getty Images; KVLADIMIRV/iStockphoto/ Getty Images. p. 119: Ridofranz/iStockphoto/Getty Images; SolisImages/iStockphoto/Getty Images; JackF/iStockphoto/Getty Images; AlenaPaulus/iStockphoto/Getty Images; Prostock-Studio/iStockphoto/Getty Images; IKvyatkovskaya/iStockphoto/Getty Images; acilo/ iStockphoto/Getty Images; Poike/iStockphoto/Getty Images; Ksenia Shestakova/ iStockphoto/Getty Images; mphillips007/iStockphoto/Getty Images; imaginima/ iStockphoto/Getty Images; turk_stock_photographer/iStockphoto/Getty Images; Anthony Boulton/iStockphoto/Getty Images; xxmmxx/iStockphoto/Getty Images; -slav-/iStockphoto/ Getty Images; mauro_grigollo/iStockphoto/Getty Images; adventtr/iStockphoto/Getty Images; Rodrusoleg/iStockphoto/Getty Images; goir/iStockphoto/Getty Images; Madzia71/ iStockphoto/Getty Images; popovaphoto/iStockphoto/Getty Images; scanrail/iStockphoto/ Getty Images. p. 120: jhorrocks/iStockphoto/Getty Images; Renata Angerami/iStockphoto/ Getty Images; kohei_hara/iStockphoto/Getty Images; mixetto/iStockphoto/Getty Images. p. 121: Paul Bradbury/iStockphoto/Getty Images; David Sacks/iStockphoto/Getty Images; Bicho_raro/iStockphoto/Getty Images; recep-bg/iStockphoto/Getty Images. p. 124: Alexey yakovenko/iStockphoto/Getty Images; Hiranmay Baidya/iStockphoto/Getty Images; Sensvector/iStockphoto/Getty Images; Trifonenko/iStockphoto/Getty Images. p. 126: SCStock/iStockphoto/Getty Images. p. 128: Shaiith/iStockphoto/Getty Images; Sergdid/ iStockphoto/Getty Images; Itos/iStockphoto/Getty Images; glaflamme/iStockphoto/Getty Images. p. 129: dubassy/iStockphoto/Getty Images; sculpies/iStockphoto/Getty Images; Mlenny/iStockphoto/Getty Images; LisaStrachan/iStockphoto/Getty Images. p. 130: Irina Cheremisinova/iStockphoto/Getty Images; eyewave/iStockphoto/Getty Images; Bohdan Skrypnyk/iStockphoto/Getty Images. p. 131: Generistock/iStockphoto/Getty Images; sanchezgrande/iStockphoto/Getty Images; Daniel Ochoa de Olza/AP Photo/Imageplus. p. 132: Pgiam/iStockphoto/Getty Images; peterspiro/iStockphoto/Getty Images. p. 133: adokon/iStockphoto/Getty Images; superjoseph/iStockphoto/Getty Images; chameleonseye/ iStockphoto/Getty Images. p. 134: Hanna Shyriaieva/iStockphoto/Getty Images; wdstock/ iStockphoto/Getty Images; Ridofranz/iStockphoto/Getty Images; pixdeluxe/iStockphoto/ Getty Images; HRAUN/iStockphoto/Getty Images. p. 135: daverhead/iStockphoto/Getty Images. p. 136: ojogabonitoo/iStockphoto/Getty Images. p. 137: GoodOlga/iStockphoto/ Getty Images. p. 139: Sohadiszno/iStockphoto/Getty Images; TomasSereda/iStockphoto/ Getty Images; RudyBalasko/iStockphoto/Getty Images. p. 140: axz66/iStockphoto/Getty Images. p. 141: Dandelion/iStockphoto/Getty Images; vbacarin/iStockphoto/Getty Images; franckreporter/iStockphoto/Getty Images; nessaflame/iStockphoto/Getty Images; JudyDillon/iStockphoto/Getty Images; Davel5957/iStockphoto/Getty Images; FG Trade/ iStockphoto/Getty Images; Francesco Ricca Iacomino/iStockphoto/Getty Images; huad262/ iStockphoto/Getty Images; Joaquin Ossorio-Castillo/iStockphoto/Getty Images; Radist/ iStockphoto/Getty Images. p. 142: Karlos Garciapons/iStockphoto/Getty Images. p. 144: Circle Creative Studio/iStockphoto/Getty Images; Basilico Studio Stock/iStockphoto/Getty Images; M-Production/iStockphoto/Getty Images; RapidEye/iStockphoto/Getty Images; Coprid/iStockphoto/Getty Images. p. 145: EvgeniiAnd/iStockphoto/Getty Images; S_A_N/ iStockphoto/Getty Images; Koh Sze Kiat/iStockphoto/Getty Images. p. 146: wckiw/ iStockphoto/Getty Images. p. 147: AJ_Watt/iStockphoto/Getty Images. p. 148: monkeybusinessimages/iStockphoto/Getty Images; ivanastar/iStockphoto/Getty Images. p. 149: Beto Celli; AlexLMX/iStockphoto/Getty Images. p. 150: luoman/iStockphoto/Getty Images; Oat_Phawat/iStockphoto/Getty Images; GoodLifeStudio/iStockphoto/Getty Images; Nikada/iStockphoto/Getty Images; a_Taiga/iStockphoto/Getty Images; Baloncici/ iStockphoto/Getty Images; davidf/iStockphoto/Getty Images; Cay-Uwe/iStockphoto/Getty Images; apomares/iStockphoto/Getty Images. p. 151: Galina Zhigalova/iStockphoto/Getty Images; Imagesbybarbara/iStockphoto/Getty Images; MesquitaFMS/iStockphoto/Getty Images; kosmos111/iStockphoto/Getty Images; Liderina/iStockphoto/Getty Images. p. 152: WitR/iStockphoto/Getty Images. p. 153: PhotoInc/iStockphoto/Getty Images. p. 155: Sjo/ iStockphoto/Getty Images; Morsa Images/iStockphoto/Getty Images; FernandoPodolski/ iStockphoto/Getty Images; MaszaS/iStockphoto/Getty Images. p. 156: monkeybusinessimages/iStockphoto/Getty Images. p. 157: EvgeniiAnd/iStockphoto/Getty Images; Basilico Studio Stock/iStockphoto/Getty Images; eyenigelen/iStockphoto/Getty Images; PeopleImages/iStockphoto/Getty Images; EvgeniiAnd/iStockphoto/Getty Images; S_A_N/iStockphoto/Getty Images; EvgeniiAnd/iStockphoto/Getty Images; Bakal/ iStockphoto/Getty Images; M-Production/iStockphoto/Getty Images; Circle Creative Studio/ iStockphoto/Getty Images; Oat_Phawat/iStockphoto/Getty Images; a_Taiga/iStockphoto/ Getty Images; apomares/iStockphoto/Getty Images; Baloncici/iStockphoto/Getty Images; Nikada/iStockphoto/Getty Images; davidf/iStockphoto/Getty Images; Cay-Uwe/iStockphoto/ Getty Images; luoman/iStockphoto/Getty Images; GoodLifeStudio/iStockphoto/Getty Images. p. 158: SerrNovik/iStockphoto/Getty Images; kateshephard1/iStockphoto/Getty Images; ImageGap/iStockphoto/Getty Images; South_agency/iStockphoto/Getty Images; nantonov/iStockphoto/Getty Images; luoman/iStockphoto/Getty Images; ad_foto/ iStockphoto/Getty Images; WitR/iStockphoto/Getty Images; FernandoPodolski/iStockphoto/ Getty Images. p. 159: chameleonseye/iStockphoto/Getty Images; lakshmiprasad S/ iStockphoto/Getty Images; Alina555/iStockphoto/Getty Images; Mirjana Ristic/iStockphoto/ Getty Images; Kharchenko_irina7/iStockphoto/Getty Images; Mumemories/iStockphoto/ Getty Images; AndreyPopov/iStockphoto/Getty Images; lisegagne/iStockphoto/Getty Images; monkeybusinessimages/iStockphoto/Getty Images; bfk92/iStockphoto/Getty Images; Morsa Images/iStockphoto/Getty Images. p. 164: SolStock/iStockphoto/Getty Images; Elmar Gubisch/iStockphoto/Getty Images; monkeybusinessimages/iStockphoto/ Getty Images; azmaners/iStockphoto/Getty Images; Courtney Hale/iStockphoto/Getty Images; wsfurlan/iStockphoto/Getty Images. p. 168: fad1986/iStockphoto/Getty Images. p.169: FG Trade/iStockphoto/Getty Images p. 170: Jorge Elizaquibel/iStockphoto/Getty Images; Prostock-Studio/iStockphoto/Getty Images; andresr/iStockphoto/Getty Images. p. 172: skynesher/iStockphoto/Getty Images. p. 174: Daisy-Daisy/iStockphoto/Getty Images; monkeybusinessimages/iStockphoto/Getty Images; NoSystem images/iStockphoto/Getty Images; South_agency/iStockphoto/Getty Images; Solovyova/iStockphoto/Getty Images; Bilanol/iStockphoto/Getty Images; Sergey Nazarov/iStockphoto/Getty Images; merteren/ iStockphoto/Getty Images. p. 175: baona/iStockphoto/Getty Images; FG Trade/iStockphoto/ Getty Images; Edwin Tan/iStockphoto/Getty Images; HRAUN/iStockphoto/Getty Images; Global_Pics/iStockphoto/Getty Images. p. 176: claudiodivizia/iStockphoto/Getty Images. p. 179: lagunabluemolly/iStockphoto/Getty Images. p. 180: Jovanmandic/iStockphoto/Getty Images. p. 182: KatarzynaBialasiewicz/iStockphoto/Getty Images; Prostock-Studio/ iStockphoto/Getty Images. p. 183: Hiraman/iStockphoto/Getty Images; Eoneren/ iStockphoto/Getty Images; eyecrave productions/iStockphoto/Getty Images; baona/ iStockphoto/Getty Images. p. 184: clubfoto/iStockphoto/Getty Images. p. 186: spooh/ iStockphoto/Getty Images; Leonid Andronov/iStockphoto/Getty Images; skyNext/ iStockphoto/Getty Images; DarthArt/iStockphoto/Getty Images; Nedrofly/iStockphoto/ Getty Images; jean-francois/iStockphoto/Getty Images; Joey Ingelhart/iStockphoto/Getty Images; eugenesergeev/iStockphoto/Getty Images; DarthArt/iStockphoto/Getty Images; Salameh dibaei/iStockphoto/Getty Images. p. 187: phaisarn2517/iStockphoto/Getty Images; Poulssen/iStockphoto/Getty Images; imaginima/iStockphoto/Getty Images; simpson33/ iStockphoto/Getty Images; Ziuk/iStockphoto/Getty Images; SensorSpot/iStockphoto/Getty Images; dml5050/iStockphoto/Getty Images; sebastian-julian/iStockphoto/Getty Images. p. 188: Prasit Rodphan/iStockphoto/Getty Images; ManunNgueampha/iStockphoto/Getty Images. p. 189: Kirkikis/iStockphoto/Getty Images; itsskin/iStockphoto/Getty Images; Filipovic018/iStockphoto/Getty Images; Elenathewise/iStockphoto/Getty Images; filadendron/iStockphoto/Getty Images; Ziga Plahutar/iStockphoto/Getty Images; Giselleflissak/iStockphoto/Getty Images; iprogressman/iStockphoto/Getty Images; dardespot/iStockphoto/Getty Images; SeanPavonePhoto/iStockphoto/Getty Images. p. 190: ilbusca/iStockphoto/Getty Images; solarseven/iStockphoto/Getty Images. p. 191: csfotoimages/iStockphoto/Getty Images; Pawel Gaul/iStockphoto/Getty Images. p. 192: Onfokus/iStockphoto/Getty Images; Cristian Storto Fotografia/iStockphoto/Getty Images; ermingut/iStockphoto/Getty Images. p. 195: AALA IMAGES/iStockphoto/Getty Images. p. 197: Brasil2/iStockphoto/Getty Images; Alexlky/iStockphoto/Getty Images; davidf/ iStockphoto/Getty Images; Johann K Johannsson/iStockphoto/Getty Images; clintspencer/ iStockphoto/Getty Images; MaxMichelMann/iStockphoto/Getty Images. p. 199: pantonov/ iStockphoto/Getty Images; tepic/iStockphoto/Getty Images. p. 201: JianGang Wang/ iStockphoto/Getty Images; Willard/iStockphoto/Getty Images; MarioGuti/iStockphoto/ Getty Images; apomares/iStockphoto/Getty Images; Ballygally View Images/iStockphoto/ Getty Images; Biogeek/iStockphoto/Getty Images; Larry Crain/iStockphoto/Getty Images; AJ_Watt/iStockphoto/Getty Images; Rixipix/iStockphoto/Getty Images. p. 203: NGvozdeva/ iStockphoto/Getty Images. p. 206: ASIFE/iStockphoto/Getty Images. p. 207: istanbulimage/ iStockphoto/Getty Images; zorandimzr/iStockphoto/Getty Images; orestegaspari/ iStockphoto/Getty Images; Graeme Coughlan/iStockphoto/Getty Images; olgt/iStockphoto/ Getty Images. p. 208: Oleksandr Hrytsiv/iStockphoto/Getty Images. p. 210: FG Trade/ iStockphoto/Getty Images. p. 211: andresr/iStockphoto/Getty Images. p. 212: CowlickCreative/iStockphoto/Getty Images; UnionStep/iStockphoto/Getty Images. p. 213: bombuscreative/iStockphoto/Getty Images. p. 214: LeoPatrizi/iStockphoto/Getty Images. p. 215: insta_photos/iStockphoto/Getty Images; Valeriy_G/iStockphoto/Getty Images. p. 216: ArtistGNDphotography/iStockphoto/Getty Images; MesquitaFMS/iStockphoto/Getty Images. p. 218: victormaschek/iStockphoto/Getty Images; Anderson Coelho/iStockphoto/ Getty Images; WitR/iStockphoto/Getty Images; anyaivanova/iStockphoto/Getty Images; stockcam/iStockphoto/Getty Images. p. 219: pkazmierczak/iStockphoto/Getty Images. p. 220: Mlenny/iStockphoto/Getty Images. p. 221: ferrantraite/iStockphoto/Getty Images; Srabin/iStockphoto/Getty Images. p. 222: Irina Cheremisinova/iStockphoto/Getty Images. p. 223: HaizhanZheng/iStockphoto/Getty Images; Tarzan9280/iStockphoto/Getty Images. p. 224: AaronAmat/iStockphoto/Getty Images; THEPALMER/iStockphoto/Getty Images; Gilitukha/iStockphoto/Getty Images; JoeGough/iStockphoto/Getty Images. p. 227: Prostock-Studio/iStockphoto/Getty Images. p. 228: D76MasahiroIKEDA/iStockphoto/Getty Images. p. 229: SyhinStas/iStockphoto/Getty Images; sasar/iStockphoto/Getty Images; ES3N/ iStockphoto/Getty Images; gece33/iStockphoto/Getty Images; Anastasiia Shavshyna/ iStockphoto/Getty Images; syolacan/iStockphoto/Getty Images; FerreiraSilva/iStockphoto/ Getty Images; Sergio Yoneda/iStockphoto/Getty Images; vbacarin/iStockphoto/Getty Images. p. 230: bernardbodo/iStockphoto/Getty Images. p. 231: eyecrave productions/ iStockphoto/Getty Images; DonFink/iStockphoto/Getty Images. p. 232: OlegAlbinsky/ iStockphoto/Getty Images; Moussa81/iStockphoto/Getty Images; Tero Vesalainen/ iStockphoto/Getty Images; Wanlee Prachyapanaprai/iStockphoto/Getty Images; Natalia Darmoroz/iStockphoto/Getty Images; pagadesign/iStockphoto/Getty Images; tadija/ iStockphoto/Getty Images; karandaev/iStockphoto/Getty Images; gremlin/iStockphoto/ Getty Images; gorodenkoff/iStockphoto/Getty Images; Maksim Prasolenko/iStockphoto/ Getty Images; Devrimb/iStockphoto/Getty Images.

Catalogação na Publicação (CIP)

(BENITEZ Catalogação Ass. Editorial, MS, Brasil)

I321 InstaEnglish 2nd edition level 1: student's book and
2.ed. workbook / Emma Heyderman...[et al]. – 2.ed. –
São Paulo: Macmillan Education do Brasil, 2022.
240 p.; il.; 21 x 29,7 cm.

Outros autores: Fiona Mauchline, Patrick Howarth, Patricia Reilly, Olivia Johnston.
ISBN: 978-65-5752-101-4

1. Língua inglesa (Ensino fundamental II).
I. Mauchline, Fiona. II. Howarth, Patrick. III. Reilly, Patricia. IV. Johnston, Olivia. V. Título. VI. Série.

07-2022/43 CDD 372.652

Índice para catálogo sistemático:

1. Língua inglesa: Ensino fundamental II 420.7

Bibliotecária: Aline Graziele Benitez CRB-1/3129

MACMILLAN EDUCATION BRASIL
Av. Brigadeiro Faria Lima, 1.309, 2º Andar
Jd. Paulistano – São Paulo – SP – 01452-002
www.macmillan.com.br
Customer Service: [55] (11) 4613-2278
0800 16 88 77

Impresso no Brasil,EGB,01 2025